ROBIN
COOK

Dr. Robin Cook. Photograph by John Earle. Courtesy of the Putnam Publishing Group.

ROBIN COOK

A Critical Companion

Lorena Laura Stookey

CRITICAL COMPANIONS TO POPULAR CONTEMPORARY WRITERS
Kathleen Gregory Klein, Series Editor

Greenwood Press
Westport, Connecticut • London

Library of Congress Cataloging-in-Publication Data

Stookey, Lorena Laura.
    Robin Cook : a critical companion / Lorena Laura Stookey.
      p. cm.—(Critical companions to popular contemporary
  writers, ISSN 1082–4979)
    Includes bibliographical references and index.
    ISBN 0–313–29578–6 (alk. paper)
    1. Cook, Robin, 1940– —Criticism and interpretation.
  2. Medicine in literature. 3. Detective and mystery stories,
  American—History and criticism. 4. Adventure stories, American—
  History and criticism. 5. Didactic fiction, American—History and
  criticism. I. Title. II. Series.
  PS3553.05545Z88   1996
  813'.54—dc20   96–5804

British Library Cataloguing in Publication Data is available.

Library of Congress Catalog Card Number: 96–5804
ISBN: 0–313–29578–6
ISSN: 1082–4979

First published in 1996

Greenwood Press, 88 Post Road West, Westport, CT 06881
An imprint of Greenwood Publishing Group, Inc.

Printed in the United States of America

∞

The paper used in this book complies with the
Permanent Paper Standard issued by the National
Information Standards Organization (Z39.48–1984).

10 9 8 7 6 5 4 3 2 1

Copyright Acknowledgments

The author and publisher gratefully acknowledge permission for use of the following
material:

Excerpts from Joseph McLellan, "The Topic of Cancer." Review of *Fever*, by Robin Cook.
Washington Post, 20 February 1982: C4. © 1982, Washington Post Book World Service/
Washington Post Writers Group. Reprinted with permission.

Published interview with Robin Cook that appeared in *Contemporary Authors*, vol. 111, pp.
117–121. Gale Research, 1984. Used by permission.

Every reasonable effort has been made to trace the owners of copyright materials in this
book, but in some instances this has proven impossible. The author and publisher will be
glad to receive information leading to more complete acknowledgments in subsequent
printings of the book and in the meantime extend their apologies for any omissions.

To James Allison

Contents

Contents

Series Foreword

The authors who appear in the series Critical Companions to Popular Contemporary Writers are all best-selling writers. They do not have only one successful novel, but a string of them. Fans, critics, and specialist readers eagerly anticipate their next book. For some, high cash advances and breakthrough sales figures are automatic; movie deals often follow. Some writers become household names, recognized by almost everyone.

But novels are read one by one. Each reader chooses to start and, more importantly, to finish a book because of what she or he finds there. The real test of a novel is in the satisfaction its readers experience. This series acknowledged the extraordinary involvement of readers and writers in creating a best-seller.

The authors included in this series were chosen by an Advisory Board composed of high school English teachers and high school and public librarians. They ranked a list of best-selling writers according to their popularity among different groups of readers. Writers in the top-ranked group who had not received book-length, academic literary analysis (or none in the last ten years) were chosen for the series. Because of this selection method, Critical Companions to Popular Contemporary Writers meets a need that is not addressed elsewhere.

The volumes in the series are written by scholars with particular expertise in analyzing popular fiction. These specialists add an academic focus to the popular success that these best-selling writers already enjoy.

The series is designed to appeal to a wide range of readers. The general reading public will find explanations for the appeal of these well-known writers. Fans will find biographical and fictional questions answered. Students will find literary analysis, discussions of fictional genres, carefully organized introductions to new ways of reading the novels, and bibliographies for additional research. Students will also be able to apply what they have learned from this book to their readings of future novels by these best-selling writers.

Each volume begins with a biographical chapter drawing on published information, autobiographies or memoirs, prior interviews, and, in some cases, interviews given especially for this series. A chapter on literary history and genres describes how the author's work fits into a larger literary context. The following chapters analyze the writer's most important, most popular, and most recent novels in detail. Each chapter focuses on a single novel. This approach, suggested by the Advisory Board as the most useful to student research, allows for an in-depth analysis of the writer's fiction. Close and careful readings with numerous examples show readers exactly how the novels work. These chapters are organized around three central elements: plot development (how the story line moves forward), character development (what the reader knows about the important figures), and theme (the significant ideas of the novel). Chapters may also include series on generic conventions (how the novel is similar to or different from others in its same category of science fiction, fantasy, thriller, etc.), narrative point of view (who tells the story and how), symbols and literary language, and historical or social context. Each chapter ends with an ''alternative reading'' of the novel. The volume concludes with a primary and secondary bibliography, including reviews.

The Alternative Readings are a unique feature of this series. By demonstrating a particular way of reading each novel, they provide a clear example of how a specific perspective can reveal important aspects of the book. In each alternative reading section, one contemporary literary theory—such as feminist criticism, Marxism, new historicism, deconstruction, or Jungian psychological critique—is defined in brief, easily comprehensible language. That definition is then applied to the novel to highlight specific features that might go unnoticed or be understood differently in a more general reading of the novel. Each volume defines two or three specific theories, making them part of the reader's understanding of how diverse meanings may be constructed from a single novel.

Taken collectively, the volumes in the Critical Companions to Popular Contemporary Writers series provide a wide-ranging investigation of the complexities of current best-selling fiction. By treating these novels seriously as both literary works and publishing successes, the series demonstrates the potential of popular literature in contemporary culture.

Kathleen Gregory Klein
Southern Connecticut State University

The Life of Robin Cook

The publication of *The Year of the Intern* in 1972 signaled the beginning of Dr. Robin Cook's long and successful career as a premonitory voice in popular culture. Writing from the authority of his position within the medical profession, Cook has secured a reputation as today's foremost practitioner of the contemporary fiction genre known as the medical thriller. To date, Cook has written seventeen novels. Fifteen of these books, most of them best-sellers, offer cautionary and suspenseful tales of conspiracy and intrigue set within the worlds of medicine or medical research. While Cook's fiction is written primarily to entertain his many avid readers, his novels, as a review of *Vital Signs* in *Publishers Weekly* aptly noted, are also "designed, in part, to keep the public aware of both the technological possibilities of modern medicine and the ensuing ethical problems" (Steinberg, 1990, 55).

Cook's career as writer of the medical thriller runs parallel to the recent growth of public interest in the field of medicine itself. For Cook's readers, a friendly and familiar figure once known as "Doc" (the bearer of the ubiquitous black bag) has faded into legend. The black bag has long since given way to medical technology, and the ancient art of healing has been broadly named—with obvious significance—the "health care industry." An industry indeed, incorporating private insurance plans and Medicare and Medicaid, emergency rooms, specialty clinics, for-profit hospitals, and medical teaching facilities. Pharmaceutical companies are part of the health care industry, as are the laboratories where medical research is conducted. Preventive medicine is an important concern within the burgeoning industry, and numerous varieties of alternative medicine have also attracted public attention. In one form or another, the health care industry commands a significant portion of the nation's economy and work force. With the high costs of medicine ever continuing to rise, the industry itself has become the subject of a national debate.

It is in the context of this general debate that Cook's literary contributions have assumed a special relevance. Other physicians, notably William Carlos Williams, Oliver Sacks, and Richard Selzer, have written insightfully about the medical profession; in both stories and essays, these writing doctors have shared poignant moments—triumphant ones or painful ones—garnered from their wisdom and experience. This literature offers laypersons an opportunity to see a side of medicine that is otherwise not generally available to them. The same can be said for Robin Cook's suspense fiction, though it is written from a different angle. In setting out to surprise, shock, and entertain his reading audience, Cook makes use of the popular narrative genres to draw the attention of an exceedingly broad reading audience. The platform of the thriller novel lets him engage ideological issues in a highly dramatic fashion. He, too, reveals dimensions of the world of medicine that lie beyond most readers' direct experience—with the express intention of encouraging them to become involved in the debates being carried out in Congress and in the press. As he stated in a 1983 interview for *Health* magazine: "The public is more powerful now. We've lived through an age of consumerism. I believe that medicine is just as amenable to that kind of approach. I would like to see more consumerism in medicine. I think it's perhaps the only way to goad this enormous inertial mass known as medicine into changing itself" (Grossmann, 57). In choosing the medium of popular literature, Cook strives to democratize an interest that many people have hitherto thought to be arcane. His timely fiction appeals to a reading audience that has grown increasingly conscious of the major role that health care issues have come to play in public life.

Cook is deeply committed to situating his interest in medical policies and practices within the larger context of contemporary culture. He is, for example, especially concerned about the effects of marketplace motivations on the health care industry. Many of his novels therefore explore, from one perspective or another, questions of the economy of medicine. When medicine's economy intersects with that of the law, as it clearly does in instances of personal injury claims or malpractice litigation, Cook focuses his social critique on the law. His overviews of the workings of social institutions such as medicine and law dramatically reveal many of the ways in which the self-interests of these professions impinge upon the public welfare.

In addition to matters of economic interest, the novels consider numerous current social problems. Cook is attentive to women's issues: to women's positions in the health science workplace and to their treatment by the medical profession. He is concerned about society's widespread use of drugs and about the health threats posed by industrial pollution. He enjoys engaging the ethical problems that medicine's new technologies have inevitably raised—questions about genetic engineering, for example, or in vitro fertilization or experiments with fetal tissue. His first best-seller, *Coma*, raises the problematic issue of organ transplants, suggesting by means of its startling plot that clearly time has come for a drastic revision of social attitudes about the collection and use of human organs. Always carefully researched, the subjects of Cook's medical thrillers offer his readers much to ponder. Because he characteristically uses the technical terminology employed by members of the medical profession, his books are also instructive, providing his reading audience with an authentic vision of the world of contemporary medicine.

Born May 4, 1940, in New York City, Robert Brian (shortened to Robin) Cook spent his childhood years in Leonia, New Jersey, a community that receives mention in a couple of his books. His father, Edgar Lee Cook, was a commercial artist and businessman. His mother, Audrey (Koons) Cook, has apparently been a particularly significant figure in Cook's life—he appreciatively dedicated both *Outbreak* and *Harmful Intent* to her. Robin Cook has an older brother, Lee, and a younger sister, Laurie. (*Mortal Fear* is dedicated to Cook's siblings with a heartfelt expression of his esteem and affection.)

As a young child, the winsome Robin Cook modeled toddler's fashions, but his first great enthusiasm was for archaeology, the subject he knowledgeably explores in his third work of fiction, *Sphinx*. As its title indicates, he was especially fascinated by the wonders of ancient Egypt, and as a youth regularly visited the mummy rooms of Manhattan's Metropolitan Museum—where he was, in fact, inspired to commit to memory the names of the rulers of all the Egyptian dynasties. This early interest in the lore of Egypt has remained a lifelong passion, one that indeed received expression in the only one of Cook's seventeen novels to date that is not set within the world of medicine.

Readers of his books will readily note that Robin Cook's first and third novels are anomalous in respect to the rest of his fiction. The largely autobiographical first book, *The Year of the Intern*, is not a thriller, and *Sphinx*, which is unquestionably a suspense novel (one that even features a double conspiracy plot), is not a medical thriller. Appearing in the wake of the popular success and critical acclaim that attended the publication of his second novel, *Coma*, *Sphinx* spent seven weeks on the best-seller list and was also adapted for the screen. The movie, in whose production Cook took no part at all, was not the success that the movie version of *Coma* had been, and reviews of the novel itself were decidedly mixed. It is quite apparent that, after writing *Coma*, Cook used his newly acquired facility with the suspense genre to write a novel that paid homage to his fascination with mysteries of the past. After experimenting, however, with a thriller that featured black market intrigue in the smuggling of Egyptian antiquities, Cook chose to return to his fictional exploration of a variety of medical issues, and it is this specialized focus that has come to distinguish his work within the body of contemporary suspense literature.

Sphinx's plot is an intricate one, providing room for Cook to play with standard conventions of the suspense novel, and the book is of general interest to his readers in two other noteworthy respects. In the figure of its central character, Erica Baron, it offers an example of a strong female protagonist, and in its "lovingly detailed and sensuous descriptions of Cairo, Luxor, and Egypt's holy places" (Aldridge, 36), it captures an atmosphere of place that can be favorably compared with the realistic effects that the writer characteristically achieves in his representations of hospital settings. *Sphinx*'s ingenious plot, based on the notion that the undisturbed tomb of another Egyptian ruler, Seti I, actually lies hidden beneath the familiar tomb of King Tutankhamen, proved to be of timely interest to many readers, for the book was published around the time artifacts from Tutankhamen's tomb were on exhibition in the United States.

Although his obsession with archaeology predated his interest in medicine, the latter passion also emerged early in Robin Cook's life. Indeed, it was at age fifteen, after he had witnessed a football injury at Leonia High School, that he determined that he would become a doctor. Cook graduated from Connecticut's Wesleyan University with a B.A. in pre-med in 1962. He then attended Columbia University's College of Physicians and Surgeons, receiving an M.D. in 1966. (Cook's summer job during his years at Columbia was a particularly interesting one: traveling each summer to Monaco, he served as a lab assistant to Jacques Cousteau; readers can see a reference to Cook's scuba diving experiences in *Vital Signs*, where one character is devoured by an immense white shark while diving off Australia's Great Barrier Reef.) While Cook found his university experiences at Wesleyan immensely stimulating, he has frequently criticized the ways advanced medical education is organized, believing that medical schools have "a tendency to stay in the past" (Grossmann, 56). The critique of medicine that is sounded throughout his literary career therefore first began to take shape while he was still a medical student.

In 1966 Cook became a surgical resident at Queen's Hospital in Honolulu, Hawaii; he remained at this post until 1968, later using his own experiences there as the inspiration for his first book, the insightful study of the institution of medical residency entitled *The Year of the Intern*. Deeply disturbed by the exhausting regimen of residency (or internship, as it was then called), and thoughtfully concerned about the ways this form of apprenticeship might in fact be counterproductive as a tool for training doctors, Cook felt compelled to find a way to express his thoughts on the subject. The opportunity arose during his stint in the U.S. Navy, where he served from 1969 to 1971 (eventually becoming lieutenant commander). Assigned to the USS *Kamehameha*, a Polaris submarine, Cook actually wrote his first novel, as he says, "under the Pacific Ocean" (*The Year of the Intern*, hereafter cited as *TYOTI*). Asked by an interviewer for *Contemporary Authors* (hereafter cited as *CA*) whether he had ever given thought to writing a novel before seizing the opportunity he enjoyed aboard the submarine, Cook acknowledged that he had wanted to begin writing while he was still in medical school, but that he had not had time. Then, the opportunity presented itself, and, as Cook said, "I didn't really know if I was going to be able to write one, but I assumed that I was" (*CA*, 119).

Although this first book, published when Cook returned to civilian life, was very well received, it did not enjoy as wide a circulation as he had hoped. Cook had a message he wanted to deliver (in fact, in 1973, the year following the publication of *The Year of the Intern*, he summarized its sentiments in "My Turn," *Newsweek*'s regular guest opinion column), and he now needed to find a way to appeal to a broader reading audience. Readers of *The Year of the Intern* had certainly included people with a specialized interest in the practice of medicine (it was recommended reading for both established doctors and doctors-to-be), but Cook was determined to write a novel that would catch the eye of the general public. With this ambition in mind, he set out to discover the secrets of successful popular fiction. Hoping to produce a best-seller himself, he spent six months in 1975 reading and analyzing best-sellers (over one hundred of them, in fact). Cook's reading suggested to him that the mystery-thriller genre would be likely to "capture the interest of the largest number of people" (*World Authors*, 183), and he therefore decided to write one, drawing upon his own special expertise through the use of a medical setting. The result of Cook's efforts was *Coma*, a best-seller that was also made into a successful motion picture.

"Learning to write a best-seller ," Cook later told *People* magazine, was "like teaching yourself to wire a house" (Jennes, 65). Having successfully published his first novel, he was unaware, until he wrote *Coma*, of how truly difficult it generally is to break into the highly competitive popular market. In fact, reflecting upon the earlier publication of *The Year of the Intern*, he commented to *Health* magazine's John Grossmann: "If I had known then what I know now—that the chances of a first-time author getting published are about as good as winning the state lottery—I don't think I would have attempted the book. I thought you simply wrote a book, sent it in, three weeks later it was in the bookstores, people ran and bought it, and then you went on the Johnny Carson show. I was very lucky" (Grossmann, 56). If Cook was lucky with *The Year of the Intern*, by the time he was ready to seek a publisher for *Coma* he had found a narrative formula that was probably guaranteed to win him success. His setting was marvelously authentic, his subject matter explosive, and, as Charles J. Keffer of *Best Sellers* observed, "I do not think anyone can beat the suspense and the story line developed throughout this novel. It is so close to the truth that one has to reinvestigate the title page to be sure that it really did say 'A novel by Robin Cook' " (*Contemporary Literary Criticism*, 131). *Coma* found readers of the thriller genre ready to embrace the possibilities of medical intrigue.

Before he was drafted into the navy, Cook had served his medical internship in general surgery. When he returned to civilian life, he decided to specialize in eye surgery, and therefore took up a residency in ophthalmology at the Massachusetts Eye and Ear Infirmary (an institution affiliated with Harvard Medical School). Cook was a resident there from 1971 to 1975. When his residency was completed, he opened a private practice near Boston and also joined the teaching staff at Massachusetts Eye and Ear. (Later, when he decided to commit more time to writing, he took a leave of absence from his Harvard teaching appointment.) Readers might be interested to note that two of Cook's villainous doctors, *Outbreak*'s Ralph Hempston and *Blindsight*'s Jordan Scheffield, are themselves ophthalmologists. Additionally, the medicine of the eye is featured in a couple of Cook's thriller plots. *Blindsight*'s central action is concerned with the great demand for cornea transplants, and, in *Mortal Fear*, where unsuspecting victims are administered a dose of a sinister "death hormone," the deadly substance is cunningly introduced into patients' bodies through the mucous membrane of their eyes. In Cook's most recent novel, *Contagion*, the central character is an opthalmologist who has been driven from private practice by a profit-oriented medical corporation.

Remarkably, Robin Cook wrote his second, third, and fourth novels while both maintaining his private practice and serving on the staff at the Massachusetts Eye and Ear Infirmary. Cook acknowledges that he writes rapidly (*The Year of the Intern* and *Coma* were reputedly drafted in six weeks and *Sphinx* in ninety days), but it is also likely that the disciplined habits he acquired while studying and practicing medicine have in fact served him well as a writer. When asked by an interviewer for *Contemporary Authors* whether it was difficult to establish a writing routine while practicing medicine full time, Cook answered that in his experience the two activities seemed to complement one another. "Medicine," he stated, "is a very episodic type of phenomenon where every fifteen minutes or so you're being faced with another problem to solve; you're making decisions, interacting with people all the time. Writing is just the opposite. You're sitting in your own room surrounded by your own objects, by yourself, for protracted periods of time. In a way I think the two things are compatible" (*CA*, 119).

After the publication of *Brain* Cook decided to take an extended leave of absence from the active practice of medicine, and it now appears that he no longer intends to return to his original occupation. He has busied himself in the meantime with the prodigious task of researching and writing thirteen additional medical thrillers, and he remains an outspoken advocate for medical reform. His favorite reading, he recently informed the editor of *Reader's Digest Condensed Books*, remains the *New England Journal of Medicine*.

Cook's reading habits and longtime interest in all manner of medical issues keep him well abreast of new developments in his field, and he delights in opportunities to speculate about future trends in his profession. Indeed, in a 1989 interview for *Omni*, Cook had some startling predictions to make:

> Although we're going to see dramatic improvements in transplantation during the next ten or fifteen years, genetic manipulation is going to make organ transplants seem terribly old-fashioned. It will also cause most of modern medicine, perhaps even doctors, to become obsolete. The real physicians, in fact, will likely be genetic engineers.
>
> I also believe that viruses are going to be useful in the genetic-engineering revolution. We're going to see a change in our perception of viruses. We'll no longer view them as some sort of inimical enemy. They may be much more helpful than we realize. (Bryant, 22)

These intriguing predictions notwithstanding, Cook knows that issues surrounding organ transplants, viruses, and genetic engineering all lend themselves to suspenseful treatment in the hands of the writer of medical thrillers, and thus takes up these matters in *Coma*, *Outbreak*, and *Mutation*. He also has some thoughtful observations to make about cancer treatment, a subject he explores in both *Fever* and *Terminal*. As he told John Grossmann, "I think the major problem in cancer research is the system: The drug firms want the cure for cancer to be a white powder they can patent. I think the solution will come through prevention and an immunological approach, which are less likely to have that kind of economic impact. This is where I'd like to see the research concentrated" (Grossmann, 57).

Besides keeping up with developments within his field and conceiving plots for chilling thrillers, Cook enjoys refurbishing and decorating houses or apartments. He maintains homes in Boston and Naples, Florida, and has recently redecorated an apartment in New York City's Trump Tower. His current interest in architecture and decor is in fact given expression in a recent novel, *Acceptable Risk*. There his protagonist discovers that she too is fascinated by old buildings and by the creative challenges inherent in tackling problems of renovation and artful decoration. When he is not busy pursuing one of his many creative inclinations, Cook enjoys playing tennis, skiing, or organizing a pickup game of basketball at Columbia University's medical school gym (which is now called the Robin Cook Gymnasium in honor of the benefactor who arranged for its complete renovation). Basketball, as it turns out, is also an interest that Cook has found means to incorporate in his fiction. In a truly fascinating way, his perceptive study of the social conventions that inform playground basketball in New York's inner city plays an important role in *Contagion*, his latest thriller.

Twice married, Cook has no children. His first wife was a young Scandinavian woman whom he had met while working with Jacques Cousteau in Europe. They were married in 1968 and divorced only a few months later. A relationship that "was more romantic than practical" (Jennes, 65), as Cook later revealed to Gail Jennes, it came to an end just before he was drafted. In 1979 Cook married Barbara Ellen Mougin, an actress and model who served as the inspiration for his characterization of Denise Sanger, a central figure in his fourth novel, *Brain*. An end to this marriage, which was apparently a very happy one for several years, is seemingly signaled on the acknowledgments page of *Mortal Fear*, where Cook thanks the many friends who offered him support during "difficult" times.

To date, two of Robin Cook's novels, *Coma* and *Sphinx*, have been made into large screen motion pictures, and three others, *Mortal Fear*, *Outbreak* (renamed *Virus*), and *Terminal* have been specifically produced for television audiences. His fiction has been translated into Spanish, and many of his books are available on audiocassettes. Cook, a widely recognized figure within the contemporary literary scene, serves on *The American Heritage College Dictionary*'s select Usage Panel.

ROBIN COOK'S AUTOBIOGRAPHICAL FIRST NOVEL

The Year of the Intern, written before Robin Cook determined that he would learn how to write a thriller novel, is intended to be an exposé of the "adverse environment" (*TYOTI*, 2) that he sees as a condition of the institution of medical internship. The novel is thus passionately earnest, indeed polemical, in its tone, and it is clear that when Cook wrote it, he had hopes that his poignant account of the ways the internship experience works to demoralize and harden idealistic young doctors might excite members of his profession to institute a change. Cook was, in this respect, somewhat disappointed, for although he was invited to be a keynote speaker at a subsequent conference on medical education, the book "didn't cause any particular movement to look into these things" (*CA*, 119). In Cook's opinion, the medical internship unfortunately remains a "kind of a hazing year" (*CA*, 119). Later on in his writing career, when he chose to master the possibilities of the suspense genre, Cook found a very different means to voice an exposé.

Dedicated to "the ideal of medicine we all held the year we entered medical school," Cook's first novel recounts the disillusioning experiences of one Dr. Peters (interestingly, a first name is never offered), intern at a community teaching hospital in Hawaii. It is the only one of Cook's seventeen novels to date to employ a first person narrative voice. The central character (generally called the protagonist) addresses the reader with an intimacy that is appropriate to the story he has to tell. The novel, which begins on the fifteenth day of Dr. Peters's internship, is divided into three sections that correspond to the different medical rotations that comprise the surgical intern's hospital assignments over the course of a year. Thus the first section, "General Surgery," relates Peters's initial experiences as an acting physician. The second section, called "Emergency Room," begins on the 172nd day of his internship, and the third section, "General Surgery: Private Teaching Service," takes up Peters's story on his 307th day of service. A concluding section, "Leaving," summarizes Dr. Peters's feelings on the 365th day, as he happily passes his responsibilities on to another beginning intern, the eager and idealistic Dr. Straus. And thus, as the book's ending suggests, the grueling, exhausting, and enervating cycle of medical internship will begin anew. The question that hangs in the air almost seems to answer itself: will Dr. Straus, after his year of internship has passed, emerge with his hopes and his high ideals intact?

The Year of the Intern marks Cook's first use of the episodic structure of plot development that he employs with such notable success within his suspense fiction. In this first novel, where plot is mainly a recounting of a series of unrelated events (events that Cook describes as "a synthesis of my own experiences and those of my fellow interns" [*TYOTI*, 2]), there is admittedly little occasion for the writer to demonstrate the skill that will later be his hallmark. Nonetheless, the story convincingly portrays the gradual transformation of an empathetic young doctor into something of a cynic, and in the closing pages of the book this change is emphatically registered upon the reader through Cook's use of a shrewd plotting device: with a wonderfully delicate touch, he repeats the moving scene with which his novel opened. This time, however, he places Dr. Peters in the position of detached observer of an event that less than a year earlier he had himself experienced with a great deal of pain and confusion. By the end of his internship, Dr. Peters has forgotten the immense trepidation he had felt the first time he "had been faced with the sole responsibility for pronouncing death" (*TYOTI*, 5).

Readers are first introduced to Dr. Peters as he is summoned in the middle of the night to confirm the death of an elderly patient. Although Peters has obviously witnessed death before, he has never before been responsible for making the "judgment call" (5). Stricken by the burden of this new responsibility and uncertain of what he should do, Dr. Peters wavers: "He was dead. Or . . . was he?" In touching detail, Cook depicts Peters's moments of uncertainty:

> I took out my stethoscope slowly, postponing the decision, and finally settled the pieces into my ears while I held the diaphragm on the old man's heart. . . . I couldn't hear the heart—yet couldn't I, almost? Muffled and far away? . . . My overheated imagination kept giving me the vital, normal beat of life. And then I realized it was my own heart echoing in my ears. Pulling the stethoscope away, I tried again for pulses, at the wrists, groin, and neck. All was quiet, yet an eerie feeling said he was alive, that he was going to wake up and I was going to be a fool. How could he be dead when I had talked with him a few hours ago? I hated being where I was. Who was I to say whether he was alive or dead? Who was I? (*TYOTI*, 5-6)

Dr. Peters applies his stethoscope again, and finally says, "He's dead, I guess" (*TYOTI*, 6), but there is more for him to do. He must now call the next of kin, and this presents him with a new set of anxieties, as he tries to determine what he should say: "I tried to think of some neutral word, one to convey the fact without the meaning. 'Dead,' 'demise' . . . no, 'passed away.' " When an experienced nurse appears and asks him to sign the death certificate, Peters wonders aloud when the old man died; the nurse's scornful reply takes him by surprise: "He died when you pronounced him dead, Doctor" (*TYOTI*, 7). Not sure even yet that the man is really and truly dead, Peters fights the urge to go back and check the pulse once again.

This poignant (and sympathetically comical) scene—wherein the young doctor confronts mortality and most reluctantly admits it, awkwardly yielding to its horrendous finality—is echoed in the concluding chapter. On this occasion the experience is Dr. Straus's, and Peters's response takes a measure of the changes he has undergone in his year as intern. Peters is packing his belongings when Straus phones him:

> "Well, what's the current crisis?" I asked.
> "An old lady died. About eighty-five years old."
> There was a pause. I didn't say anything, expecting to be told more about the problem. Straus's breathing could be heard on the other end of the line, but he apparently had nothing to add. (*TYOTI*, 198)

As the telephone conversation continues, punctuated with many hesitations on Straus's end, it becomes quite apparent to the reader (though not to Peters) that Straus is suffering uncertainties very similar to those that earlier confounded Peters. Straus does not know what to say to the family or how to handle the necessary paperwork. Indeed, he seems to need someone else to confirm the death, but Peters refuses to help him out. Thus Straus is left to undergo alone the intern's traditional rites of initiation, and Peters, for whom a full-fledged "medical practice was at last within sight" (*TYOTI*, 189) wonders whether he should purchase a Mercedes or a Porsche. (He knows that the Cadillac is a favorite car with surgeons, but this conspicuous status symbol is not—at least not yet— quite to his taste.)

Offering the first of Robin Cook's highly authentic depictions of life within a hospital setting, *The Year of the Intern* examines hospital politics, outlining the hierarchical order that defines staff members' relations to one another. It emphasizes the competition that exists among the interns—all striving to catch the attention of the hospital's most important doctors. It portrays occasional incompetence in medicine, often the result (at least in cases involving interns) of exhaustion or confusion. The novel takes a measure of the psychological wear and tear that naturally occurs when people witness others' suffering or death, and it even notes the various physical discomforts that are a doctor's lot: for example, the irritation of being unable to scratch an itch within the operating room's sterile conditions. The hospital setting brings with it associated problems, those of dealing with drug companies or handling insurance claims. All of these details and others (debates, for instance, about the relative advantages and disadvantages of Medicare) are significant to Cook, who is interested in capturing as realistic a portrait as possible of both the intern's typical experience and the general flavor of hospital life. (Before submitting his manuscript for publication, he asked eight other young doctors to read it and confirm his observations.) Indeed, for the reader who is curious about the inner workings of the medical profession, *The Year of the Intern* provides an excellent introduction. Gail Jennes describes the work as the "rather sour tale of the harsh life led by doctors in training" (Jennes, 65), but *World Authors* notes the book's importance, claiming that "it can be seen as part of a growing protest against the processes of depersonalization built into medical training" (*World Authors*, 182).

Robin Cook's
Medical Thrillers

As George N. Dove observes on the opening page of *Suspense in the Formula Story*, "One of the best things that can happen to a novel is for it to gain the reputation of A Book You Just Can't Put Down." He goes on to describe this book as the one "we sit up reading until two A.M., despite the necessity of being up again at seven, or read on the plane and train and at dinner. . . . The persistence of effect of such books is remarkable, because we are driven not only to continue reading this one but also to watch for the next one by the same author." Interested in understanding the "holding power" of such a book, Dove uses a reader-response approach to analyze a variety of novelistic effects that work to compel readers to keep turning the pages. While he acknowledges that "a book may have any one of several features that make it hard to put down (style, ideology, informational content, humor)," he sees the use of suspense as one of the strongest of these features.

The terms "suspense" and "thriller" are perhaps most commonly used to denote specific categories of popular formula fiction. While the terms can be used interchangeably—as they frequently are in this study—to designate the kinds of stories that are built upon the tension evoked by the presence of a terrifying danger, they can also be used to define particular subgenres of popular fiction. In this technical application, "suspense" refers to the plot wherein an innocent character is somehow threatened, and "thriller" to a plot's use of a conspiracy motif (wherein the very fabric of the social structure is threatened by the schemes of evildoers). Because Robin Cook draws upon both these plotting strategies—often, in fact, intermingling the two—the distinction is not particularly useful in reference to his work.

Additionally, "suspense" and "thriller" are terms sometimes used to characterize certain subgenres of the mystery novel. The mystery, a popular fiction genre featuring a story that recounts the solution of a crime (generally murder), obviously employs strategies designed to evoke suspense; when the mystery is combined, however, with features of the suspense novel, or with the conspiracy plot of the thriller, the mystery connoisseur is afforded an opportunity to make useful distinctions among the various kinds of mystery plots. (In *Great Women Mystery Writers*, Kathleen Gregory Klein distinguishes fourteen different subgenres of the mystery novel.) Because Robin Cook's suspenseful stories generally include instances of murder, elements of the mystery genre are significant in his work. Interestingly, however, murder is itself usually incidental to the kind of suspense that lies at the center of his plots, and his novels cannot therefore be classified as purely mystery fiction. Indeed, Cook's medical thrillers are often quite generally categorized as special instances of the mystery-suspense genre.

Cook's idiosyncratic contribution to popular suspense fiction is, of course, his unsettling use of the worlds of medicine and medical research as the sites for the assorted nefarious schemes envisioned in his work. The extraordinary authenticity with which he realizes the details of his settings cannot but contribute to the jarring effect his novels produce on readers who are necessarily horrified by the scenarios offered in his plots. That criminal activity of the most devious order might occur within the hallowed halls of medicine unquestionably serves to jolt readers out of complacent assumptions they might hold about the medical profession. As one reviewer notes: "Eye surgeon Robin Cook writes best selling medical mystery thrillers that are admired for their topical themes and technical facts concerning the medical world. It is important to Cook to be able to relay information about the moral and social issues in the medical profession to the general public through his stories" (*Contemporary Authors, New Revision Series*, 77). Or, as Joseph McLellan observes in the *Washington Post*, "What makes you start reading Cook, at least since his spectacular success with *Coma*, is the expectation of horror and of a glimpse behind the scenes at the medical establishment" (McLellan, C4). Because setting and theme are thus intrinsic to the suspenseful effects Cook achieves within his work, the generic label that most appropriately defines his fiction is one that acknowledges these crucial elements: indeed, Cook is largely responsible for shaping the subgenre of mystery-suspense fiction that has come to be called the medical thriller.

Dating from the 1830s, when the family story paper (a publication printed in newspaper format) first began to flourish, the thriller genre has been a popular one with American reading audiences. Featuring serial fiction that offered "romance with some kind of exotic setting, episodes of threat to a helpless heroine from lawless brigands or pirates or the like, fates worse than death, separations of families and lovers, scenes oozing with sentiment, and the distribution of just deserts followed by a grand reunion at the close" (Panek, 10), the family story paper excited general interest in intrigue and suspense. Following the success enjoyed by family story papers, inexpensive pamphlets called mystery and misery stories began to appear in large American cities. Dropping the exotic settings used by family story papers, the mysteries and miseries replaced them with "the sensational background of the corrupt city" (Panek, 10). Crime, of course, was an important feature of corruption within the city and thus grew to play an important role in emerging thriller fiction. By the time the dime novel, prototype of modern paperbacks, appeared in the 1870s, the thriller was a well established genre within popular literature.

Interestingly, the first doctor to enjoy unqualified success when he turned his hand to writing suspense fiction was none other than Arthur Conan Doyle. In introducing Sherlock Holmes with his 1887 publication of *A Study in Scarlet*, Doyle began to emphasize the use of scientific method in pursuit of solving crimes. This move opened an interesting connection between suspense and the world of science, one that other writers were quick to exploit. It might further be noted that in choosing a physician, Holmes's sidekick Dr. Watson, to serve as narrator for his stories, Doyle also established an early link between detection and the world of medicine. (A contemporary of Doyle's, R. Austin Freeman, almost immediately followed this lead, also using a doctor as narrator within his suspense fiction.)

Although he is by no means the only contemporary writer of medical thrillers (see, for example, Elizabeth Trembley's study of Michael Crichton's work, also published in this series), there is no doubt that Cook's name is the most readily recognizable among novelists in this somewhat specialized field. Reasons for this are perhaps obvious: Cook is prolific (over the past decade he has published a new book almost every year).

His novels, most of them best-sellers, are carefully researched, highly informative, and undeniably entertaining. Cook has, in short, developed a reputation as a writer of those books you just can't put down. Ardent devotees of medical suspense might search out Michael Carson's *The Experiment* or *Pain*, or they might well enjoy Carl Djerassi's *Cantor's Dilemma*, Maureen Duffy's *Gor Saga*, or *The Medusa Syndrome* by Ron Cutler. Robin Cook, however, has succeeded in creating an audience of his own, and many readers of popular fiction keep an alert eye open for his latest book. Interestingly, it is highly likely that Cook's success in popularizing the medical thriller will have the effect of opening the field for other writers with similar interests.

The degree to which Cook has in fact popularized the medical thriller should not go unremarked. Readers might not be aware that medical mysteries of one sort or another have been published for over one hundred years. One of the earliest writers interested in mixing medicine with mystery was British author Elizabeth Thomasina (L. T.) Meade, whose fiction was published in the 1890s. In spite of its relatively long history, the suspense novel now known as the medical thriller has really come of age during the two decades that have witnessed the publication of Robin Cook's fifteen popular thrillers.

If Cook's medical thriller can generally be seen as presenting an amalgamation of plotting strategies drawn from formulas recognizable within the suspense, thriller, and mystery genres, it should also be noted that much of his work intersects with yet another popular genre, namely, science fiction. Particularly in the novels where Cook explores the domain of medical research, or in those that feature plots centered upon the use of some cutting-edge technology, the futuristic turn that is the hallmark of science fiction is readily apparent. Indeed, Robert Reginald's 1992 bibliography of science fiction and fantasy literature lists *Brain*, *Coma*, *Harmful Intent*, *Mindbend*, *Mortal Fear*, and *Mutation* among its entries. While Cook is not, as he has more than once maintained, interested in writing science fiction per se, he does want to draw readers' attention to the possible implications of certain trends within medicine's use of scientific technology. Serving as cautionary tales, the novels in which Cook speculates about the future directions of medical research envision worst-case scenarios that reflect the writer's characteristic wariness about any kind of science that is driven more by economic considerations than by a concern for the public good. In speculating about the future, Cook himself performs a special kind of public service: he informs a general reading audience about developments within the field of medicine that, if not exactly professional secrets, are nonetheless not always readily accessible to laypersons. Cook's fiction has done much to demystify the arcane world of medical science.

In at least three of his medical thrillers, *Godplayer*, *Mutation*, and *Acceptable Risk*, Cook incorporates suspense strategies borrowed from the horror novel. (*Outbreak*, whose plot features viral epidemics, could also plausibly be seen as an instance of the horror subgenre that Michael Wood has recently termed the "mutant-disaster story" [Wood, 54].) The horror novel, featuring a special kind of suspense that derives from the manifestation of hideous psychological or supernatural forces or events, is best exemplified in the work of another popular contemporary writer, Stephen King. In Cook's fiction, the horrific emerges in the form of monstrous villains who inhabit the worlds of medicine or experimental research. *Godplayer*, a novel of psychological terror, features a psychopath whose egomaniacal tendencies are exacerbated by his important role as a leading surgeon. Tension in the novel mounts as other characters remain oblivious to the fact that there is a murderous monster in their midst. In both *Mutation* and *Acceptable Risk*, monsters are the result of scientific experiments that go wrong: the "mutation" is a Frankensteinian creature conceived in his father's lab, and the zombies who haunt the night in *Acceptable Risk* are researchers who have conducted their experiments on themselves. In all three books the presence of monsters turns the general effect of Cook's strategies for suspense in the direction of the horrific.

Cook, who successfully established his reputation as leading writer of the medical thriller with the publication of *Coma*, his first truly gripping novel, continues to experiment with a variety of suspense strategies. In one of his most recent books, *Acceptable Risk*, he plays with elements of the gothic, exploring questions about witchcraft, from both old and new perspectives. Readers who are fascinated by his ability to incorporate plotting strategies derived from a variety of genres should remember that, in teaching himself to write the popular novel, Cook carefully analyzed a large collection of best-selling novels. Drawing inspiration from these, he finds a way to blend elements of suspense, mystery, science fiction, and horror.

ROBIN COOK'S SUSPENSE STRATEGIES

In his close analysis of the suspense strategies commonly employed by writers of popular formula fiction, George N. Dove offers useful insights about the characteristics of novels that readers just can't put down.

(He also debunks certain myths about the ways suspense works.) Dove's understanding of the nature of suspense is based upon the pact he sees as existing between a reader and a writer. The writer, he believes, must actively involve the reader in the unfolding of a novel's action; the reader must, in other words, be brought to care about what happens next. To establish a framework for his definition of suspense, Dove offers three statements of principle for use as guidelines to support his readings of specific texts. These guidelines, which are applicable to an understanding of Robin Cook's success as writer of suspense fiction, are as follows:

1. Suspense takes place only when the reader is involved in the story.
2. Suspense is dependent to a far greater extent upon thrust than upon delay.
3. The will to read on—that is, intensification of interest in what happens next, or *suspense*—is dependent to a greater degree upon what the reader has been told than upon what he wants to find out. The more the reader knows (without knowing everything), the more he wants to know. (Dove, 4)

Dove acknowledges that "the involvement of a reader naturally takes many forms" (Dove, 4), but one device that seems to work especially well for Robin Cook is his frequent use of a prologue to introduce his novels. This device, which Cook actually uses for a variety of different purposes (to foreshadow events, to plant clues, to afford his readers a dramatic view of microscopic events taking place within the human body), has the effect of immediately plunging readers into the world of the novel. A device he uses to set the stage, as it were, the prologue instantly excites readers' curiosity. Joseph McLellan waxes poetic about the theme he finds embedded in *Fever*'s prologue:

> Here the primary evil force is microscopic, a cancer cell, and the best section of the book is probably the first two pages where Cook describes the creation of that cell. He takes his "inside story" perspective to some kind of logical ultimate: We are inside the bone marrow of Michelle Martel, watching the carcinogenic molecules of benzene pour in "like a frenzied horde of barbarians descending into Rome." There follows a

massive rape of cells, most of which die in the process. But
one is only damaged so that it begins to reproduce as cancer
cells. No longer responsive to "the mysterious central control,
... they had become parasites within their own house."
(McLellan, C4)

McLellan's use of "we" is telling. "We," of course, are the readers, who
have an interior view from a privileged position of a medical phenomenon. "We" can see how cancer originates, and through graphic analogy,
can see how it will spread. The reader of *Fever* thus begins the experience
of reading with immediate engagement in the process that will shape
the content of the story.

In arguing his second point, that suspense depends more "upon thrust
than upon delay," Dove takes issue with critics who hold the view that
"the key to effective suspense lies in the number of obstacles a writer
can place in the way of successful resolution, that is, in using the strategy
of delay." (Dove, 5) Dove believes that it is not the "delays and obstacles
placed" before readers that impel them to read on, but rather the "messages" and "almost surreptitious signals" provided by a writer who is
interested in sustaining "the state of tension that creates successful suspense" (Dove, 5). Robin Cook, indeed, is a master of the use of "surreptitious signals," generously distributing hints and clues as he unfolds his
tightly woven plots. Almost ironically, it is the very fact that he so deeply
involves the reader in the unraveling of his schemes that he is able to
spring unexpected surprises (as he does in *Brain* and in *Harmful Intent*)
that turn out, from the reader's perspective, to make perfect sense in the
end.

Dove's third point is the logical extension of his second principle. As
he observes, "One thing that keeps us interested in a story is our access
to privileged information, whereby we know something that has been
withheld from the characters themselves" (5). Cook shrewdly employs
this principle, almost always granting his readers an angle of vision
broader than that commanded by his characters. Because so much of his
suspense depends upon his readers' apprehension of the ways his protagonists (or other characters) have unknowingly become ensnared in
dangerous circumstances, Cook must find means to provide his readers
with information to which the characters are not privy. (The suspense of
a scene of entrapment is enhanced when the reader can anticipate that
the trap will indeed be sprung.)

Cook's common theme of entrapment is nicely realized through his occasional use of a technique for developing suspense that might be referred to as the "Cassandra motif." This motif, which evokes a distinct chill within the reader, is realized when one character suddenly recognizes an imminent danger, but is unable to convince others that the threat indeed exists. The reader, who also perceives the impending crisis, sharply experiences the terrible sense of entrapment that is the lot of a character who sees clearly but cannot, for one reason or another, persuade others to accept her (or his) privileged form of knowledge. In *Godplayer*, Cook uses this motif to dramatic effect. When his central character, Cassandra Kingsley, finally understands that her husband, who has murdered several other people, has also set his sights on her, her position is one of absolute helplessness. Recovering from an eye operation, she lies in a hospital bed, blindfolded and sedated. Her requests to be transferred to another room are not honored because she has in fact already been moved twice. Her fears are dismissed as expressions of paranoia resulting from the operation itself or from the drugs she has been given. Horrifyingly, Cassandra Kingsley knows exactly what is going to happen, but she has no means to forestall it. She is completely and certainly trapped.

As Cassandra's name signals, she occupies the position held by the Cassandra of Homeric legend, the daughter of Priam who warns against acceptance of the Wooden Horse and who foresees that Troy will fall. She is the character who possesses a knowledge that others cannot be brought to believe. Cook uses the motif he introduces in *Godplayer* in other novels as well, but often it is the reader who seems to hold the Cassandra position in respect to his plots. In *Outbreak*, *Mortal Fear*, and *Mutation*, for example, it is the reader who must helplessly look on as central characters move closer and closer to a danger that the reader has already identified. Suspense, then, builds, while readers, mesmerized in horror, observe protagonists approaching the traps that certainly await them.

In *Suspense in the Formula Story*, Dove goes on to elaborate the nature of the pact that exists between readers and a successful writer of popular fiction. One important expression of this implicit agreement, he notes, can be seen in popular literature's use of genre formulas, or conventions. When readers choose to read in a particular genre, they meet with a writer on a common field of expectations. As Dove observes, it is "those accepted conventions of formula fiction, those proved, almost endlessly durable devices so familiar to the experienced reader," that initially "serve to establish a common ground between writer and reader, so that communication between them is facilitated" (Dove, 6). Those critics who complain that writing in the popular genres is too formulaic, have, Dove insists, entirely missed the point. Readers, who delight in finding the conventions they have expected to encounter, do not tire of the inevitable repetitions that are a given part of formula fiction. While many of Cook's conventional ploys are derived from the suspense genre (his chase scenes, his hired thugs or hitmen, his use of psychopathic maniacs), it is, as Joseph McLellan noted, the anticipation of horror, combined with a behind-the-scenes look at the medical establishment, that draw readers to his books.

OTHER FEATURES OF COOK'S PLOTS

Robin Cook does not lack a sense of humor, and clearly enjoys concocting wicked plots and sporting with the conventions of his genre. His quite serious intentions of informing his reading public about the inner workings of the medical profession do not, happily, cancel out his playful side. Many of Cook's conventional chase scenes are presented tongue-in-cheek; clearly the writer is exercising his imaginative faculties, looking to amuse his faithful readers with a variation they have never seen before. The chase scene in *Terminal* is one such example. Exploiting a spy versus spy motif, Cook lines up sets of characters, each following someone else, until he has created a veritable parade of cars streaming across the expanses of central Florida. (To add to the fun, Cook shows the vehicles all executing a U-turn, one after another.) In *Harmful Intent* he enjoys great sport with a minor character, a sometimes bad guy, sometimes good guy whose quirky mannerisms and great facility for being Johnny-on-the-spot finally endear him to the novel's readers. In *Acceptable Risk*, where he whimsically transforms a whole passel of cocky, self-serving, and impatient researchers into grunting, snorting, fire-fearing brutes, the invitation is laid wide open for readers to join in his hilarity: those arrogant researchers unquestionably got their just deserts!

Beginning with *Coma* and *Sphinx*, Cook demonstrates a keen interest in women's positions within the professional world. *Coma*'s Susan Wheeler and *Sphinx*'s Erica Baron are the first of the many strong, resourceful women characters that Cook casts in the role of protagonist. (Eight, which is to say nearly half, of Cook's seventeen novels to date feature female protagonists. And in *Fever*, *Terminal*, and *Fatal Cure*, important women characters work closely with male protagonists to resolve the novels' central conflicts.) Although characterization is not one of Cook's particular strengths (he generally prefers to present his character studies in vignettes that serve the larger purpose of plot development), his most fully developed characters are, speaking generally, his several female protagonists. Cook is sympathetically alert to the kinds of problems women meet in attempting to assume positions of equality to men (when readers first meet *Sphinx*'s Erica Baron she is being manhandled by a leering adolescent youth in the streets of Cairo), but his resilient women protagonists unfailingly fight back (Erica turns around and slugs the offending youth, much to the approval of cheering onlookers in the crowded bazaar).

To elaborate a little on the question of characterization within the suspense genre, it is useful to reflect upon some insights offered by Thomas J. Roberts in *An Aesthetics of Junk Fiction*. Noting that "readers and writers agree—too quickly, I think—that the people in paperback fiction are simply drawn," Roberts argues that "readers' interest in fictional characters" need not "depend upon their complexity" (24). Indeed, because "role identities are fundamental social realities for urban humanity" (25), this critic of the popular genres sees the strategy of characterizing fictional figures in terms of the roles they play within novels as a thoroughly appropriate one. Robin Cook, occasionally criticized in reviews for his "simplistic" handling of characterization, is nevertheless greatly skilled at drawing characters who fill the roles envisioned by his own conceptions of institutional or social realities. Thus, "truth of character" (Roberts, 26) for many of Cook's heroines and heroes can be found in the strikingly realistic roles they play within the worlds portrayed by the books.

COOK'S CENTRAL THEMES

To Robin Cook, what you don't know *can* hurt you. Since the publication of the initial exposé that he offered in his only nonthriller, *The Year of the Intern*, Cook has consistently sought to democratize knowledge of the specialized interests related to the medical profession. (The only exception, noted earlier, is *Sphinx*—which nonetheless does expose a different set of special interests, those involving the illegal marketing of immensely valuable Egyptian antiquities.) All of Cook's major themes, his visions of entrapment and the victimization of innocent people, his scenarios of secrecy in research and the deadly secrecy of conspiracy, can be linked together by the recognition that in knowledge resides a power to confront the designs of special interests that do not serve the public good. Within Cook's novels, the villains who ruthlessly exploit others are invariably motivated by vanity or greed.

Central to Cook's concerns about recent changes in the field of medicine is his fear that its gradual transformation into a form of business enterprise leaves it vulnerable to the manipulations of people too strongly motivated by economic considerations. Where there is big money to be made, he suggests, greedy people will seek out opportunities to promote their special interests. Part of Cook's purpose in writing thrilling tales of intrigue and suspense is to demonstrate for readers just where those interests lie. Thus, in exaggerating their dangers through his use of a conspiracy motif, he is able to inform his reading audience about trends within the complex social institution that is the object of his focus. His presentation of ordinary people (that is, patients) as the victims of these trends speaks dramatically to readers who immediately recognize that they, too, as ordinary people, necessarily have a strong interest in understanding developments within the medical profession.

One significant trend within the health care industry is the recent growth of subscription plans for medical services. The emergence of health maintenance organizations (HMOs) has effected changes in the ways medicine is practiced, and Cook examines the implications of these changes from a couple of interesting angles. When HMOs first began to claim a noticeable portion of the medical market (in the 1980s), some doctors in private practice began to worry that this new health care delivery system might jeopardize their own positions. In *Outbreak* Cook shows how the beginnings of a shift from a general reliance upon private practice to organized group practices created shock waves that reverberated throughout the medical profession. Basing his plot on an actual conspiracy by private physicians to discredit HMOs, Cook conceives of the wicked scenario wherein a cartel of private doctors arranges to eradicate certain self-funded clinics by unleashing upon them the dreaded Ebola virus. In this Battle of the Titans, this clash between opposed economic interests within the medical profession, innocent victims lose their lives and the society in general is recklessly threatened with the danger of contagion. In *Outbreak* the arrogant assertion of the desires of greedy vested interests endangers the welfare of the public.

Outbreak's HMOs are themselves victimized by influential members of the traditional medical establishment, but Cook recognizes that, as business entities, HMOs also have vested economic interests. In *Mortal Fear* and *Fatal Cure* he turns his attention to these very interests, showing how it profits the HMO to keep its medical costs down. (Obviously, an HMO's ability to operate is threatened if expenditures exceed the amount of money its membership brings in.) One way to keep costs down is to somehow avoid handling those patients who require unusually expensive treatment, and the hospital administrators depicted in these novels devise fiendish plots to realize this end. In *Mortal Fear*, middle-aged patients who engage in health-threatening personal habits (excessive drinking, smoking, overeating, etc.) are secretly injected with a "death hormone" that speeds up the aging process. In *Fatal Cure* another costly group of patients, those who suffer from such chronic illnesses as cystic fibrosis, are irradiated in a hideous hospital bed specially installed by the Board of Directors. In these plots that feature "rationed medicine" by design, the economic interests of the health care industry once again override the medical interests of the public, and innocent people are victimized.

Cook exposes the strong self-interests of the pharmaceutical industry in *Mindbend*. In an utterly extravagant plot, one that features a scenario wherein Arolen Drugs attempts to gain control of the entire medical profession by "bending" doctor's minds, Cook cleverly uses a strategy of exaggeration to acquaint readers with the very real kinds of power and influence that large pharmaceutical companies command. (The pharmaceutical industry, after all, spends $1 billion more each year on product promotion than it does on research.) Similarly, *Harmful Intent* reveals the special interests of the law as they apply to medical malpractice litigation, and both *Vital Signs* and *Terminal* focus on the emerging trend within specialized branches of medicine to mount attempts to corner a market. In *Vital Signs* an international conglomerate seeks to dominate the field of fertility clinics, and in *Terminal* a research center tries to gain an inside track on cancer treatment. In all of these novels greedy malefactors advance their selfish causes by victimizing an innocent public.

If medicine's alliance with business interests opens opportunities for the greedy, its traditional status as a privileged profession presents special temptations for the vain. Among Cook's gallery of villains is a collection of doctors or medical researchers who also prey on the public in their endeavors to serve their own private ends. In the cases of *Coma*'s Dr. Howard Stark, *Brain*'s Dr. William Michaels, *Godplayer*'s Dr. Thomas Kingsley, or *Mutation*'s Victor Frank, Jr., an arrogance born of their special calling leads characters to set their personal goals above the interests of other people. Working in secrecy, these characters do not stop at murder in their singular pursuit of their private ambitions and desires.

Cook's purpose in presenting villains of this sort is part of his general critique of the medical profession. As members of a socially honored occupation, doctors are, in his view, sometimes too conscious of their own importance. This is particularly true, he believes, of physicians engaged in scientific research:

> Researchers feel they're doing something so important that they don't have to be held to the same guidelines that other people are. In a way that's one of the general problems in medicine, researchers feeling that they're doing the most important thing of all and that it gives them a sort of license to do what they think is right. They start making minor or major ethical decisions on their own. . . . The ethical problems of dealing with this kind of thing are horrendous. (*CA*, 120)

In plotting stories that depict the repercussions of doctors' or researchers' arrogance, Cook emphatically alerts readers to the existence of the ethical problems he has cited.

In Cook's conspiracy plots, where, as Joseph McLellan observes, "the horrific situation is one of helplessness in the face of a vast, impersonal and malevolent force" (C4), readers perceive that some awareness of contemporary cultural trends seemingly offers the only available means to address their possible implications. The malevolent force to which McLellan refers is, in Cook's vision, the very human evil that arises from vanity or greed; through the plots of his medical thrillers, Cook endeavors to impart knowledge of the present dangers of this evil. Knowledge, he believes, is as important to the reader as it is to the characters in his books. Most of the protagonists of Cook's novels become entrapped because they lack some crucial piece of knowledge, and the innocent patients in the books are the victims of what they do not know (and have no reason to suspect). Cook sees the medical thriller as an ideal forum for educating people about developments within his profession because, as he states, "not only can fiction gain you a much larger audience than, say, if you wrote a serious essay about these problems, but you also get people to experience the emotional aspects of the problems and reach an understanding which they couldn't have otherwise, short of actually participating themselves" (*CA*, 120).

AN INTRODUCTION TO THE MEDICAL THRILLER: *FEVER* AND *FATAL CURE*

Robin Cook's fifth and fifteenth novels, *Fever* (1982) and *Fatal Cure* (1993), are illustrative of some of the refinements the writer has made in the medical thriller over the years. For example, in both *Fatal Cure* and *Terminal*, two of his most recent novels, Cook experiments with form by introducing subplots to accompany the central action. Designed to provide his readers with extra thrills and chills, the subplots function to reinforce the medical thriller's ties to a broader suspense genre. (*Fatal Cure*'s subplot features the menacing presence of a serial rapist who haunts Bartlet Community Hospital's parking lot.) Heightening suspense by enhancing the aura of danger, Cook's subplots contribute to the non-stop action of his thrillers.

In two of his most recent novels, *Fatal Cure* and *Acceptable Risk*, Cook introduces another (and quite fascinating) innovation. Although the evil-doers in Cook's fiction are not always brought to justice (as in *Fever*, for example), in both of these recent books the plots ensure—in an altogether Dantesque fashion—that the villains are meted wonderfully appropriate punishments to redress their terrible crimes. *Acceptable Risk*'s elitist researchers are transmuted into primitive beasts, and *Fatal Cure*'s monstrous Board of Directors is irradiated by its own lethal bed. (Thus, as an old saw would have it, the Board must lie in the bed it has made.) With these daringly whimsical flourishes, wherein fictional retribution is visited upon fictional malfeasance, Cook weaves a strand of surrealism into the fabric of his thrillers' plots.

Although eleven years and certain innovations in technique separate *Fever* and *Fatal Cure*, the two novels do have much in common. Both books feature plots wherein protagonists find themselves pitted against the power held by the medical establishment, and both are set in rural communities, where local inhabitants are strongly protective of the business interests that support the regional economy. Unlike any of Cook's other plots, those in these two novels are sharply focused on family life, for in *Fever* and *Fatal Cure*, the lives of the protagonists' children are in danger.

Fever's protagonist, Dr. Charles Martel, is a researcher at the Weinburger Research Institute, a facility that specializes in developing treatments for cancer. Martel's special expertise lies in the area of immunology (which, as Robin Cook actually believes, offers the best hope for finding a means to control the dreaded disease), but his job is in jeopardy because his research does not offer the promise of producing a patentable or marketable drug. Martel, therefore, finds himself opposing the special interests of his company at a time when it is especially important that he preserve his job, for his young daughter Michelle has been stricken by leukemia. Under pressure to change the direction of his research, Martel resists, largely because he firmly believes that his own line of inquiry offers the best chance of finding a cure for Michelle. (Michelle is undergoing traditional chemotherapy while her father races against the clock in his efforts to find a way to trigger an immune response within his child.)

Charles Martel is furthermore convinced that his daughter's leukemia (the disease, in fact, that killed his first wife) was brought on by the benzene that Recycle, Ltd., the most important factory in his rural New Hampshire community, has dumped into the local river.[1] Therefore, in addition to battling his superiors at the Weinburger Institute, he is waging war with the industrial powers who are recklessly polluting the environment—and his actions in this regard have incurred the wrath of the local citizenry, whose very livelihood depends upon Recycle, Ltd. (Martel is himself viciously beaten and the members of his family are harassed by disapproving neighbors.)

Thus Charles Martel is a man beset, and the novel's theme of besiegement reaches its crescendo after he has, in a desperate effort to save her life, actually kidnapped his declining daughter from her hospital bed and boarded up his house. With his family united around him, and police and armed citizens surrounding his home, Martel applies his treatment to Michelle.

Fever nears its climax when Martel is brought to the recognition that his actions have endangered his entire family. A man manages to enter the house during the early morning hours (descending from the attic), and when Martel apprehends him, and finds that he is armed with a Smith and Wesson .38 special as well as concussion grenades, he realizes that the man is a professional agent of some kind. Checking his wallet, Martel finds a business card identifying the intruder as one Anthony Ferrullo, a security guard for Breur Chemical. Knowing that Recycle, Ltd., is a subsidiary of Breur Chemical,

> Charles felt a shiver of fear pass over him. Up until that moment he had felt that whatever risk he was taking in standing up against organized medical and industrial interests could

be resolved in a court of law. Mr. Anthony Ferrullo's presence suggested the risk was considerably more deadly. And most disturbing, Charles realized that the risk extended to his whole family. In Mr. Ferrullo's case, "security" was obviously a euphemism for coercion and violence. For a moment the security man was less an individual than a symbol of evil, and Charles had to keep himself from striking out at him in blind anger. Instead he began turning on lights, all of them. He wanted no darkness, no more secrecy. (*Fever*, 298)

The novel's climax is dramatic. Martel's hope, when he removes his barricades, is that the presence of many newspaper and TV reporters among the hostile crowd will serve to forestall any further violence, but this hope is in vain. Martel is indeed shot, by one of his angry neighbors, as he emerges from his house. (Seriously wounded, Martel nonetheless survives, and Michelle, too, goes into remission—although it is impossible to determine whether this is a result of her father's treatment or of her traditional therapy. In the book's concluding scene, the Martel family has, most understandably, packed up and left Shaftesbury, New Hampshire. It is time for the family to begin life anew, in distant California.)

In challenging the special interests of the medical establishment (the Weinburger Institute), big business (Breur Chemical), and local enterprise (Recycle, Ltd.), Charles Martel faces daunting odds. Although the malefactors in *Fever* are never fully brought to justice, the protagonist does extract some compromises. Fearing unfavorable publicity should the story of Martel's shooting arouse the sympathies of the public, Breur Chemical agrees to make an anonymous compensatory payment to a family that lost a member to benzene poisoning, and the Environmental Protection Agency (EPA) agrees to investigate Shaftesbury's pollution problems. Nevertheless, Martel's victory is a partial one, and in *Fever* Cook once again illustrates the power of big business to protect its vested interests.

Like *Fever*, *Fatal Cure* is set in a small New England town. Angela and David Wilson, the novel's joint protagonists (casting a couple in the role of central character reinforces the centrality of family in this novel's story), have left university hospital jobs in Boston to assume positions at the Community Hospital in Bartlet, Vermont. Desiring both to escape their frantic city life and to find a suitable environment for their young daughter, who suffers from cystic fibrosis, the Wilsons believe that they have finally found an ideal setting in Bartlet's homey community. (David is an internist and Angela a pathologist; both have been hired to work under Bartlet Community Hospital's new "managed care" system.)

Readers quickly find that all is not well behind Bartlet's romantic facade, for in the prologue they learn of the existence of the town's mysterious rapist, and they also witness the vicious murder of the hospital's former director (a retired doctor who is severely critical of Bartlet Community's present operation). Positioned, then, to anticipate the unpleasant surprises that await the Wilsons, readers are immediately drawn into the novel's recounting of their disillusionment. Indeed, the Wilsons' disappointment is quickly manifested, when Angela is sexually harassed by her new supervisor, and when David is roundly reprimanded for spending too much time with individual patients. Soon new hospital rules follow, restricting the use of the emergency room to HMO patients and limiting the number of diagnostic tests or medical consultations that staff doctors can order. Bartlet Community Hospital, it turns out, has severe financial problems, in part the result of overexpansion, and in part the effect of the Board of Directors' decision to underbid the health care contract it carries with the HMO holding company.

Both Angela and David Wilson believe in health care reform, but Bartlet Community's draconian measures seem to them to be detrimental to the patients. When they begin to express their reservations, they, like *Fever*'s Charles Martel, excite the ire of their neighbors—the hospital, as it happens, is the largest employer in their region. (Fiercely competitive, Bartlet Community has driven two nearby hospitals out of business.) Finally, after significant numbers of hospital patients die (including a young friend of their daughter who also happened to have cystic fibrosis), the Wilsons become suspicious.

The Board of Directors' diabolical scheme to eliminate patients whose treatment is too expensive is known by the acronym DUM (Drastic Utilization Measures)—Cook's little joke. The Wilsons' own daughter Nikki is of course scheduled to receive these drastic measures, but at the novel's climax, when the Wilsons have finally realized what is happening at Bartlet Memorial, they rescue their daughter from her deadly hospital bed. (Needless to say, this family also leaves the community it had hoped to claim as home.)

Fatal Cure is dedicated to "the spirit of health-care reform and the sanctity of the doctor-patient relationship." To this dedication Cook adds his "fervent hope that they need not be mutually exclusive," as indeed they are in the scenario *Fatal Cure* envisions. In the novel Cook has outlined some of the problems that attend recent changes in health care policies. That these problems are important ones is testified to by a U.S. senator's request that copies of *Fatal Cure* be distributed to all members of Congress. As always, Cook's novel informs his readers—and also leaves them with questions to ponder.

NOTE

1. The April 5, 1982 edition of the *New York Times* printed a story detailing a lawsuit filed after the publication of *Fever*. In the suit, another writer charged that Cook's depiction of benzene poisoning resembled a plot proposal that she had submitted to Putnam, Cook's publisher. Responding to the charge, Cook called the legal action "a totally groundless nuisance suit" (Blumenthal, B3).

Coma
(1977) and
Terminal
(1993)

Robin Cook's second novel, *Coma* (1977), is the book that successfully launched his writing career. The first of his fifteen medical suspense thrillers to date, this novel quickly caught the public's eye. With *Coma*, Cook began to define a popular genre that has attracted more and more attention as people have become increasingly interested in health care issues and in technological and ethical developments within the practice of medicine. Using the rapid-fire action of Fletcher Knebel and Charles Bailey's *Seven Days in May* as his model for *Coma*, Cook was able to give the classic suspense thriller a new home in his own field of expertise.

Widespread interest in Cook's new version of a novel of medical intrigue deepened in 1978 when MGM released a movie adaptation of *Coma* starring Genevieve Bujold and Michael Douglas and with a supporting cast that included Richard Widmark, Elizabeth Ashley, and Rip Torn. Although Cook's *Sphinx* has also been adapted to the screen, and several of his other books have been filmed as movies made for television (including *Terminal*, in fact), *Coma* has probably been the most successful of these ventures. The dramatic appeal of Cook's novel was well realized in the movie version. (Few people who have seen the film will ever forget the stark horror of its representation of patient facilities at the Jefferson Institute: there row after row of comatose bodies hang eerily suspended in midair.) Michael Crichton, of *The Andromeda Strain* and *Jurassic Park* renown, wrote its screenplay and then directed this successful film.

Cook's fourteenth novel, *Terminal* (1993), picks up and plays out variations on the same structural design for a medical thriller that served him so well in *Coma*. Although the two books focus on different questions of medical ethics—*Coma* examines the problems associated with the scarcity of organs available for transplantation, and *Terminal* the difficulties related to the funding of cancer research—there are striking similarities between their characters and plots. In quite interesting ways, therefore, Cook uses *Terminal* to revisit, after sixteen years have passed, the scheme that he devised in his original best-seller.

PLOT DEVELOPMENT

In both *Coma* and *Terminal*, bright (and brash) young medical students must draw upon their newly acquired research skills to first discover and then prove malfeasance on the part of senior hospital officials. In *Coma*, Dr. Howard Stark, Chief of Surgery at Boston Memorial Hospital, operates in cahoots with the Jefferson Institute to sell human organs on the medical black market. Under his arrangement with the Institute, Dr. Stark provides the steady supply of brain-dead patients needed for organ transplants. Dr. Randolph Mason, Director of *Terminal*'s Forbes Cancer Center, presides over a hospital that proudly boasts a 100 percent remission rate in its treatment of medulloblastoma, a rare form of brain cancer. This astonishing statistic, however, means nothing when the nefarious scheme behind it is finally brought to light: the center itself has artificially introduced into its patients the very cancer that it cures.

The skullduggery practiced at both Boston Memorial and the Forbes Center originates in two equally important considerations on the part of its masterminds; on the one hand, the evil plots generate significant extra income for hospitals hard pressed by rising costs, and, on the other, they advance the medical experimentation conducted at the research facilities associated with the hospitals. Cook's fiction frequently calls attention to problems related to the spiraling cost of health care. Indeed, the temptations inherent in this circumstance strike him as being an ever-present danger, one that he readily exploits in his plots. In *Coma* and *Terminal* he adds to his antagonists' economic motivations a desire to achieve medical breakthroughs, "to crack the mystery" (*Coma*, 299; hereafter cited as *C*) of the workings of the human body. This additional element offers readers more than a hint of the familiar "mad scientist" motif. The frightening irony, of course, is that the doctors' noble goal to benefit the many requires that they heartlessly sacrifice the few. *Terminal* quotes Rabelais in its all too appropriate epigraph: "Science without conscience is but the ruin of the soul."

Both hospitals select their victims from among patients who have sought treatment for relatively minor complaints. Those at Boston Memorial (always assigned, ominously, to operating room number eight) are invariably young and healthy, eminently suitable as organ donors. After they have undergone anesthesia, these patients never again wake up. When they have been stabilized, they are conveniently transferred to the Jefferson Institute, a storage warehouse for body parts that masquerades as an intensive-care facility devoted to the comatose.

The scheme in *Terminal* is a little more elaborate than that portrayed in *Coma*. The Forbes Cancer Center runs a secret computer program that correlates insurance claims from across the country with Social Security numbers and other personal information. With these data, the villains are able to selectively pinpoint multimillionaires to serve as victims. An agent from the Forbes Center visits the hospitals where patients are recovering from minor surgery and injects a cancer-causing mixture into their intravenous (IV) bottles. Within months, these patients all appear at the Forbes Hospital seeking its sure-fire cure for their disease. Deeply appreciative, these patients too are "donors," generously endowing the Forbes with "over sixty million dollars in essentially unrestricted donations" (*Terminal*, 364; hereafter cited as *T*).

In several of his novels Robin Cook quotes a maxim popular within the medical profession: "When you hear hoofbeats you should think of horses, not zebras" (*T*, 19). If this precept is, in general, applicable enough, it nevertheless will not work for the protagonists of *Coma* and *Terminal*. The conspiracies these characters encounter are so cynically devious and so carefully disguised as projects designed to serve the public welfare that at first it is not at all apparent that conspiracies exist. Furthermore, the perpetrators of both books' malicious deeds are themselves highly respected medical professionals, seemingly beyond reproach and having well-established reputations. It is perhaps for this reason that Cook chooses as his central characters two young, perceptive, and stubbornly inquisitive medical students. Not important people within the rigid hierarchies of their hospitals or research centers, these characters are able to see and question what remains invisible to others. In *Coma* and *Terminal* it takes the rash and indignant innocence of youth to recognize that, in these instances at least, the sound of hoofbeats signals zebras—and not the anticipated horses at all.

As do many Cook novels, *Coma* and *Terminal* open with a short prologue in which the writer introduces his hospital setting. Both prologues feature patients who are undergoing treatment, and Cook carefully details their trepidations and concerns. The effect of this device is to acquaint readers with patients who will be victims and to establish early a grim, foreboding tone. He achieves this in *Coma* by engaging readers' sympathies for the plight of Nancy Greenly, a young college student who needs a routine dilation and curettage (D&C). Lying in the operating room, she feels vulnerable and frightened: "She hated and feared the hospital at that moment and wanted to scream, to run out of the room and down the corridor" (C, 1). Knowing that Greenly's impulse is a very common one, Cook uses it to build suspense. Indeed, complications occur during her operation, and when it is over her anesthesiologist fears that "something was wrong . . . something was very wrong" (C, 11). Similarly, in *Terminal* the prologue provides early moments of suspense. In four brief scenarios, Cook describes patients in serious trouble. When informed of his diagnosis, one of them moans, "Oh God! It's terminal, isn't it?" (T, 4). This patient's fear dramatically introduces the ominous word that Cook has chosen for his title.

After striking his prologues' initial suspenseful notes, Cook introduces readers to the protagonists of his novels. In Chapter 1 of *Coma*, Susan Wheeler awakes after a restless night filled with "bizarre, disturbing dreams in which she found herself wandering through foreign mazes searching for horrible goals" (C, 14). Although this anxiety dream expresses her nervous anticipation of the first day on her assigned clinical rotation, it also serves well to presage the terrifying events of the next three days of Wheeler's life.

Susan Wheeler has just completed the first two years of her medical training, "the basic science part taught in the lecture halls and science labs with books and other inanimate objects" (C, 12). Although she has excelled in her academic work, she realizes that it is "hardly proof against the uncertainties of actual patient care" (C, 14). These uncertainties are quickly manifested when Wheeler encounters, on her first morning, the limp form of Nancy Greenly, lying quietly in her vegetable state. Because her medical chart indicates that Greenly is twenty-three years old, exactly Wheeler's age, and that she was admitted to the hospital for treatment of vaginal bleeding, a condition Wheeler has also suffered, Susan Wheeler immediately feels a rush of empathy for this first patient. Although her colleagues dismiss her quite personal response as unprofessional, characteristic, perhaps, of a woman's feelings (she is the only female in her group), Wheeler is deeply troubled by Greenly's condition. The operating room "accident" seems to her too great a tragedy, too dear a waste of human life.

Coma's action is undeniably fast-paced, and Cook quickly adds further developments to his unfolding plot. Later on during her first day, when another patient Wheeler has assisted emerges from his minor knee operation in a comatose state, the sorrow Susan Wheeler felt over Nancy Greenly abruptly turns to anger. Horrified at what has happened, and determined to explain, at least to herself, the startling coincidences she has witnessed, Wheeler hastens to the medical library. Drawing upon her well-honed academic skills, she begins to gather information about coma and its incidence. When she realizes that the statistics at Boston Memorial are an anomaly, that the occurrences of anesthesia complications there are far more frequent than the norm, she begins to wonder if she is, perhaps, "on the track of a new disease or syndrome or drug reaction at the least" (C, 209). Intrigued by her preliminary investigations, Wheeler decides to use the medical problem she is now studying as the subject of her third-year research paper; she therefore turns to various doctors and hospital officials seeking advice and assistance in obtaining necessary medical records and charts. The treatment she receives at this point both bewilders and dismays her. Harshly reminded that she is but a mere student, and subjected, moreover, to the openly sexist attitudes of male doctors, Wheeler is ungraciously rebuffed by nearly everyone. Only the ordinarily gruff Dr. Stark affords her the courtesy of expressing interest in her project.

Undaunted by the generally unpromising responses to her inquiries, Wheeler remains convinced that her project is worth pursuing. When, on the third day of her short tenure at Boston Memorial, she is dismissed from her position at the hospital, and later stalked, threatened, and assaulted by a hired killer, it is quite clear that someone does not want her to investigate the coma cases. Of course, at this point it is also clear that the mystery that intrigues her is not a medical puzzle. Climbing up into the maze of pipes and ducts that lie above the ceiling of the hospital's operating rooms, Wheeler finds an extra valve attached to the oxygen pipe that leads to number eight.

Understanding now the possible means by which Nancy Greenly and other patients might have suffered cerebral hypoxia, Wheeler is nonetheless mystified as to motive. What could possibly explain these planned instances of coma in unrelated patients? It takes only a visit to the weirdly futuristic Jefferson Institute for her to find her answer. There she sees "more than a hundred patients" who are destined to be body parts. Lined up in a gigantic hall, they hang suspended from the ceiling, looking like "grotesque, horizontal, sleeping marionettes" (C, 267).

As *Coma* reaches its startling climax, Susan Wheeler knows how and why Boston Memorial's patients have been turned into vegetables. She does not, however, know who is responsible for these monstrous crimes. Remembering Dr. Stark's interest in her work, she decides to confide in him. In a nightmarish scene that takes place in Stark's office, horrifying realization dawns just before Wheeler falls into a drugged stupor. Dr. Stark, who has hastily decided that Wheeler needs an emergency appendectomy, has scheduled the operation for room number eight.

Coma ends in suspenseful ambiguity. When Susan Wheeler first discovered the special valve on room number eight's oxygen line, she told a friend, Mark Bellows, both what she had found and what its significance might be. Since she could not explain why anyone would wish to maliciously tamper with the oxygen line, he had then scoffed at her suspicions. Nevertheless, when Wheeler begins to experience cardiac irregularities during her operation, Bellows sees to it that the piped-in oxygen supply is suddenly cut off. Luckily, the anesthesiologist is able to move quickly to an emergency cylinder, and that is when Dr. Stark begins to grow nervous: "Of the operating team, only Stark knew that the patient's cardiac irregularities meant that she had received carbon monoxide with the mainline oxygen. But when that oxygen source failed, he couldn't be sure whether Susan had received enough of the deadly gas for his purposes" (C, 304). Whether or not Susan Wheeler regains consciousness, Dr. Stark is caught red-handed. It is an unhappy irony that Wheeler herself serves as the proof of his complicity.

Terminal's brilliant and cocky protagonist, Sean Murphy, thrives on the cutting edge of medical research. Twenty-six years old, he is in his third year of medical school at Harvard. Energetic and deeply in love with his work, he is, in addition to his medical training, completing a Ph.D. in molecular biology. His field, he believes, is the wave of the future: " 'This is an exciting time in biological science,' Sean said. 'The nineteenth century was the century for chemistry; the twentieth century was the century for physics. But the twenty-first century will belong to molecular biology; it's when all three—chemistry, physics, and biology— are going to merge. The results will be astounding, like science fiction come true' " (T, 219).

Terminal's plot depends upon Murphy's use of his intelligence and research skills, but it also requires other talents that he possesses; growing up in Boston's rough working-class neighborhoods, he has mastered such useful arts as picking locks and jump-starting cars. Emotionally as well as physically tough (he was an outstanding hockey player during his undergraduate years) and ever resourceful, Sean Murphy is ideally suited to stir up a great deal of trouble for the Forbes Cancer Center.

That Murphy might well turn out to be a source of trouble is readily apparent to both Dr. Mason and Dr. Deborah Levy, Head of Research, when he arrives in Miami, the site of the Forbes. (Murphy has arranged to secure a two-month research elective at the Forbes after hearing about its successful treatment of brain cancer.) Although Murphy informs them that his current research "involves the molecular basis of cancer" (*T*, 23), Mason and Levy assign him to a project that has nothing to do with the successful cancer treatment. Explaining that its experimental protocols are still under study and that the cancer-treating agent has not yet been patented, they forbid him entry to their special labs and access to their project. Indeed, the center's high-profile security staff keeps a close eye trained on Murphy.

As it happens, the security men are not the only people interested in watching Murphy. Sushita Industries, a gigantic Japanese electronics firm, has recently begun investing in biotechnology. Because it holds an interest in the Forbes, this corporation keeps an industrial spy on the premises. The Forbes employs its own industrial spy as well, and both of these characters are assigned to conduct background checks on Murphy. When they discover that Murphy and some of his associates have already owned and sold one successful biotech company, and, in fact, are trying to arrange financing for another, their watchfulness intensifies. (Sushita Industries, when it suspects instances of espionage, is in the habit of spiriting people off to Japan in the dead of the night.)

Unenthusiastically welcomed, carefully watched, and shunted off to a deserted lab, Sean Murphy is naturally puzzled by his reception. All in all, the Forbes Cancer Center strikes him as an exceptionally odd place. His curiosity is piqued, however; these obstacles are all that he really needs to excite his fighting Irish instincts. Although he has no intention of stealing the Forbes's cancer cure, he is very much interested in discovering how it works. Using samples acquired by his girlfriend, a nurse who has taken a job at the Forbes Hospital, Murphy begins to run analyses in his own lab. Like *Coma*'s Susan Wheeler, Sean Murphy certainly does not at first suspect that the hospital might be up to dirty tricks. There is no question, of course, that Mason and Levy have secrets to hide, but their behavior is thoroughly comprehensible if it is understood that they are protecting their claims to a major medical breakthrough.

The breakthrough, as he eventually discovers, is a hideous one indeed: "what makes this medulloblastoma cancer so different is that not only is it manmade, it's curable" (*T*, 340). Murphy's suspicions are aroused when his lab work indicates that each of the Forbes's brain cancer patients is immediately treated with the same specific agent. This procedure clearly contradicts all of his previous understanding of immunotherapy, for generally, as he notes, "It takes time to develop an antibody and everybody's tumor is antigenetically unique" (*T*, 340).

It remains for Sean Murphy to disclose his findings publicly, and in *Terminal*'s thrilling climax he does this in dramatic fashion. In *Coma*, the unnecessary operation performed on Susan Wheeler offered authorities clear proof of Dr. Stark's wrongful deeds. Murphy, too, needs physical proof to support his unlikely charges, and in *Terminal* this takes the form of a brain he has stolen from the body of one of the Forbes's victims. (One patient did not receive the center's treatment in time to save her from the complications resulting from her cancer.) Murphy relinquishes this evidence to authorities after he has attracted their attention (bomb squad and SWAT team included) by kidnapping Dr. and Mrs. Mason. Although his flamboyant actions have landed him in serious legal trouble, his brother is a lawyer, and possible charges of kidnapping, mayhem, or breaking and entering are eventually reduced to "disturbing the peace and malicious mischief" (*T*, 365).

CONVENTIONS OF THE THRILLER PLOT

Interested as he is in probing the ramifications of modern medical technology and, of course, in inviting readers to contemplate these issues themselves, Robin Cook finds the thriller genre a particularly appropriate forum. A mode of fiction that is, with its thrills and chills, written primarily to entertain, the thriller can also serve to enlighten readers about the possible importance of political, economic, or social trends around them. (George Orwell's classic thriller, *1984*, is an early example of one such cautionary tale.) Cook's choice of medical issues as subject matter lends itself well to the art of suspense, for the field of medicine has long been mysterious to the uninitiated. Even more essential, however, is the element of danger that Cook's subject inevitably invites. In the thriller there is always danger, and Cook has recognized its presence in the very practice of medicine, which rests upon a pact of trust: in his novels characters place their lives and well-being in the hands of doctors who then violate that trust. A truly terrifying danger, betrayal on this scale is indeed the stuff of thrillers, the more shocking when it occurs where it has been entirely unexpected. Certainly Cook's novels do remind readers that even the hallowed practice of medicine is, after all, a human (and hence corruptible) institution.

The thriller novel is a type of formula fiction, which is to say that it draws upon a repertoire of common strategies or conventions. Its design generally calls for fast-moving action, and Cook guarantees this effect in both *Coma* and *Terminal* by including subplots in addition to his suspenseful central action. In *Coma* an unsavory hospital maintenance worker has been stockpiling stolen drugs in doctors' lockers, and in *Terminal* another maintenance man, this time a true psychopath, has been "helping" patients with advanced breast cancer by putting them out of their misery. In both cases these lesser hospital mysteries link up with Cook's central plots while generally serving the purpose of heightening suspense as it builds within the novels.

Because thrillers draw from common formulas (including their frequent use of stock figures such as thugs or hired guns), writers who wish to avoid presenting readers with entirely predictable plots often work unusual variations on the standard ploys or even use them tongue-in-cheek. The thriller's conventional chase scene, for instance, provides Robin Cook with occasion for exuberant whim in *Terminal*. Sean Murphy has heard that a former brain cancer patient from the Forbes lives in Naples, on Florida's western coast. He and his girlfriend, Janet Reardon, therefore decide to take the road across the Everglades to interview this man. Meanwhile, Tom Widdicomb, the psychopath who kills breast cancer patients, has come to believe that Janet Reardon has grown suspicious of him; determined to kill her, he sets off in hot pursuit. Janet does not suspect Widdicomb, but Robert Harris, chief of Forbes's security, does, and he therefore joins the chase. The Japanese investors, having concluded that Murphy is a threat to their interests and thus looking for an opportunity to kidnap him, quickly get in line. (The chase vehicle, in this instance, is a large limousine.) Finally, Sterling Rombauer, the industrial spy hired by the Forbes to prevent Murphy's abduction, takes his place in the hilarious procession. Far indeed from an ordinary chase scene, Cook offers *Terminal*'s readers a Chinese box of chases. (Unfortunately, the television adaptation of *Terminal* omits this amusing scene.)

In *Coma*, Cook entertains readers with a similarly imaginative variation on a conventional thriller scene. Pursued by Dr. Stark's hired killer, Susan Wheeler seeks refuge in the medical school's deserted cadaver room.

She slips into the freezer, where the rows of "hanging bodies appeared like an army of ghouls" (C, 244). When the killer follows her, she sets a line of corpses moving along the track from which they are suspended: "Like a row of dominoes the entire group of bodies slid forward on their ball bearings." The horrified killer wildly fires his gun to no avail, for "two hundred pounds of frozen human meat slammed into the hit man, sending him crashing into the side of the freezer. In rapid succession the other corpses tumbled after the first, several falling from their hooks, creating a huddle of corpses, a tangle of frozen extremities" (C, 245). With this most unusual means of diverting the killer's attention, Wheeler is able to effect her escape while Cook offers his readers a spot of what can only be called graveyard humor.

Writers of suspense fiction aspire to keep their readers guessing and to provide them with plenty of surprises in their thrilling twists of plot. Robin Cook's use of subplots in *Coma* and *Terminal* is a device that serves this end. Readers of thriller novels, accustomed to the presence of imminent danger, to exciting chase scenes and hair-raisingly narrow escapes, expect writers to draw upon these familiar devices. Without question, Cook's ingenious manipulation of standard thriller conventions adds high entertainment value to his books. The subject matter of his novels, suggesting as it does the treachery of those sworn to the Hippocratic oath, must leave his readers wondering, "Could it happen?"

CHARACTER DEVELOPMENT

Writers of thriller fiction typically use characterization to support the narration of their suspenseful tales. Although Robin Cook elicits readers' sympathies for some of the patients portrayed in *Coma* and *Terminal* by providing sketches of their backgrounds and circumstances, the secondary characters in most of these novels are one-dimensional figures whose function in the books serves development of plot. *Coma's* Dr. Stark and *Terminal's* Dr. Levy, for example, can both be seen as types: like other fictional "mad scientists," these characters are ambitious and arrogant. They are representative of a misguided and unrestrained desire to achieve their singular goals, no matter what the cost to others. As Dr. Stark, enveloped in his massive egoism, remarks to Susan Wheeler, "We need people like myself, indeed like Leonardo da Vinci, willing to step beyond restrictive laws in order to insure progress" (C, 299). *Terminal's* psychopath, Tom Widdicomb, is clearly another character of this type.

Enclosed within his own paranoid delusions, communicating only with the dead mother he keeps preserved in his freezer, he can be regarded as a foil to the figures of the equally self-serving doctors.

While in their social standing characters like Dr. Stark or Dr. Levy are poles apart from the deranged Tom Widdicomb, they nevertheless share with him a twisted, antisocial purpose. Widdicomb, one of society's unfortunate misfits, has known only the "close, secret world" he has shared with his mother since his father died when he was four. Excluded by others ("his schoolmates had teased him mercilessly about his crossed eyes, chasing him home nearly every day" [*T*, 40]), his mother always reassured him, "We don't need other people." And thus the solitary Widdicomb has never found through the society of others a means to check his terrible delusions. Ironically, Dr. Stark and Dr. Levy are, for quite different reasons, also estranged from those around them. Their exiles, however, are self-imposed, born of their ambitions. At the pinnacle of their professions, the respected surgeon and researcher have become obsessed with their purely private goals. Unwilling to trust others (indeed, Stark believes that "he had to attend to everything if he wanted it done right" [*C*, 168]), these characters essentially remain aloof, treating their colleagues with disdain and their subordinates with contempt. Tom Widdicomb, the madman, does seem to sense that he is acting outside the law, but, in their own minds, Dr. Stark and Dr. Levy have clearly placed themselves above the law.

For Dr. Randolph Mason, Director of the Forbes, drastic measures seem the only means to salvage the financially troubled hospital that is at the center of his life. (Dr. Mason, who married the wealthy and promiscuous daughter of the cancer center's founder, quite obviously does not enjoy a fulfilling private life.) A sociable man, a glad-hander and dedicated fundraiser who is at ease on the speaker's circuit, Mason clearly enjoys the job of advancing his institution's interests. Bolstered therefore by Dr. Levy's assurance that the cancer she has created can easily be cured, he decides to take a calculated risk with the lives of individuals; in his mind, this risk is worth the greater good that his hospital and research center promise to achieve. A character who does seem, finally, to possess the social conscience that Dr. Levy lacks, Mason implicitly acknowledges, in his astonishing and public suicide, that the risk he took was wrong.

As the protagonists of *Coma* and *Terminal*, Susan Wheeler and Sean Murphy are the most fully developed characters in these books. Stock characters, such as the villains, can be usefully presented as stereotypical figures, but because readers' attention to the action within thriller novels centers on the perspectives and experiences of the main characters, writers generally invest these figures with individual attributes. Robin Cook usually affords his readers insights into the psychological makeup of his heroines and heroes. This strategy, which enables him to portray their personal interests and motivations, works effectively to establish a ready rapport with readers.

Susan Wheeler and Sean Murphy have much in common. Unquestionably intelligent, and eager to learn all they can from their medical training, they are both assertive figures: they both manage to thoroughly offend their superiors quite shortly after arriving on the job. Cook makes quite clear that their brash behavior, more than simply the impudence of their youth, results from the slight chips they carry on their shoulders. Susan Wheeler feels a special need to prove herself because she is highly aware of her status as a woman in a field thoroughly dominated by men. Sean Murphy, who was something of a juvenile delinquent, wants to earn the professional success that his alcoholic, working-class father was never able to achieve. Determined, therefore, to take full advantage of their educational experiences, these characters do not hestitate to ask prying questions, or, when the answers are not forthcoming, to seek those answers for themselves.

Although Susan Wheeler and Sean Murphy are both ambitious to prove themselves in their chosen fields, they plainly possess the high-minded idealism of the young. In this respect, their ambitions are to be seen in sharp contrast to those of their cynically self-serving hospital superiors. It is, of course, because she has been so moved by the plight of the coma patients that Susan Wheeler decides to study what has happened to them. And Sean Murphy has similarly altruistic reasons for wishing to learn the secret of the Forbes's cancer cure. As he explains to his girlfriend:

> This is what bugs me about the private funding of medical research. The goal becomes a return on investment instead of the public interest. The public weal is in second place if it is considered at all. This treatment for medulloblastoma undoubtedly has implications for all cancers, but the public is being denied that information. Never mind that most of the basic science these private labs base their work on was obtained through public funds at academic institutions. These

private places just take. They don't give. The public gets
cheated in the process. (*T*, 144)

Insightfully, Robin Cook links Wheeler's and Murphy's youthful idealism to a strong sense of indignation. Their anger at the injustices they
have witnessed inspires them to do all they can to expose the wicked
schemes devised by their elders.

Although they are not as fully developed characters as Wheeler and
Murphy, two other figures play significant roles in *Coma* and *Terminal*.
Mark Bellows, a surgical resident at *Coma*'s Boston Memorial Hospital,
and Janet Reardon, the nurse who follows Sean Murphy to the Forbes
in *Terminal*, are Wheeler's and Murphy's romantic partners in the books.
Within the design of the plots, these characters serve as sidekicks, as-
sisting the protagonists in their investigations. Bellows covers for
Wheeler when she skips scheduled lectures to pursue her library research. Although he is at first skeptical about the plot she believes she
has uncovered, he quickly changes his mind when she is abruptly rushed
into the operating theatre. It is thus Bellows who comes to her rescue by
closing off the pipe that is carrying carbon monoxide to her lungs. Janet
Reardon, who is assigned to care for some of the medulloblastoma patients at the Forbes, proves to be most helpful to Sean Murphy. Engaging
in a bit of espionage herself, she is able to obtain the medical charts and
treatment samples that he needs to study the cancer cases. Fascinated by
what she has learned about medical research, Reardon decides, at the
end of *Terminal*, that she too would like to go to medical school.

Besides serving as assistants to the novels' protagonists, their romantic
partners contribute much to Cook's strategies for characterizing the central figures in the books. In both *Coma* and *Terminal*, the overly confident
young male partners learn through experience to recognize the strengths
of their female companions. *Coma*'s Mark Bellows, who is a bright and
determinedly ambitious fellow, already shows in his medical career a
marked tendency to regard his patients as scientific problems rather than
as people. This failing stands in sharp contrast to Susan Wheeler's attitude, and when events bear out the value of her inquisitive form of
attention to others, Bellows comes to learn a hard lesson about the cost
of depersonalizing the patients that he serves. In *Terminal*, it is the stead-
fast presence of Janet Reardon that eventually serves to bring about the
emotional maturation of the novel's central character. Intellectually wise,
Sean Murphy is nonetheless reluctant to finally grow up, to accept the
responsibility of a personal obligation. Reardon, who understands the

inclinations of both her heart and her mind, provides Murphy with a
model of commitment. In quietly following her own firm resolves, Reardon instructs Murphy in the value of a personal loyalty, one that he
finally recognizes he does wish to share.

THEMATIC ISSUES

Robin Cook closes *Coma* with an author's note in which he states: "This
novel was conceived as an entertainment, but it is not science fiction. Its
implications are scary because they are possible, perhaps even probable"
(*C*, 306). Cook is here referring, of course, to the scenario of the black
market trade in human organs that he has envisioned in his novel. His
remark, however, can be generally applied to the themes of most of his
books. Worried about the ways in which economic interests increasingly
control or even drive policies within the practice of medicine, Cook is
interested in probing the depths of human arrogance or greed. (Simply
because medicine is a field dedicated to the welfare of the public does
not, as Cook knows, guarantee that its practitioners will be immune to
these human faults.) His novels expose technological possibilities that
are mainly held in check by assumptions of good will. The law, he believes, has not adequately addressed a growing need for transplant organs, and the long lists of those who currently await transplants suggest
that he is right. Cook fears that when demand is far greater than supply,
the risk of audacious entrepreneurialism becomes ever higher. This process is, to some degree, already under way, for, as he points out,
"blood—which may be considered as an organ—is routinely bought and
sold" (*C*, 306).

In *Terminal* Cook continues to explore the dangers associated with a
market economy in medicine. Here, however, in a fiendish twisting of
the ordinary laws of supply and demand, he presents a scenario similar
to the one he earlier proposed in *Vital Signs*: the Forbes Cancer Center
supplies the medical services for which it has created its own demand.
The Forbes Center's motive in doing this speaks, of course, to another
economic pressure that today troubles the medical profession. As costs
have risen and funding sources have grown more scarce, independent
hospitals and research centers have struggled to survive. The Forbes's
diabolical scheme to acquire financial support signals the severity of this
problem. Sean Murphy realizes this near the end of *Terminal* when he
observes that "specialty hospitals and associated research centers have
become increasingly desperate as NIH grants are getting harder and

harder to come by. Creating a group of wealthy, grateful patients is a good way to make it through to the twenty-first century" (*T*, 342).

In *Coma*'s author's note, Robin Cook recommends books and articles that might interest readers who wish to pursue further the themes that his novel introduces. In addition to studies of the social and legal problems associated with organ transplants, he recommends a book that treats general issues of medical policy and an article that examines the particular problems women face when they choose medical careers. Although the reference works Cook describes are perhaps somewhat dated by now, the medical issues they explore most certainly are not. *Terminal*, written sixteen years after *Coma*, continues Cook's ongoing study of medical policy problems in its focus on the secrecy that so often cloaks medical research. As Sean Murphy is aware, the kind of breakthrough in cancer treatment that the Forbes Center pretended to have discovered should have been made available to other interested researchers. Instead, the desire to patent and then reap the financial rewards of medical technology exerts an economic pressure that results in widespread practice of the kind of secrecy that is so carefully maintained at the Forbes.

As to Cook's interest in the problem of sexism within the medical profession, this is a theme that recurs throughout the body of his fiction. Although some of the problems Susan Wheeler encounters when she is assigned to Boston Memorial have no doubt been ameliorated since *Coma*'s publication (Wheeler discovers early in the novel that the hospital provides no changing room for female physicians), Robin Cook remains highly aware of women's efforts to improve their positions within the professional workplace. For his part, he has written sympathetically about the ways women in medicine have experienced gender discrimination, and he has introduced in his fiction a long line of strong female protagonists, among whom Susan Wheeler is merely the first. When, at the end of *Terminal*, he describes Janet Reardon's newfound resolution to pursue the challenges of advanced medical study and research, he offers yet another note of encouragement to women. Imagining the intellectually stimulating possibilities that now lie before her, Reardon says, "I think I want to be a part of it" (*T*, 367).

ALTERNATIVE PERSPECTIVE: CULTURAL CRITICISM

It is through cultural criticism that the field of literary studies has in recent years begun to approach the formal study of popular novels like those written by Robin Cook. Over the last thirty years, literary critics and theorists have paid increasing attention to the work of many writers who use the popular genres to explore contemporary social interests while entertaining their readers. While a great number of these studies have focused on the work of those writing in the detective/mystery genre, the books in this series of critical companions also consider writers of romance, science fiction, and suspense. Because one of the cultural critic's fascinations lies in questions about what it is that people do read, the popular genres are an obvious site of interest.

In its opposition to a highly traditional and therefore elitist attitude toward definitions of what constitutes a society's culture, cultural criticism works to break down the old boundaries that in the past have separated "high culture" from so-called popular culture. Cultural critics, in fact, challenge the very notion that any society possesses a single, uniform tradition that might be defined as its culture. Rather, cultural critics see societies as being composed of multiple, interactive, and constantly changing elements of cultural significance.

In questioning traditional assumptions of what defines a culture, those cultural critics who focus on the study of literature have rejected the categorical elevation of the group of literary works that has frequently been called "the classics" or "the Great Books." These texts, defined by Matthew Arnold toward the end of the nineteenth century as "the best that is known and thought in the world," were for many years singled out as representative of Western society's "high" literary culture and were therefore placed at the center of most school curricula. Interested in a broader conception of culture than that typically defined by school experience, cultural critics study the ways in which a great variety of texts play interesting roles within society in general. Indeed, these critics see literary works in the cultural context of a highly complex society, and in doing this they are able to frame extremely provocative questions about people's reading: Why, for example, do medical thrillers attract significant numbers of readers? Why is the suspense novel so satisfying a source of entertainment? What does this genre (or, for that matter, any of the other popular genres) say to readers about the values, beliefs, or economic/political conditions of the society in which they live? Can what people read speak to who they are or where their society is going— or what they desire or, perhaps, fear?

Interested in all these questions and many others, cultural critics do not practice a single methodology in their efforts to identify expressions of meaning within the culture. Rather, they draw upon a variety of analytical strategies and, as is appropriate to their interests, they address a broad range of subjects. Cultural critics have written about the pop star Madonna as a capitalist icon, and they have used literary theories of drama to scrutinize the effects produced in television commercials. From their perspective, all aspects of culture, past as well as present, are legitimate subjects for analysis and critique.

As cultural criticism has established itself within academic institutions, it has clearly articulated the interdisciplinary nature of its focus. Courses in film studies, for example, have been introduced on many college campuses, and these have been offered by a wide variety of departments (communications, sociology, and English departments, among others, have designed courses that explore the significance of film as cultural artifact). Women's studies is generally an interdisciplinary field whose central concern is cultural criticism.

As is perhaps obvious, many of the questions cultural critics ask lead to the examination of issues of political interest. In attempting to understand the complex workings of culture and its institutions, critics interrogate the assumptions that shape social behavior. This questioning reveals patterns of power distribution among social organizations and often unmasks, in particular, the nature of the authority vested in long-standing institutions. The law, education systems, and traditional gender roles are among the many institutions that have been subjected to the critiques of cultural analysis. In his fiction, Robin Cook offers readers a most interesting critique of medicine as institution. Looking at the culture of medicine within the context of society's economy of needs, he expresses concerns about the development of certain trends within its practice.

Like the law, medicine in Western societies has long been regarded as an austere profession, one that seems automatically to command both respect and admiration. Indeed, it is one of the small number of professions about which the word *mystery* is used in the special sense that denotes, in the words of *The American Heritage College Dictionary*, "the skills, lore, or practices that are peculiar to a particular activity or group and are regarded as the special province of initiates." Traditionally, it has been the knowledge of this special lore (or even art) that, along with medicine's professed dedication to the service of the common good, has set apart its practitioners as members of an honored occupation. Those with positions held in high esteem by their societies are often accorded special privileges or powers, and this has certainly been true of the field of medicine, for physicians in Western societies have long enjoyed both privilege and power.

Along with the privileges that respect and trust afford, however, come expectations of responsibility, and about his sense that doctors have begun to abrogate their responsibilities Robin Cook has much to say. He knows that if doctors fail to acknowledge the obligations implied by their bargain with society, they will surely squander the respect and trust that they have traditionally enjoyed.

The dangers that Cook sees are twofold, related to both the privilege and the power that doctors have been granted. As medicine increasingly claims a place in today's market economy, Cook fears that physicians themselves are becoming more and more absorbed with the material benefits that naturally accrue by dint of their special status. Taking their privileges for granted, the doctors who succumb to greed are mainly interested in capitalizing on the mysteries of their elect profession. (Doctors, of course, are not alone in a culture that values the material so highly. They are, however, clearly positioned to exercise control over a necessary commodity.) For those who become enchanted with the power of their position, the secret knowledge that they possess becomes a source of untoward pride and satisfaction. Cook believes that through their arrogance these doctors too can break their social contract. In distancing themselves from the immediate obligations defined by their profession, physicians like Dr. Stark enter into the Faustian bargain that is portrayed so often in science fiction.

In his efforts to draw public attention to current developments within the field of medicine, Robin Cook has done much to demystify its practice. In his novels he employs the medical terminology that doctors actually use. His assumption, clearly, is that this vocabulary should be available to all and not the preserve of a select few. His specific subject matter, so often dramatically presented in the form of conspiracy plots, acquaints readers with current technology while inviting them to ponder the ethical implications of its use. Cook obviously believes that policies determining the use of new technologies should be completely open to public debate. His depiction of villainy within the sacred halls of medicine serves as a caveat to those who would forget that it, too, is a very human institution. Finally, Cook's revelations about women's experiences within the medical profession are not to be overlooked; as he demonstrates in *Coma*, the field of medicine can no longer be regarded as a paternalistic cult.

For additional discussion of insights available through cultural criticism, see the concluding sections of Chapters 6 and 8.

Brain
(1981)

Robin Cook's fourth novel, *Brain* (1981), marks his return after a brief hiatus to the successful suspense formula he first devised in *Coma*. After taking time out to write a very different kind of thriller, *Sphinx*, Cook decided to settle on the medical mystery as his chosen genre. (*Sphinx*, a modern intrigue featuring new revelations about King Tut's tomb, spoke to one of Cook's several personal interests, Egyptology; however, his long series of subsequent medical thrillers has most characteristically expressed his continuing fascination with medicine, his own original profession.) Sometimes called the "techno-thriller," or even the "medstery" (medical mystery), Cook's work has been deeply influential in shaping a new subgenre of the suspense novel. Besides regularly entertaining his many avid readers, Cook has used the medium of popular fiction to address a variety of social problems associated with health care issues.

Brain features one of Robin Cook's several conspiracy plots; whereas many of the later novels portray conspiracies largely inspired by corporate greed, his earliest medical thrillers, *Coma* and *Brain*, present readers with conspiracies centered upon the visions of egomaniacal scientists grasping for Faustian knowledge and power. *Brain*'s Dr. William Michaels, a brilliant young computer wizard, seeks the ultimate achievement within his field, the creation of true artificial intelligence. To obtain his ambitious goal, Michaels is perfectly willing to sacrifice living human subjects in the name of science. When his early work provides remarkably promising results, results applicable to the field of weaponry, the U.S. government's Defense Department quickly responds, sending teams of government agents to blanket the project, as Michaels says, "with the highest level of security they've ever amassed, even more than the Manhattan Project back when the atomic bomb was being created" (293). Thus it happens that *Brain*'s unsuspecting protagonist, neuroradiologist Dr. Martin Philips, finds himself enmeshed in a nightmarish government conspiracy to cover up the use of unacceptable research protocols.

THE APPEAL OF THE MEDICAL THRILLER

Robin Cook's genre combines the mystery (most of his novels feature murders) with the suspenseful action offered by novels of political intrigue (his early plotting strategies are modeled on those of the popular thriller *Seven Days in May*). The conspiracy motif he frequently employs introduces the frightening sense of helplessness his novels generally evoke, and his use of the world of medicine as his setting eerily enhances that effect. Medicine is by its very nature a profession that rests upon the public's trust, and Cook's grim reminder that such trust is by no means inviolate naturally leaves his readers ill at ease. As Joseph McLellan has aptly noted, "Cook discovered some time ago that for the average person an active, well-lit modern hospital is infinitely spookier than a dark old abandoned house" (McLellan, C4). *Brain*, like *Coma*, effectively uses Cook's persuasively realistic depiction of hospital routine to engulf readers in a fictional scenario that is, as *Los Angeles Times* reviewer Rosalind Smith asserts, "unnervingly plausible, deeply frightening—and possibly prophetic" (R. Smith, 10:1).

Skillfully manipulating suspense strategies that blend elements of mystery, the political intrigue of conspiracy, and the horrors of medical technology run amok, Cook presents *Brain*'s readers with a thoroughly engrossing tale. The novel's mystery involves the strange disappearance of young women who, after receiving gynecological care at Hobson University Medical Center's women's clinic, have developed severe neurological problems. Dr. Philips, who wonders if these women's brain scans might indicate the presence of early stages of multiple sclerosis, attempts in vain to track them down. When he finally locates one of them, a young woman who died while undergoing a temporal lobectomy, he finds, to his great astonishment, that her brain has been removed. The novel thus offers plenty of puzzles to confound the mystery fan: what is the fate of seventeen young women who seemingly have vanished? What is the link between the women's visits to the clinic and the medical problems they later develop? And finally, yet one more perplexing problem—what has become of Lisa Marino's brain?

Preoccupied with the hospital mysteries he is attempting to unravel, Dr. Martin Philips has no suspicion whatsoever of government complicity until the horrifying realization dawns, during an especially gripping chase scene, that the FBI intends to kill him. Through this shocking plot development (for both protagonist and reader), *Brain*'s suspense deepens as Cook reveals the political intrigue that underlies the action. In an author's note that accompanies the text of the story, Cook comments on the circumstances that inspired the conspiracy angle. Citing numerous examples of recent medical experiments that have violated the ethical standards that obtain to human subjects, Cook encourages his reading audience to take an interest in this problem. Although, as he clearly states, "it would be irresponsible to suggest that the majority of research involving humans in the United States is based on unethical standards," nonetheless, "the fact that there is a significant minority is frightening and demands attention from the public" (305). Because most of the actual experimental studies Cook describes "were knowingly supported by U.S. government agencies" (304), the appearance of the FBI in *Brain* does not, unfortunately, strike the reader as being too far-fetched. As is his common practice, Cook includes a short bibliography for those interested in further reading on this topic.

In addition to mystery and conspiracy, *Brain* offers its reading audience a close-up view of authentic medical issues and procedures. This third dimension of the medical thriller is one that particularly fascinates Robin Cook's many devoted readers. While his novels are unfailingly informative about the larger world of current health care practices, they also address personal apprehensions about illness, mortality, and the welfare of the body. In other words, Cook understands that portraying the position of the layperson (or the patient) vis-à-vis the specialized perspective of medical professionals lends a special drama to his suspenseful hospital scenes. For example, the fourth chapter of *Brain*, which presents a technically accurate step-by-step account of Lisa Marino's delicate brain surgery, opens by vividly depicting the patient's thoughts and understandable trepidations: as she prepares to face her "upcoming ordeal," Marino recognizes that "her central being was going to be rudely cracked open and violated. Not just a peripheral part of her, like a foot or an arm, but her head . . . where her personality and very soul resided. Would she be the same person afterward?" (38).

The frightening question Lisa Marino poses for herself is very much to the point within the plots of Cook's first two medical thrillers, for both *Brain* and *Coma* startle readers by envisioning the terrifying prospect of the loss of sense of self. When Robin Cook chose the word *coma* as the title of his first medical thriller, he drew upon a term guaranteed to inspire dread in the imaginations of his readers. *Coma*'s plot, presenting the spectacle of patients who never again awake after undergoing anesthesia, brings to horrible realization an ever present fear that haunts those who face the experience of anesthesia. Similarly, *Brain*'s plot exploits a not uncommon morbid anxiety about the loss of conscious control: the unfortunate victims of Michaels's experimental research suffer frighteningly sudden (and often embarrassingly public) seizures. While the spectacle of these seizures is terrifying in itself, Michaels's ultimate design calls for possession of the victims' brains—and thus possession as well of the autonomous identities their owners once enjoyed. *Coma*'s victims lose their selfhood through the course of their brain deaths, but in *Brain*'s shocking twist of plot, victims are reduced to nothing more than brains.

Cook takes his novel's epigraph from Hippocrates, the Greek physician who has been called the "Father of Medicine": "From the brain, and from the brain only, arise our pleasures, joys, laughter and jests, as well as our sorrows, pains, griefs and tears." This epigraph, as it happens, serves a deeply ironic purpose within the context of the plight of Michaels's victims. Suspended in cylinders of cerebrospinal fluid, these brains that once were people are stimulated by electrodes embedded in their pleasure centers. Existing, then, only to respond to pleasure, the unwitting research subjects have been cruelly denied the full range of human experiences enumerated by Hippocrates. They too, in a fashion quite different from *Coma*'s patients, have lost their sense of selfhood.

PLOT DEVELOPMENT

Like *Coma*, *Brain* is shrewdly plotted to maintain its nonstop suspenseful action. Most of the novel's events occur within a large university research hospital, and the first scene takes place on the steps of that hospital, where Katherine Collins, reluctant to enter the building, reads the inscription above the door: "For the Sick and Infirm of the City of New York" (1). Filled with dread about the prospect of revisiting the hospital's "impersonal and cold" (5) women's clinic, Collins reflects that the sign "should have read, 'Abandon All Hope Ye Who Enter Here' " (1). Indeed, the atmosphere within the hospital is expressed in hellish images that lend their weight to the heavy cloud of foreboding that hangs over Collins. She sees about her "distorted faces, scaly rashes and oozing eruptions" in a crowd that brings to mind a "painting by Brueghel" (5). Readers are thus quickly immersed in the ominous aura that surrounds Hobson University Medical Center, and by the end of the first chapter, when she is swept away by two men dressed in white, it is readily apparent that readers must certainly abandon all hope for Katherine Collins—who, as it turns out, is fated to be one of the young women mercilessly sacrificed on the altar of scientific progress.

Brain's plot employs the episodic narrative structure that is commonplace in suspense fiction. Moving back and forth between scenes that feature the harrowing experiences of the novel's hapless victims and those that focus on the protagonist's continuing efforts to piece together the curious puzzle that he has happened to uncover, Cook unfolds a tale that grows increasingly sinister as its mysteries deepen. When, in the thrilling climax, Michaels's horrendous secret is at last revealed, readers recognize that all the clues Cook has cleverly planted within the story at last fall neatly into place.

Chapter 3 introduces readers to all the novel's most important characters: the protagonist and his lover, and the computer scientist who is finally revealed to be a rogue. *Brain*'s central character, Dr. Martin Philips (Assistant Chief of Neuroradiology at Hobson), is an exceptionally busy man. In picturing Philips's constant movement among his administrative duties, his regular hospital work (as a neuroradiologist, Philips reads and interprets X-rays and CAT scans), and his teaching responsibilities, Cook successfully captures the ambiance of a bustling research hospital. As if Philips's work were not enough to occupy his full attention, the hospital's various political intrigues also make their demands upon his time.

Whenever he can find a spare moment, Philips turns his attention to the research project that has recently become his central interest. Working with Dr. Michaels from the hospital's computer center, Philips is attempting to design a computer program that can analyze and interpret X-rays. The hope is that such a program, one capable of performing pattern recognition, would prove to be more efficient than human interpretation—which, unfortunately for patients, is sometimes fallible. (In fact, Philips himself estimates that the diagnostic work of exceptionally skilled radiologists is accurate only about 75 percent of the time.) Obviously, a computerized reading technique that could produce 100 percent efficiency would be tremendously valuable to medical science.

It is while he is testing the new computer program that Philips, quite ironically, takes note of the anomaly that recurs in the brain scans of the young women. The program, constructed to learn from Philips's expert input, requests additional information about variations in the X-rays it is reading; the particular density pattern in question is very subtle, but Philips quickly realizes that he (even with his immense experience and expertise) does not recognize its significance. He is, therefore, extremely eager to find a satisfactory explanation for himself. What he does not know, of course, is that his computer program is registering the effects of Dr. Michaels's experiment: the women's brain scans show the traces of the radioactive glucose with which they have been secretly injected during their visits to the women's clinic.

Chapter 3 also offers readers a fleeting encounter with Dr. Michaels, the novel's ruthlessly purposeful villain. Michaels is presented in the early pages of the book as a brilliant, hard-working, and ambitious figure. Readers, of course, have no means to calculate the full range of his ambitions until *Brain*'s startling climax reveals that his collaboration with Dr. Philips focuses, in fact, on only one of the many applications of his much larger project. To create a computer that thinks, that learns and reasons and generally functions on the model of the human brain, Dr. Michaels requires extensive knowledge of the neural pathways of the brain. By connecting the victims' peripheral sensory nerves to electrodes, Michaels uses their brains as feedback systems that can report on their own various functions. As he says about the design of his experiment, "We've used the human brain to study itself" (288). The novel's climactic scenario unquestionably presents the vision of a scientific experiment that echoes a literary tradition established by Mary Shelley; the crucial difference, however, between the gruesome work performed by William Michaels and that of Victor Frankenstein is strikingly noteworthy: unlike Frankenstein, who gathers the requisite body parts from the graves of the dead, Michaels assembles his artificial creation by using living human organs. Mary Shelley chose to leave a vision of the details of her scientist's lab to her reader's imaginations. The hideous laboratory scene that Cook describes in *Brain* is one that few readers would ever be able to imagine—and one that they almost certainly will find impossible to forget.

The final character who plays an important role in plot development is Dr. Denise Sanger, a young resident in radiology who is Dr. Philips's lover. Like the other young women featured in *Brain*'s plot, Dr. Sanger is eventually victimized by William Michaels. Although she is not subjected to his macabre experiment, she does fall prey to the deadly conspiracy that unfolds around it. It is Denise Sanger who is held hostage while the FBI team searches for Dr. Philips, and when, at the novel's climax, Philips is forced to promise that he will not reveal what he now knows about the origin of Michaels's scientific breakthrough, it is Sanger's very life that hangs upon that promise.

With *Brain*'s climax, then, a monstrous trap closes upon Dr. Philips. He learns, among the other dramatic revelations of this scene, that he has been under close government surveillance for over a year; he unwittingly endangered himself (and, of course, Dr. Sanger) when he began to conduct inquiries into the nature of the peculiar brain scans of the missing women. Now that he has found the remains of the women and thus solved the mystery he once doggedly pursued, the time has come for him to face the moral consequences that attend upon his knowledge. The choice Michaels offers him is clear. As he says, "You're going to have to decide if you can live with this whole affair" (293). If Philips cannot promise to swear himself to silence, then he and Sanger, perceived to be national security risks, will both be "liquidated" by the FBI.

Philips is utterly repulsed by the great sacrifice of individual lives that he has witnessed, but, ironically, it is his turn to weigh the value of a single human life. Acknowledging his responsibility for the well-being of Denise Sanger, he clearly recognizes that "if individual life was important, then so was hers" (297). He therefore acquiesces to the demands of those who hold him in their power, but even as he does this, he reminds himself that "they had him shackled for the moment, but he would find a way to break their hold someday, even if it took years" (287). Dr. Philips's private resolve thus affords him some small means to combat his suffocating sense of entrapment.

Brain's narrative action concludes with its startling climax, but one final chapter presents readers with a dramatic newspaper story attributed to the *New York Times*. With a headline that reads "Scientist Shocks Scientific Community; Seeks Political Asylum in Sweden" (299), the news account announces that Dr. Philips has indeed kept the vow he has made to himself. Cook's use of the fictional news report, which serves as a kind of epilogue to the novel, allows him finally to untangle the web of conspiracy in which he has enmeshed his protagonist. Readers learn that both Dr. Martin Philips and his new wife, Dr. Denise Sanger, have been granted political asylum with the Swedish government's protection and that "within twenty-four hours a document written by Dr. Philips will be released for the international community outlining a gross abrogation of human rights perpetrated under the aegis of medical experimentation" (300). The document, when it is released, will undoubtedly create an immense political uproar, for rumors are rampant that Dr. Philips will likely be the recipient of a Nobel Prize for Medicine.

For its first 240 pages, *Brain*'s ingenious plot assumes the shape of the murder mystery. Robin Cook, however, is a writer who notably delights in finding occasion to take his readers by surprise. Drawing upon one of suspense fiction's traditional conventions, he uses a thrilling chase scene to turn the direction of his plot. When Dr. Philips, who has witnessed the murder of a hospital employee, realizes that the killers from whom he is fleeing are indeed agents from the FBI, he understands at once that there is more afoot than murder. Readers, who have to this point in the novel puzzled over possible motives for the murders of a group of unrelated women, are quite ready to agree. Thus Cook's shocking twist of plot turns out to make its own startlingly unexpected sense. With the novel's dramatic chase scene, Philips steps directly into the terrible trap that awaits him.

CHARACTER DEVELOPMENT

Brain's jarring impact clearly resides in the story that the novel tells and in the drama inherent in its strikingly realistic setting. Rather than investing readers' attention in the narrative development of multidimensional characters, Cook chooses in this novel to draw upon stereotypical figures whose attitudes and actions reflect the roles they play within the tale. Thus Dr. Philips is an embodiment of the scientist who possesses an ethical sensibility, and Dr. Michaels is the embodiment of literature's mad scientist, the Faustian figure who values knowledge and mastery above all else. Although several reviewers comment on Cook's use of stereotypical characters in *Brain* (the *San Francisco Chronicle*'s William Hogan states that "the characters here tend to be 'Dr. Kildare' stock"), most agree with Rosalind Smith, who noted that "superficial characterizations do not significantly detract from the impact of *Brain* because the characters in mysteries are traditionally just devices to advance the plot." Indeed, Smith goes on to make a most interesting observation when she claims that "medical procedure assumes the importance of character and so dominates the narrative that absence of believable human beings is not terminal" (R. Smith, 10:1).

Robin Cook's ability to render the details of his hospital settings with extraordinary accuracy has been remarked throughout the course of his writing career. Capturing both the point of view of the patient and that of the medical professional, he presents a world whose rich texture is vibrant with the drama of human fears, ambitions, and moral dilemmas. In many of his novels, and certainly in *Brain*, Cook is more interested in depicting the larger worlds of medicine and medical research than he is in exploring the personal stories of the characters who populate those worlds. In other words, a character like Dr. Michaels, *Brain*'s villain, is necessary to a plot that portrays the excesses of scientists driven by their inordinate ambitions, but the character himself merely represents these impulses within the world of science—readers are not privy to Dr. Michaels's inner thoughts or motivations, and *Brain* does not narrate the story of his personal quest for knowledge. Instead, casting Michaels in the role that has already been defined by such well-known literary figures as Faust or Frankenstein, Cook concentrates on the repercussions of the presence of a Faustian desire within the context of the modern world of science.

Similarly, the other characters in *Brain* represent additional features of the world characterized by the novel. The childish and tyrannically arrogant brain surgeon, Dr. Mannerheim, is a readily recognizable type: a preening prima donna, Mannerheim is the man of medicine who glories in the special power that his skill and position quite naturally afford him. (For a full-blown study of this character type, see Cook's novel *Godplayer*.) The hospital administrator, conservative and sensitive to all appearances of trouble or impropriety, represents the bureaucratic interests that work to maintain authority over the distribution of power and privilege within the medical establishment. Other figures—Philips's competent and sympathetic secretary, the rude receptionist in the women's clinic, or the attentive and conscientious anesthesiologist, Dr. Ranade—are all character types that together give shape to the microcosm that Cook methodically fashions in *Brain*.

Although Dr. Philips's most significant role is serving as the voice that speaks for scruples in the practice of scientific research, he also plays a part in the world of hospital experience that is configured by the book. A dedicated professional who is entering early middle age (he is forty-one years old), Dr. Philips has reached a discomforting stage in his medical career. Overburdened by his many bureaucratic responsibilities and tired of the relentless routine he has practiced for many years, he is distinctly interested in finding a new direction for his life. He has begun to feel, in other words, that the constant demands of his work have come to occupy his time completely. Dr. Philips's first marriage fell prey to his commitment to his work, and he is therefore determined that his relationship with Sanger should not suffer a similar fate. Although hospital authorities are obviously grooming Philips to eventually step into a high administrative post, he has begun to imagine a new life focused on his research: "Philips occasionally let himself dream of having his own research department, and even the Nobel Prize" (22). Cook's portrait of his protagonist thus affords readers a glimpse of the workings of hospital politics as well as an understanding of some of the personal costs the conscientious medical professional must often pay in service to a particularly consuming occupation.

In keeping with the sympathetic roles they play within *Brain*'s mesmerizing plot, Martin Philips and Denise Sanger are drawn as exceptionally attractive characters. Rosalind Smith summarizes Cook's portraits of these figures well: "Philips is as brave, dedicated and uncorruptible as he is handsome. Philips' colleague and lover, Dr. Denise Sanger, looks and acts like a Charlie's Angel in a lab coat. Their relationship is literally too good to be true but it does have simple romantic appeal" (R. Smith, 10:1). Part of the appeal of this relationship clearly lies in the fact that Philips and Sanger, in both their private and professional relationships, respond to one another as equals. Working closely together each day, the two doctors make a thoroughly well-matched team, and even though Sanger is several years younger than Philips, her professional credentials (she was first in her graduating class) are as impeccable as his own.

Dr. William Michaels is *Brain*'s contemporary incarnation of Victor Frankenstein. (Interestingly, the Frankensteinian impulse to bestow being upon a newly constructed form of intelligence is also central to the plot of Cook's tenth novel, *Mutation*.) Michaels desires to be the creator, the mastermind behind the fashioning of an artificial intelligence. In a striking reversal of Mary Shelley's original scheme, Cook's scientist uses living organs to produce his inanimate creation—whereas Frankenstein, of course, creates a living creature from an assemblage of completely inanimate parts. Like Victor Frankenstein, however, Michaels envisions his creation as a boon to humankind, and, like Frankenstein as well, he fails to anticipate that his creation might turn out to be a monster. Michaels's particular monster takes the form of the conspiracy that enshrouds his wicked work; in the end, his monster must destroy him— just as surely as Frankenstein's handiwork ineluctably becomes the instrument of his undoing.

Readers actually see little of Dr. Michaels until the climactic scene wherein he introduces Dr. Philips to the horrors housed within his secret lab. Like Philips, readers are thus unaware, until *Brain*'s climax, of Michaels's willingness to sacrifice human lives in the name of science. Appropriately enough, Michaels remains a disturbingly shadowy figure, an enigmatic presence whose evil actions can be perceived as speaking conclusively for themselves. The few idiosyncratic details Cook provides (his puckish sense of humor, for example) only add to the disconcerting impression that Dr. Michaels leaves. Philips, who has previously known nothing of Michaels's private life, does learn in the novel's final scene that it was Michaels's wife, the woman who runs the gynecology clinic, who selected the healthy patients who were then doomed to be used in her husband's secret experiment. (It was also this woman, the sinister Ms. Blackman, who injected the young women with a radioactive substance during their visits to the clinic.)

In interesting ways, Robin Cook's use of stereotypical characters well suits his objective of rendering a memorably authentic hospital scene. As types, his characters all play useful roles within their setting without distracting from the integrity of its overall effect. A microcosm, after all, is composed of elements of the typical, and the fullness of the slice of hospital life that Cook offers his readers depends upon his populating his fictional world with figures who broadly represent features of the common hospital experience. Cook is deft at depicting characters of this sort—with the result, as Rosalind Smith has suggested, that the medical world he portrays seems itself to assume the status of character within *Brain*'s pages.

THEMATIC ISSUES

As Cook's author's note indicates, *Brain* focuses on some of the modern implications of humankind's age-old quest for knowledge, for an understanding and a mastery of the workings of the physical environment. Research scientists today carry on the quests earlier envisioned by writers who explored the dreams and the ambitions of a Faust or a Victor Frankenstein, and Cook knows that the notes of warning sounded by such writers have not become outdated. *Brain* thus issues its own warning, about the alluring power that knowledge so often seems to promise and about the dangers of the temptation to pursue knowledge beyond the moral and ethical limits established by societies.

The literary character Faust recognized that knowledge can bring with it a ready claim to power. In *Brain* it is indeed that claim to power that blinds the representatives of government to the unethical means by which the scientist has obtained his knowledge of the functions of the human brain. Michaels himself argues that his "results justify the methods", and the Defense Department apparently agrees. Michaels's technological breakthrough in artificial intelligence thus offers, for the price of the lives of the seventeen young women, the "guarantee of the defense superiority of the United States" (293). The loss of the few, then, can be rationalized by Michaels and others as the gain of the many, but to a scientist (and moralist) like Philips, the government's conspiracy is nothing less than a true Faustian bargain: in his view, the government that sanctions Michaels's work in its eager bid for power has also quite clearly forfeited its soul. With this in mind, Philips's departure from the country—obviously a necessary safeguard—can also be read as a symbolic gesture.

Cook's fictional exaggeration of government complicity in unethical scientific research points to a very real social problem, one that governments (and also businesses) endeavoring to master new technologies must sometimes face. The risks inherent in many scientific enterprises—the development of nuclear technologies, for example—have made it difficult for scientists to obtain necessary knowledge without endangering human lives. When atomic energy was first unleashed, scientists possessed imperfect knowledge of the effects of varying amounts of radioactivity on the human body; subsequent studies, including those conducted in the aftermath of the explosions at Hiroshima and Nagasaki, have, of course, yielded crucial information. As an early leader, however, in the development of technologies that employ nuclear power, the United States government has been distinctly interested in closely investigating the effects of radiation, and Cook cites numerous experiments wherein radioactive materials have been introduced into the bodies of "unsuspecting people" (304)—most commonly, retarded people housed in institutions. Acknowledging that certain kinds of knowledge can only be obtained by taking some degree of risk, Cook argues strenuously for a scrupulous observation of the practice of "informed consent." People who volunteer to participate in medical experiments, he claims, should be well advised as to possible effects or risks. Certainly, he proclaims, human subjects should never be used as unwitting guinea pigs.[1]

Interestingly, a small furor arose within the scientific community shortly after *Brain* was initially published. In the novel, Cook posits that the young women who have begun to suffer seizures are manifesting the effects of the high doses of radioactive deoxyglucose secretly administered to them. As it happens, such a substance is indeed used by "researchers who have been mapping brain functions in volunteers" (Miller, 156), and thus the March 7, 1981 edition of *Science News* devotes an entire page to a rebuttal of Cook's fictional proposition. Defending the practices of "the real-life scientists who use the deoxyglucose technique in their research," science reporter Julie Ann Miller quotes one such researcher who firmly maintains that "We stay well within the federal guidelines for safe use of radiactive material." Apparently, the *Science News* response to *Brain* was inspired by researchers' concerns that Cook's fictional extrapolation could "make people afraid to participate in experiments using deoxyglucose" (Miller, 156).

That a science news publication would choose to open a debate with a work of fiction over this technical detail clearly suggests that *Brain*'s themes and message might well have touched a sensitive nerve within the world of medical research. Cook himself, when asked about the scientific community's rapid response to *Brain*, observed that those engaged in the research at issue did not welcome the public attention generated by his book. The unwanted publicity, he further claimed, probably had the effect of inconveniencing researchers who would in all likelihood be forced to respond to increased public pressure to prove that their experiments were safe. Believing that researchers should fully explain their experiments and any attendant risks, and that the public should be encouraged to take an active interest in matters relating to research protocol, Cook, in fact, consistently welcomes occasions to discuss openly issues of the sort raised by *Brain*. It might be noted, furthermore, that Robin Cook is a sharp critic of the general practice of secrecy in research; he directly voices an array of concerns about the problems he sees in secrecy in such novels as *Mortal Fear*, *Terminal*, and *Acceptable Risk*.

Brain's vision of the world of scientific research affords readers a view of the different kinds of science practiced by two very different scientists.

Martin Philips and William Michaels are indeed collaborators on their computer image-reading project, but that is where their common interests end. These characters hold quite different views of science and its purposes and therefore represent some of the divergent interests that can be seen within the research community today. Largely speaking, Philips pursues a science that serves a public purpose, while Michaels, only incidentally interested in the applications that might result from his discoveries, strives to conquer nature's secrets. The differences in these scientists' objectives are clearly reflected in their methods, for Michaels, who operates outside a sense of social obligation, does not, correspondingly, consider himself bound by society's rules.

Dr. Philips practices his medical research within the context of science's socially defined altruistic purposes. Hoping to improve the general outcome for future hospital patients, he focuses his work on the development of an extraordinarily useful tool for diagnosis. (That this project, which offers obvious benefits for patients, is nonetheless not beyond controversy should not go unremarked. Fearing that Philips's innovation would dramatically change the entire field of radiology, powerful hospital administrator Dr. Harold Goldblatt strongly opposes the research.) It is because both the aims and the methods of Philips's research enterprise fall well within the boundaries of socially sanctioned scientific inquiry that he can dream that his contribution might invite the ultimate recognition for service to humankind, the Nobel Prize.

In sharp contrast to Philips's practice of a public science, one that promises clearly defined practical applications, William Michaels's pursuit of knowledge is a distinctly private matter. Confronting one of nature's most inviting mysteries in his quest to understand the workings of the human brain, Michaels desires to solve a puzzle that hitherto remained unsolved. This form of inquiry, sometimes called "pure science" or "pure research," expresses humankind's deepest impulses to know fully the nature of the universe it inhabits. Williams wants both to possess a new form of knowledge and to exhibit his mastery of it by building a new kind of machine. He rationalizes the nature of his research by citing numerous beneficial applications (a contribution to the planet's weaponry?), but it is clear that he is motivated by his obsessions with knowledge and control. Always working behind the scenes, not in the least interested in socially sanctioned forms of recognition, Michaels by no means dreams of winning a Nobel Prize. Pitting his genius against what is yet unknown, he seeks a private satisfaction.

Reiterating themes from the stories of Faust and Frankenstein, Cook offers Michaels as an image of the researcher who exhibits hubris, or excessive arrogance and pride. Although the will to knowledge is not an evil in itself, Michaels is the figure who transgresses limits in his quest to understand the nature of the brain. These limits, established by a society that places high value on an individual life, are also transgressed by the government that supports and protects Michaels's research. Tempted by the knowledge that Michaels has to offer, the government in *Brain* readily betrays itself.

In addition to his consideration of the politics that drive scientific research, Cook presents in *Brain* a characteristic study of the world of hospital life. The hospital, too, is an arena for a variety of political struggles, and Cook details for his readers the kinds of forces that are typically at work there. As Rosalind Smith observed in her review of *Brain*: "The milieu of a large university hospital is rendered with exquisite accuracy, from the bureaucratic regulations victimizing both patients and personnel to the atmosphere of the operating rooms and laboratories" (R. Smith, 10:1). Readers will certainly note that the selfish ambitions of such lesser characters as Dr. Mannerheim or Dr. Goldblatt tellingly mirror those of Michaels. Hence Robin Cook reminds readers that the world of medicine, like the world of research, is home to figures whose goals are far from altruistic.

ALTERNATIVE PERSPECTIVE: MYTH THEORY AND CRITICISM

Myth criticism in the field of literary studies generally focuses on analysis of the symbols, characters, or patterns of action that strike readers as deeply resonant of shared human experience or apprehension. This shared or communal experience, understood to be at once particular and yet general, is at the heart of all human myths and rituals; myth critics are interested in the ways communal experience manifests itself in literature, in an individual work or in the recurring patterns that can be identified in many different works.

Offering one of the "affective" responses to literature (affective criticism focuses its attention on readers' reactions) myth theory is interested in why certain literary themes, characters, plots, or images evoke especially strong emotional responses in readers. Assuming that mythic elements indeed arouse these powerful responses, myth critics speculate about the symbolic significance of various mythic formulations. Those myth critics who subscribe to Carl Jung's theory of universal human experience commonly explore literature's uses of "archetypes," defined as "universal images that have existed since the remotest times" (Jung, 288). While Jungian critics are specifically interested in the many recurring patterns and images that speak to the universality of the most fundamental human experiences, other myth critics are alert to the ways the historical myths of particular cultures can also be embodied in literary art. Readers of *Brain*, for example, can see in Robin Cook's tale of science run amok the recurrence of themes expressed in two of Western society's most significant cultural myths, those that surround the figures of Faust and Frankenstein.

Myth criticism, also frequently known as archetypal criticism, incorporates a variety of critical methods and modes of inquiry that generally seek to investigate the interesting relations between literature and myth. Some theorists, distinguishing between general myth criticism and the archetypal approach, separate those mythic elements that can be related to individual cultures from those that appear to express common psychological conditions, conditions suggested by the primordial images that Jung has called archetypes. Perceiving that specifically cultural myths can and often do address archetypal experience, most myth critics are inclined to disregard fine distinctions.

An essentially interdisciplinary activity, literary myth criticism has freely borrowed insights from such divergent fields as anthropology, psychology, structural linguistics, and cultural history. Because scholars or theorists in all of these specialized areas of interest—and others as well, such as folklore studies or even philology—have in various ways investigated the nature of myth, the work of these disciplines has shed light upon many of the questions posed by the theorists or critics who study the uses and effects of myth in literature. (A notable exception to the common practice of grounding a reading of literary myth in interdisciplinary theories about the nature of myth itself can be seen in the work of Northrop Frye, who has devised a mythic scheme to account for the organizational principles at the heart of all literature.)

All myth critics, including Frye, are attentive to the various recurrent patterns and images that are embodied within literature.[2] Stories of quests or initiations, for example, or stories that feature descents to the underworld, can be seen as constituting narrative patterns symbolic of significant human experiences. As well as drawing upon these archetypal themes, literary works can invest characters with the qualities of traditional mythic types. The great mother, the hero, the wise old man or the fatal woman, the fool, the doppelgänger, all are archetypal figures representing features of people's psychological experience. Images, too, can reverberate with suggestiveness: Jung saw water as a symbol for the unconscious, and in some literary contexts water clearly signifies a baptismal rebirth or renewal. The color green implies growth and fertility, while red, the color of blood, is often associated with violent passion, sacrifice, or disorder. Black, featured in nurse Blackman's name, generally evokes mystery, evil, death, or chaos (all appropriate manifestations of Ms. Blackman's sinister presence in *Brain*).

Contemporary myth critic René Girard has conducted a wide-ranging investigation of the central role of ritual sacrifice in many cultures. Indeed, the ritual victim of sacrifice, the "scapegoat," is a widely recognized archetypal figure. Robin Cook's plot does present readers with an obvious instance of sacrifice, one in which the victims perform the role of scapegoat. In the case of *Brain*, a mythic approach that draws upon some of Girard's perceptive insights can offer an interesting reading of Dr. Michaels's elaborate justification for exacting the lives of seventeen young women in the cause of national defense.

The figure of the scapegoat is quite commonplace in myth. Typically, the welfare of a tribe or nation rests upon the ritual sacrifice of a scapegoat who is offered as propitiation to the gods. In his book *Violence and the Sacred*, however, Girard argues that the ritual of sacrifice "is society's effort to deflect upon a relatively indifferent or 'sacrificeable' victim the violence that would otherwise be vented on its own members" (Reeves, 522). Girard sees, then, the rite of sacrifice as an enactment of a communal violence where the idea of "the gods" merely represents the needs of the society itself.

Interestingly, in a long speech that rationalizes his experimental procedures, Michaels points out to Philips that "these seventeen young women have added something to society." Acknowledging that the women's lives have certainly been "sacrificed" (293), Michaels sees what they have "added" as some kind of social necessity. In Girard's terms, the sacrificial victims have provided their society with a measure of protection against its own impulses to violence, and the thrust of Michaels's argument supports this reading very well. Quite literally, the sacrifice has made possible the development of weapons, traditional tools of violence; nevertheless, the weapons themselves are understood to be defenses, sources of protection against an assumed possibility of violence—

for in the conventional logic of defense, the more powerful the weapon, the smaller the likelihood it will be used. In affording their society the means to claim tools of violence more powerful than any others (in guaranteeing "the defense superiority of the United States"), the scapegoats have truly been used to deflect the impulse to violence. That the members of society deemed "sacrificeable," and therefore expendable, are all young, single women (Vestal Virgins, as it were) offers a passing comment on the perceived value of the victims' social roles.

NOTES

1. Today the Food and Drug Administration (FDA) oversees the implementation of federal guidelines for scientific experiments involving human participants; current regulations, based on a principle of "autonomy," do require the informed consent of all human subjects. Nevertheless, at the time of this writing, the FDA is considering waiving its "rule of autonomy" in cases of medical emergencies, particularly where experimental procedures might actually save a human life. The public has been invited to respond to the proposed change, and has been granted forty-five days in which to do this. Those who are opposed to a change in the regulations fear that any exception to the rules leaves open the possibility of their violation.

2. In his identification of the defining characteristics of literary genres, Frye suggests an analogue to people's experiences of the cycles of the seasons (a common archetypal pattern that embodies the stages of a human life). Thus spring is the mythos of comedy, summer that of romance, autumn that of tragedy, and winter that of irony.

5

Godplayer
(1983) and
Mutation
(1989)

Robin Cook's sixth and tenth novels can best be described as horror stories. Narratives that offer frightening parables of arrogance and vanity, *Godplayer* (1983) and *Mutation* (1989) both tell tales of monsters. Although these two books obviously incorporate a number of the features characteristic of Cook's other work (the use of the hospital and the research lab as settings, for example), they are nonetheless somewhat distinct in reference to their genre. Admittedly, Cook's themes and plots generally evoke a response of horror from his readers, but it is apparent that in these two books he purposefully sets out to employ aspects of the horror genre (as exemplified, for instance, in the popular fiction of Stephen King). Cook's more typical medical thriller, mixing elements of the mystery with the suspense of the conspiracy plot, is carefully designed to both surprise and shock its reader. By contrast, however, *Godplayer* and *Mutation* are shaped to produce a different kind of effect and therefore also to invite a very different kind of response from the reader.

Godplayer and *Mutation* were not well received by some reviewers, and one possible explanation can be seen in a consideration of the apparent shifts in plotting strategies employed by Cook within these works. Reviewers who complained that the novels did not provide mysteries, that the identity of their villains was in fact readily apparent, clearly expected the kinds of puzzles that Cook usually plots for readers. *Godplayer* and *Mutation*, however, are quite well served when they are classified as tales of "techno-horror," for Cook intends in them not so much to surprise, as to mesmerize his readers. That the identity of the novels' monsters can come as no surprise is, in fact, immediately established by the titles of the books: in each case there is only one character who serves the role clearly implied by the title.

In *Godplayer* and *Mutation*, Cook sets out to fascinate his readers through a recounting of a series of horrifying revelations. His strategy in these novels is to make full use of a particular technique for developing suspense that he only occasionally employs in other books (*Blindsight*, for example). The device, usefully called the Cassandra motif, predicates that one character possesses knowledge of dangerous circumstances of which others are completely unaware. This character naturally attempts to enlighten others, but all words of warning—like those of Homer's Cassandra—fall upon deaf ears. Clearly, the dramatic effects of this motif are most fully realized in *Godplayer*, where the central character, tellingly named Cassandra, cannot make others believe that her husband is trying to kill her. In *Mutation* Cook uses his technique in a somewhat subtler fashion, for there his protagonist's knowledge is actively repressed by her own will to deny what she knows. (A thoroughly understandable impulse, when *Mutation*'s monster is her young son.) In both novels, however, the protagonists' uneasy suspicions are shown to grow to certainties, and thus suspense in these stories mounts as the characters move toward full recognition of what the reader already knows to be true. In other words, as the revelations within *Godplayer* and *Mutation* are gradually unfolded, readers find themselves also occupying the position of a Cassandra-like observer. Spellbound by their fascinated horror, readers readily perceive the dangers that the novels' characters cannot or will not see. Indeed, reviewer Adam Paul Hunt expresses this effect well when he describes the experience of reading *Mutation* as "almost like going to a horror movie in which everyone knows there's a monster behind the door and futilely screams at the hero not to open it" (Hunt,124).

GODPLAYER AND *MUTATION* AS VARIATIONS OF THE MEDICAL THRILLER

Although *Godplayer* and *Mutation* can be appropriately classified as horror novels (and Robert Reginald lists *Mutation* as a work of science fiction in his bibliography, *Science Fiction and Fantasy Literature, 1975-*

1991), Cook's medical thriller proves to be an extraordinarily flexible form, incorporating the novelistic strategies of a variety of popular fiction genres. Thus both books share many of the features of Cook's other work, including the author's interest in providing readers with a highly realistic view of life within the hospital and the research lab.

Godplayer, in which the action is set at Boston Memorial Hospital (recognized by readers as the setting for *Coma* and *Harmful Intent* as well), offers one of Cook's most detailed studies of the intricacies of hospital politics. Politics, in fact, plays an important role within the plot, for Dr. Thomas Kingsley, Memorial's star cardiac surgeon, is a man who is obviously feeling the strain of trying to compete at the top of his field while fighting internal hospital battles. The political pressure Kingsley is under, combined with the tension inherent in his stressful occupation, contributes to his growing paranoia and to his emerging habit of drug abuse— not, as Cook makes clear, an altogether uncommon problem among the ranks of overworked medical professionals.

Many of the political battles at Boston Memorial take the shape of "turf wars." As an academic medical center, the hospital provides surgical facilities both for private doctors and for its own staff of teaching surgeons. Disputes therefore rage over whose patients should be given priority and, in fact, over what kinds of patients the hospital should serve at all. The teaching doctors favor admitting significant numbers of unusual cases, on the theory that medical students and residents need to be exposed to a wide range of surgical problems. Dr. Kingsley, who maintains a private practice, strongly believes that use of the hospital's limited resources should be restricted to those patients whose prognosis is good and whose lives can be seen as valuable to society. Encouraging, then, a form of rationed health care, Kingsley is willing, as some other doctors are not, to play the role of God. Cook's readers will probably note that *Godplayer*, in probing the ethical questions that arise from the specter of rationed medicine, takes up a health care issue that he also addresses in *Mortal Fear* and *Fatal Cure*.

Godplayer's vision of the bureaucratic hierarchy that operates within a hospital closely resembles the portrait Cook presents in *Brain*. Capturing the flavor of the personalities that wield the power, those who have "learned early that for success it was more important to study Machiavelli than Halstead" (*Godplayer*, 59; hereafter cited as *G*), Cook offers an insider's view of the political alignments and of the various antagonisms that commonly define hospital life. Readers learn, for example, that members of the hospital staff are expected to routinely express appropriate deference to the hospital's surgical personnel. As the occupants of an elite position within the medical world's social structure, the surgeons can expect to command the automatic respect of all. Nevertheless, it is quite clear that the medical professionals who treat physical health problems are greatly inclined to express their contempt for the staff members who work in Memorial's psychiatric ward—although Cassandra Kingsley, who is a first year resident in psychiatry, is, of course, more or less immune to this treatment by dint of her marriage to the hospital's most famous surgeon.

Godplayer, finally plotted more to thrill and frighten than to excite a mystery reader's interest, actually does appear at first to offer its readers a murder mystery to solve. Over the course of several years, seventeen of Memorial's patients have unexpectedly died while recovering from their cardiac surgery. Cassandra Kingsley, who was a student in pathology before transferring to the psychiatric ward, has, with her pathologist friend Robert Seibert, tracked these unusual cases. Although the two investigators do not at first suspect that the patients' deaths were murders, readers already know otherwise, for *Godplayer*'s prologue vividly depicts the eighteenth of these killings. Readers also know, very early in the novel, that Thomas Kingsley must be responsible for these deaths. Yet Robin Cook, who plants clue after clue directly pointing to Kingsley, nevertheless withholds final revelation of his killer's identity until the closing pages of the book. An explanation for this strategy can be found in the understanding that Cook's story is indeed interested in a mystery, although it is not the mystery of the traditional whodunit. Rather, *Godplayer*'s attention is focused on the terrible mystery of Kingsley's unspeakably monstrous behavior.

Cook's portrait of Thomas Kingsley finally presents readers with a case study of borderline personality disorder, a condition that can be exceedingly difficult to recognize in people who do not obviously exhibit psychotic episodes. As one of Memorial's psychiatrists observes in describing a borderline patient admitted to the hospital: "He's vicious, and he's smart. Somehow he knows just how to get at people: find their weaknesses. That power, combined with his pent-up anger and hostility, can be devastating" (*G*, 27).

These words, as it turns out, could well be applied to Thomas Kingsley. Manipulative and treacherously deceptive in his relations with other people, Kingsley nonetheless has an elusive character: in public moments he seems to be well in control of his actions and his purposes. He is, as the psychiatrist would say, well compensated, highly successful, and to all outward appearances an adequately socialized human being. Yet readers get chilling glimpses of a darker side of his nature and must ask themselves from time to time, "Can he be truly mad?" On the other hand, different explanations also present themselves (as they certainly do to the other characters within the book): perhaps Kingsley is experiencing unfortunate reactions to the drugs he takes, or maybe the pressures of hospital politics are finally wearing him down. The effect of withholding final revelation of the depth of Kingsley's madness is to mirror the elusive nature of his personality disorder; like other borderline cases, his behavior is "inconsistent"—thereby inviting more than one interpretation. Suspense in *Godplayer* largely resides in Cook's strategy of gradually unmasking the cunning dissemblances of a malicious maniac.

While *Godplayer* visits Cook's familiar hospital setting, *Mutation* leads readers into the more remote world of medical research. This is the realm of futuristic possibilities—where scientists, rather than surgeons, can play the role of God. Cook's general interest in health care issues has consistently encompassed the specialized area of research in medical science, and he has found within many of today's startling technological achievements the germ of an idea for a suspenseful plot. It is thus upon books like *Brain*, *Mortal Fear*, *Mutation*, *Terminal*, and *Acceptable Risk* that his reputation as the master of the techno-thriller rests.

As noted earlier, many readers are conscious of the ways the techno-thriller overlaps the science fiction genre. Indeed, it is useful to regard the techno-thriller as a melding of science fiction and suspense. Like other writers of science fiction, Cook sees within the genre a ready opportunity to address contemporary social problems as well as some of the ethical questions that the development of new technologies can certainly be expected to raise. *Mutation*, therefore, takes up the issue of genetic engineering to offer its readers a cautionary fable about the scientific breakthrough that today's researchers are clearly poised to make. In boldly recasting Mary Shelley's now legendary account of the foiled ambitions of one Victor Frankenstein, Cook once again delivers its familiar warning: the wondrous dreams of science can sometimes turn to nightmare. Nightmare, of course, is the stuff of the thriller genre, and in *Mutation* provides Cook with haunting means to fuse science fiction with horror and suspense.

When Cook chooses to explore the world of science, he does so with full consciousness of the potency of its mystique. If, as *Washington Post* reviewer Joseph McLellan has observed, Cook's common hospital setting strikes readers as "infinitely spookier than a dark old abandoned house" (McLellan, C4), the same can certainly be said for his use of the research scientist's lab. (See, for example, *Mortal Fear*'s description of Dr. Hayes's hideous lab.) *Publishers Weekly*'s review of *Mutation* makes this point nicely in noting that "the metaphor of the lab as the site of malignantly hatched creative schemes is here presented in its most extreme version" (Sweeting, 107). *Mutation*'s sinister lab is none other than Victor Frankenstein's rebuilt, and that the creature who emerges from this lab might assume a monstrous shape is the message of *Mutation* and another recent thriller, *Acceptable Risk*.

The lab is the domain of the research scientist, and in drawing upon the common literary or cultural conception of the scientist as a figure who is obsessed—sometimes, of course, to the point of madness—Cook implicitly advances his familiar note of caution: the work of science, he consistently maintains, is most potentially dangerous when it is conducted in deepest secrecy (when, serving some private ambition or conceit, it is not subjected to a public consensus or critique). This is indeed the case in *Mutation*, where Dr. Victor Frank, brilliant biophysicist and joint owner of a large, independent biotechnology company, performs his genetic experiment on his son with no one else's knowledge or consent. This act of secrecy breeds further secrecy, for following the model provided by the father (whose secret only he has discovered), ten-year-old Victor Frank, Jr., known as VJ, builds, in turn, his own secret lab. This lab, in fact, serves as the home base in VJ's private world. A genetically engineered prodigy, VJ knows that he is a "chimera, and that he had animal genes fused into his chromosomes" (*Mutation*, 92; hereafter cited as *Mu*). Born carrying the secret of his father's act of vanity, and fully cognizant of his difference from other people, the child has in fact chosen to lead his life in secrecy.

Mutation recounts Marsha and Victor Frank's growing awareness of the true nature of their son's hidden life. Through a series of increasingly horrifying revelations, the parents come to a final recognition that the monster they have never really known must somehow be destroyed. VJ's secret world is an empire built on science. Using his amazing mastery of biotechnology, he has found a means to commit murder by introducing a rare form of liver cancer in his victims. He has raised money for costly equipment and building projects by producing cocaine in his lab. And, a genetic engineer himself, he is following in his father's footsteps: in the depths of his secret kingdom, VJ is breeding a new race of protohumans to serve him in all the future enterprises he has planned. Indeed, his ambitions know no limits, for, as he boldly declares near the climax of the book: "I am what science can be. I am the future" (*Mu*, 298).

Presenting a distinct variation in the design of the medical thriller, *Godplayer* and *Mutation* can be seen as instances of the subgenre of horror fiction that Michael Wood has identified as the "mutant-disaster story" (Wood, 54). Perceived in these terms, Thomas Kingsley and VJ Frank are both mutants in the midst of others (as is Stephen King's widely recognized character, Carrie—the example Michael Wood discusses). Kingsley, the embodiment of a psychological mutation, and VJ, the embodiment of a genetic one, actively engage in acts of deception designed to disguise the central truth about their natures. Within Cook's novels, the layers of deception that enshroud these characters are gradually stripped away until readers find themselves in the presence of the atavistic evil that always seems to lie at the heart of the horrific.

PLOT DEVELOPMENT

Both *Godplayer* and *Mutation* make use of the episodic pattern of plot development that is commonplace in thriller fiction. Following introductory chapters that serve to familiarize readers with the main characters' backgrounds and circumstances, Cook begins in each novel to unfold the series of revelations that will ineluctably lead the protagonists to terrifying recognition of the evil close at hand. For Cassandra Kingsley and Marsha Frank, the novels' main characters, each new revelation provides a small piece of a larger puzzle whose general shape at first eludes them. Readers, therefore, who very early can discern the outlines of this puzzle, are positioned to watch with horrified fascination as each new piece is put in place.

In *Godplayer* and *Mutation*, the prologue presents readers with their first clear signals as to the direction the plot can be expected to take. The prologue is an extra-narrative novelistic device that Cook, in fact, regularly employs to situate his readers. Sometimes, as it does in *Godplayer*, the prologue serves to provide clues or pertinent information whose significance is only clear in hindsight. At other times, as in *Mutation*, the prologue prefigures or foreshadows events that are to come.

As mentioned earlier, *Godplayer*'s prologue presents a scene of murder. Late at night, when the hospital's halls are deserted, an unidentified figure tampers with a patient's IV bottle. The patient, a relatively young man who has been making a satisfactory recovery after his cardiac bypass operation, quickly suffocates. When she discovers that her patient is not breathing, the night nurse signals an emergency alarm. The hospital's "crash cart" instantly arrives, and efforts are made to resuscitate the patient. In the midst of this flurry of activity, Boston Memorial's most famous cardiac surgeon suddenly (and quite unexpectedly) appears. Taking matters in hand, Thomas Kingsley opens up the patient's chest and, with a display of expertise that greatly impresses the emergency staff, skillfully massages the patient's open heart.

Kingsley's masterful efforts, are, of course, in vain, and thus the prologue serves two readily obvious purposes: it introduces the novel's first note of suspense, alerting readers that mysterious murder is afoot, and it also affords readers a first acquaintance with the famous Dr. Kingsley, who will quite shortly show himself to be an enigmatic figure. While the obvious insights provided by the prologue usefully set the stage for the action that will follow, it is not long before readers realize that this introductory device has in fact presented more information than was at first apparent. In Chapter 1, for example, where readers meet Cassandra Kingsley and learn about her encounter with Colonel Bentworth (the troublesome borderline patient), the staff psychiatrist firmly asserts, "If you had to pick one word to characterize a borderline patient, I think 'inconsistency' would be the most appropriate" (*G*, 23). This observation, of course, carries suggestive significance for the reader who ponders why a man who had (perhaps) murdered a patient might then attempt to revive him. And, later on, when readers discover that Dr. Kingsley holds extremely strong views about the kinds of patients who should be treated at the hospital, the fact that the cardiac patient also suffered from multiple sclerosis suddenly seems important. Dr. Kingsley, it appears, is always at the hospital on the nights when the patients in recovery die.

While *Godplayer*'s prologue offers clues the significance of which eventually dawns on the reader, the device serves a different purpose in respect to plot development in *Mutation*. This novel opens with the birth of VJ Frank, preparing readers for the subsequent action, which takes place more than ten years later. VJ is painfully delivered by a surrogate mother who has undergone artificial insemination. (Marsha Frank had a hysterectomy after the birth of David, the Franks' first child.) This, however, is only one of the complicating circumstances that attend upon the birth. Dr. Victor Frank, the father-to-be, is exceptionally nervous throughout the course of the delivery. When he silently prays to himself, "Please make the baby normal," readers must wonder what it is that he so desperately fears could go wrong. Then, when he inwardly chides himself, "I shouldn't have done it. But please, God—let this baby be all right" (*Mu*, 8), it is perfectly clear that something untoward has in fact already taken place. Readers will learn soon enough about the details of Victor Frank's secret experiment in genetic engineering, but the evidence is already present when VJ himself finally appears.

An angelic-looking baby (bright blue eyes, blond hair, and rosy cheeks), VJ does not cry when he is born. An attendant attempts to suction his nose, but to the observers' great surprise, the infant clearly resists this effort; seizing the suction bulb from the hand of his doctor, the astonishingly dextrous newborn drops it to the floor. Amazingly, too, the baby establishes direct eye contact with those around him, and, as Victor Frank gazes into his new son's eyes, he finds that "their turquoise depths were as cold and bright as ice. Unbidden, Victor felt a thrill of fear" (*Mu*, 10). That thrill of fear is intensified for readers when the baby is brought home to join his brother David and the live-in nanny, Janice. As the ominous last words of the prologue note, "Neither realized that they only had a few more years to live" (*Mu*, 13).

The plots of *Godplayer* and *Mutation* are both episodically advanced through a series of disclosures. Cassandra Kingsley and Marsha Frank, each vaguely worried about a loved one, begin to notice small details, minor discrepancies in their husband's or their son's behavior. As Marsha Frank initially describes her concerns about VJ, "It's a number of little things. Like it bothers me that he has so few friends" (*Mu*, 23). She is also puzzled as to why VJ appears to let others win when he participates in competitive activities. And Cassandra Kingsley, who hears from her mother-in-law that Thomas had been born with a clubfoot, wonders why he so vehemently denies that this is true. Someone, she realizes— either Thomas or his mother—is not telling the truth about the past.

In both books, the small deceptions that are initially uncovered quickly lead to revelations of much greater ones. Cassandra Kingsley discovers that her husband is secretly taking drugs (ordering them through the name of a doctor who is deceased), and readers learn that he is also conducting a secret affair with his receptionist. VJ Frank, who, as his mother finds, has regularly been skipping school, has also pretended to stay with friends when, in fact, he has been elsewhere. As it turns out, VJ, since the age of three, has carefully hidden his amazing intelligence from the knowledge of all others—including his own parents. (To do this he has successfully outsmarted the batteries of IQ and personality tests administered by his mother, who is by profession a psychiatrist herself.)

Needless to say, VJ has been busy in his time away from school. He is convinced that he has a "mission, just like his father. And he could not let anything interfere" (*Mu*, 39). To equip his secret lab, VJ has broken into his father's company computer, readjusting accounts and planting evidence suggesting that certain employees have been guilty of embezzlement. (It was in his father's private computer files that VJ found a record of the genetic experiment that led to his own birth.) More than all this, VJ has, of course, dispassionately disposed of all the people who have seemed to him likely to interfere with his "mission." The list includes David and Janice and a helpful school teacher—all dead of liver cancer; two young child prodigies who, like himself, were products of his father's genetic experiment; and the entire family of one of his father's employees—wiped out in a gangland slaying contracted by VJ.

Robin Cook makes most dramatic use of his Cassandra motif just before *Godplayer* and *Mutation* reach their climaxes. At the suspenseful point where the protagonists of each of these novels have recognized the truths that they hitherto have been reluctant to admit, there is no one else who can comprehend the danger in their plights. Cassandra Kingsley, for example, puts all the pieces of her puzzle together while she is recovering from a necessary eye operation (a complication of her diabetes). Resting in Boston Memorial, she has time to think over the pattern of recent events—with a shock, she realizes that Thomas was quite likely the last person to see her friend Robert Seibert alive (he too, after having his wisdom teeth removed, has become a victim of the hospital's nighttime killer). With this frightening thought in mind, she perceives her own immediate danger: "All at once she became aware of her utter dependency and vulnerability. She was alone in a private room with an IV running, blindfolded and sedated. There was no way for her even to know when someone came into the room. There was no way for her to defend herself" (*G*, 264). Filled with terror, Cassandra does summon help. Seeking reassurance, she speaks with a nurse, her eye doctor, a friend; all try to calm her, persuading her that she is disoriented and simply requires sleep. Thus, she has been silenced with another sedative when Thomas indeed slips into her room to add an extra dose of insulin to the fluid in her IV: it is just before she falls into a coma that Cassandra recognizes the familiar scent of his cologne.

Mutation's Marsha and Victor Frank are similarly entrapped when they confront their son in his secret lab. No one, not even his parents, can come between VJ and his mission. Employing a ruse, Victor Frank leaves his wife as hostage while he goes off in search of help. While waiting to meet with a policeman,

> Victor's mind went over the conversation he was about to have with Officer Murphy. He could see himself telling the policeman that he has a son who is an utter genius and who is growing a race of retarded workers in glass jars and who has killed people to protect a secret lab he built by black-mailing embezzlers in his father's company. The mere fact of putting the situation into words convinced Victor that no one would believe him. (*Mu*, 314–315)

It is at this moment, finding himself in Cassandra's position, that Victor Frank understands that "he alone had to deal with VJ. It was to be father against son, creator against creature" (*Mu*, 316)—a reenactment, in other words, of the responsibility grimly carried to his death by Mary Shelley's original Frankenstein.

Fittingly, the climaxes in *Godplayer* and *Mutation* are both sudden and catastrophic. The hospital staff does revive Cassandra after her severe insulin reaction. Confused about what happened to her, she supposes that "her fear of Thomas had been imaginary and that a good deal of their problems were at least partially her own fault.... Anxious," therefore, "to get home and try to put her marriage back on course" (*G*, 285), she is tricked by her treacherous husband yet again. The manipulative Thomas is a most convincing liar, persuading his wife that he needs her help to overcome his recent problem with drug abuse (his first admission that such a problem exists). When the truth of his intentions finally comes out—Cassandra finds in his possession a vial of U500 insulin, "five times her normal dosage" (*G*, 312)—the two are speeding along the freeway in Thomas's powerful Porsche. Seized by her sudden anger at both Thomas and herself ("How could she have been so blind?" [*G*, 313]) Cassandra grabs the steering wheel in an attempt to force the car off the highway. Overcompensating, Thomas steers to the left, and the Porsche rams into an abutment "in a crescendo of broken glass, twisted metal, and blood" (*G*, 314).

Thomas Kingsley does not survive *Godplayer*'s climactic crash, and, as it happens, VJ is crushed out of existence too, though in a somewhat more apocalyptic fashion. Before making his way back to VJ's hidden lab, his father plants an explosive device near an old sluice gate on the

Merrimack River. Determined to "come up with some sort of cataclysmic event that would get rid of the entire mess in one fell swoop" (*Mu*, 318), Victor Frank lands on the plan of diverting the river, raging with its spring runoff, through the deserted building that houses the lab. Everyone escapes before the sluice gate breaks except VJ and his father. Because the river demolishes all traces of VJ's hideous experiments, his hidden world remains a secret, and Marsha Frank, "preferring the nightmare to end with a seemingly accidental tragedy" because "it was so much simpler than the truth" (*Mu*, 332), does not try to explain what really happened to her husband and her son.

Readers of *Frankenstein* will recall that Victor Frankenstein, having pursued his creature to the remote arctic wastes, finally expires in Robert Walton's arms. The creature, however, lives on, and in a final surprising move, Cook once again pays homage to the book that inspired the plot of *Mutation*. In an epilogue whose action takes place a year after the destruction of VJ's lab, Marsha Frank meets with a new patient in her office. When the patient, a child, gazes at her with his "piercing, ice-blue eyes" (*Mu*, 336), she suddenly recognizes that her nightmare is not yet over. Indeed, all but one of the zygotes produced in Victor Frank's original experiment were accounted for at the time of the deluge. Now, seated before her is the product of the missing zygote, yet another child created from her own ova. "Somehow," she knows, she will "have to face this last demon-child" (*Mu*, 338).

CHARACTER DEVELOPMENT

The characters of greatest interest to *Godplayer*'s and *Mutation*'s readers are the villains central to these novels. While it is intriguing that the protagonists are both psychiatrists, and therefore positioned to offer their profession's explanations for the evil they uncover, Cassandra Kingsley's and Marsha Frank's perspectives finally do not seem to account fully for the utter depravity Cook has envisioned within his demonic plots. This problem is addressed when readers regard Thomas Kingsley and VJ Frank (and, of course, also Victor) as figures who are emblematic of the worst excesses possible in medicine and science. As representatives of the vanity and arrogance of all who would play God, Kingsley and VJ embody dangerous tendencies that Cook sees at work in these professions. This reading of the purposes his villainous characters serve is indeed one that Cook invites, when he has VJ present himself as the

"future" of science itself, and when, in *Godplayer*'s epilogue, another surgeon, acknowledging that "some of Thomas's objections to our teaching
cases were valid" (*G*, 319), chooses to play God himself.

Cook's consistent use, in both *Godplayer* and *Mutation*, of stock character types offers further argument that these stories can be appropriately seen as fables. While Cook frequently draws upon stock figures for
his novels' minor roles, his general practice is to focus readers' attention
and sympathies on the more fully developed characters who are central
to his plots. Within these two stories, however, the villains clearly command center stage (as indeed the titles indicate), and the protagonists,
both stock characters, are—unlike most of Cook's other protagonists—
survivors more than heroes.

As *Godplayer*'s rendition of the typically arrogant (and often childishly
selfish) surgeon, Thomas Kingsley plays, within the world of Cook's
medical thriller, a role that the writer initially identified in his first book,
The Year of the Intern. There, thoughtless and vain surgeons make life
especially difficult for the residents on duty. This type of character also
reappears in other Cook novels, in the figure of *Brain*'s pompous Dr.
Curt Mannerheim, and in that of *Blindsight*'s unscrupulous Dr. Jordan
Scheffield. (Readers might take note that Cook, a surgeon himself, has
doubtless witnessed the behavior whereof he speaks.)

In *Godplayer*, where the portrait of the vainglorious surgeon is full-
blown, readers witness the thrill that his power over life and death produces. For Thomas Kingsley, "the excitement was like a fix." Thus the
act of surgery itself evokes in Kingsley a narcissistic pleasure. When he
reaches into his patient, "touching the heart, defying death with his own
two hands—it was like playing God" (*G*, 51). Grown accustomed to playing God, Kingsley extends the role beyond the operating theatre. As he
at last reveals to Cassandra just before the car crash, "All I want to do
is surgery on people who deserve to live, not a bunch of mental defec-
tives or people who are going to die of other illnesses. Medicine has to
understand that our resources are limited. We can't let worthy candidates wait while people with multiple sclerosis or gays with autoim-
munal deficiencies take valuable beds and OR time" (*G*, 313). As the
godplayer, Kingsley would bestow life and exact justice—both, of course,
by his own lights.

Godplayer employs an interesting device to characterize the psychological roles played by Cassandra and Thomas Kingsley. As noted earlier,
the strong parallels between Thomas's behavior and that of Cassandra's
patient, Colonel Bentworth, invite readers to see in him also an example

of borderline personality disorder. In another of her patients, Maureen Kavenaugh, Cassandra herself sees personality traits that are strikingly similar to her own. Kavenaugh, generally "hopeless, timid, and fearful" (*G*, 136), is the victim of spousal abuse. Cassandra, who knows that she too is fearful of abandonment and overly dependent upon her relationship with Thomas, strongly identifies with Kavenaugh's predicament. As readers will probably note, Cassandra's vulnerabilities in this respect do seem to leave her susceptible to her husband's manipulative strategies.

As *Mutation*'s prime example of the stock figure that readers readily recognize as the mad scientist, VJ Frank epitomizes science's obsession with rationality. A creature without feelings, and therefore lacking any moral sensibility, VJ believes that the "only thing that is immutable in this world are the laws of nature" (*Mu*, 299). It is, then, those laws alone that fascinate him and to which he has dedicated his life; as a character who has no interest in human relationships, he clearly stands in sharp contrast to his mother, whose working life is devoted to a study of the "laws" of human nature. When she reminds her son that "science runs amok when it shakes loose from the bonds of morality and consequence" (*Mu*, 299), he replies that "science" stands "above morality." "Reason," he vehemently maintains, "is the ultimate arbiter, not moralistic whims" (*Mu*, 299).

VJ's position is similar to the one held by *Brain*'s William Michaels, who also practices a conscienceless science grounded in rationality. Robin Cook, however, strongly believes that the practice of science must be grounded in morality—and thus uses characters like these to illustrate his point. Indeed, *Mutation*'s epigraph speaks to scientists like Michaels, VJ, and Victor Frank—scientists who have forgotten that science is a human (and therefore humane) enterprise. Borrowing from Mary Shelley's *Frankenstein*, Cook's epigraph reads: "How Dare You Sport Thus with Life."

Robin Cook takes pains to present the villains of *Godplayer* and *Mutation* in a frighteningly sinister light. The cunning and ruthless qualities of Thomas Kingsley's and VJ Frank's characters are unfolded for readers in purposefully chilling detail. Thomas Kingsley, an almost Byronic figure (with his childhood clubfoot and his terrible swings of mood), is the kind of person with whom other people must always be on guard. Absolutely unpredictable, he can be charming and beguiling one moment, and surly or spiteful another. Even his wife, who assumes she knows him best, constantly monitors his state of mind, deferring to his nasty temper. His selfishly calculating nature is fully revealed to readers when, early in the book, they witness his adulterous rendezvous with his doting receptionist. As to *Mutation*'s wunderkind, readers quickly understand that VJ's cherubic appearance (the blond hair, blue eyes, and rosy cheeks) belies his actual nature. Humorless and cold, the boy shuns both physical and emotional contact with most other people. His mother, who has indeed observed this lack of feeling in her son, at first tells herself that he is an unusually "independent" boy, but as VJ seems to her to grow ever more secretive and remote, her vague misgivings quickly turn to worry. This dispassionate and solitary character spends most of his time with a retarded man who is, in fact, the model for the race of slaves he is planning to create.

While the novel's villains undeniably fascinate readers, the main characters command their sympathies. Cassandra Kingsley, intelligent and deeply alert to other people's feelings, is well suited to her career in psychiatric medicine. It is, of course, this perspicacity that leads her to begin to entertain suspicions about her husband. (At the same time, naturally enough, her devotion to him promotes the strong desire to explain away or to even deny any suspicions.) Much like Cassandra Kingsley, Marsha Frank is torn between what her professional instincts tell her and what she fervently desires to believe is the truth. Above all, she is a deeply concerned mother, one who has lost one cherished son and does not know how she could bear to lose another; unfortunately for her, her struggle to find a way to understand and to help VJ eventually leads her to the ironic realization that he has always been lost to her.

Victor Frank, the scientist whose reckless arrogance has unleashed a monster, is a character tormented by the guilt he bears. Early in the novel this guilt takes the form of denial—Frank fiercely dismisses his wife's worries, insisting that VJ is a perfectly normal boy—but as evidence of his son's aberrations mounts, guilt is transformed into the acknowledgment of responsibility that also haunts Shelley's Victor Frankenstein. It is thus appropriate that the father/creator finally takes it upon himself to find a means to bring VJ's vicious career to an end.

THEMATIC ISSUES

In a good many of Cook's novels (*Outbreak*, *Vital Signs*, and *Terminal*, among others) greed motivates malefactors to ruthlessly take advantage of innocent people. This is true too, in *Godplayer* and *Mutation*, where Thomas Kingsley and VJ and Victor Frank are all insatiably greedy for personal power. Cook's analysis of this special kind of greed, this will to indulge in absolute self-satisfaction, proves it to be no less insidious a motivating force than other forms of lust.

Cook's novels offer many studies of the promotion of self-interests or ambitions that violate the common good. Greed, then, in one form or another, can be seen to be a concern that runs throughout his fiction. In several novels he exposes corporate greed: in these instances the self-interests of powerful groups are enforced, often through conspiracies. In other novels greed shapes people's political alignments, revealing the competing interests at work within society. However, in *Godplayer* and *Mutation*, which are largely family stories, Cook affords readers a singularly close-up view of the pathology of greed. *Godplayer* and *Mutation* are, in fact, horror stories precisely because in them Cook embodies his vision of monstrous intemperance in individual characters.

Thomas Kingsley and VJ Frank both lead lives of duplicity. Wearing masks to deceive those who live in an exterior world, these characters actually inhabit worlds that are entirely their own. Their secret lives are, horribly, their real lives, and in their hidden realms of self they leave no room for any others. *Godplayer*'s and *Mutation*'s shadowy villains are egoists whose greed takes the form of a supreme vanity. Interestingly, both characters define their personhood (and thus express their vanity) in terms of what they do rather than in terms of who they are. Thomas Kingsley gives expression to his sense of selfhood when he dramatically asserts, "I'm the best goddamn cardiac surgeon in the country" (*G*, 314), and VJ Frank most fully identifies himself when he announces to his mother, "I am what science can be."

Kingsley's and VJ's monstrous vanity proves to be dangerous to others in two respects: on the one hand, each character's restricted sense of personhood demands that any external challenge to identity be extinguished or overcome. Kingsley kills Robert Seibert and attempts to kill Cassandra because he is determined that "no one is going to sit in judgment of me" (*G*, 314). VJ murders the two young prodigies born to surrogate parents because he fears that their intelligence might present a challenge to his own. As he finally confesses, "I didn't want the competition" (*Mu*, 297). And Kingsley and VJ are also dangerous in another way. In addition to their willingness to murder to protect a sense of selfhood, they are, by dint of their occupational roles, positioned to exercise great power over others. The masterful surgeon's arrogance leads him to suppose that his ability to restore life also grants him the privilege to extinguish it, and the creative scientist's vanity impels him to create a race of servants willing to follow their master blindly. (VJ's distinctive Aryan appearance is chillingly suggestive of the kind of world he would eventually create.)

Kingsley's and VJ's greed for power and possession is evident in everything they do. Kingsley, for example, chooses to marry (and thus possess) Cassandra simply because she is attractive to many others. In fact, the surgeon he thinks of as his greatest rival first desired to marry her; in sweeping her away he has managed to defeat his competition. It is because his father, his "creator," runs a gigantic lab that VJ strongly feels that he must run one too. Using his cocaine deals and other swindles to purchase state-of-the-art equipment, he has managed to assemble a facility that outshines his father's. (And, to add to his triumph, he has solved a scientific puzzle that has mystified his father.) Defined by personalities that drive them to excel, and dangerous because they recognize no moral constraints at all, *Godplayer*'s and *Mutation*'s villains are the monsters of their own vanity.

ALTERNATIVE PERSPECTIVE: JUNGIAN ARCHETYPAL CRITICISM

Contemporary myth criticism, whose interests include studies of the literary expression of humankind's common or communal experiences, is greatly indebted to psychologist and philosopher Carl Jung for his theory of archetypes. Indeed, one branch of myth criticism specifically focuses on the use of Jung's archetypal motifs or images to approach an understanding of certain powerfully evocative patterns that recur in literature. These archetypal patterns do recur, Jung asserts, because they reflect or express deeply recognizable features of humankind's psychological condition. A one-time student of Freud and therefore interested in Freudian theories about the unconscious, Jung nevertheless came to believe that Freud himself too greatly emphasized the neurotic aspects of the human psyche. He therefore set out to theorize an alternative model for the unconscious.

Jung's modification of Freud's conception of the unconscious posited in human beings the existence of certain psychic predispositions, or "racial memories," that he saw as part of a "collective unconscious." Thus archetypal patterns, images, or characteristics of human personality all reside within the unconscious. These theories are particularly relevant to studies of myth and other narrative arts because Jung believed that it is through these forms of expression that the archetypal materials of the unconscious become accessible to the conscious mind. Recurring images and patterns are readily recognizable, in dreams and myths, as well as in stories, as symbolic representations of the experience of being human.

Jung's psychological theory of "individuation" has been particularly useful to myth critics interested in both literature and film. Individuation, Jung's term for the process of psychological maturation, requires that an individual consciously recognize both the favorable and unfavorable characteristics of the self. Particularly crucial to a well-balanced sense of self is the individual's acknowledgment of the archetypal components of the unconscious that Jung has termed the "persona," the "shadow," and the "anima." Although Jung suggests that these characteristics of personality are part of everyone's unconscious, readers will probably recognize that they are often embodied in individual characters within literature or films. In many movie plots, for instance, the hero can be seen as representative of the persona, while the heroine and villain express the anima and shadow. In Robert Louis Stevenson's *The Strange Case of Dr. Jekyll and Mr. Hyde*, the psychological aspects of the persona and the shadow are embodied in one figure.

Borrowing his term from Greek drama, Jung postulated that the persona is the mask that an individual wears to show a face to the world. It is, as archetypal film critic James F. Iaccino describes it, "simply a facade that one exhibits publicly, both for the benefit of others and for self-advancement." A social aspect of personality, the persona "is not real; it is a deception that the human uses to convince others that he can conform to society and be an upright and law-abiding citizen" (Iaccino, 6). Jung believed that for an individual to attain psychological maturity it was necessary that the persona be brought into harmony with other characteristics of personality. Those other characteristics include the shadow, the dark or unfavorable side of the unconscious, and the anima, the life-force, or source of spiritual energy. In Stevenson's much cited novel, Dr. Jekyll is persona, the public self, and Mr. Hyde is shadow, the unconscious's repressed self.

Godplayer and *Mutation* are both interested in questions of the psychological makeup of personality, as Robin Cook clearly demonstrates in choosing psychiatrists to serve as his protagonists. Using contemporary theoretical models to explain their deviant behavior, Cassandra Kingsley and Marsha Frank regard Thomas and VJ, respectively, as instances of borderline personality disorder (a condition that *Godplayer*'s psychiatrists claim is rarely curable) and severe alienation (because he is a chimera and very different from others, VJ feels estranged from the experiences of "normal" people). The villains' maladjustments are further explained in the details provided about their personal family lives. The father that Thomas emulates is dead, and his mother is a domineering and coldly critical woman. VJ also emulates his father, but he is confused about his mother(s). Readers learn, in the concluding pages of the book, that he has searched out his surrogate mother and employed her in his lab. Perhaps most important, VJ—the chimera—thinks of himself as the child of science. While these explanations serve Cook's purposes within the context of his novels, it is also possible to explore these works from a Jungian perspective.

Jekyll and Hyde personalities, Thomas Kingsley and VJ Frank are characters in whom persona and shadow do not exist in harmonious relationship. These characters have repressed their shadow selves, separating the shadow from the persona and relegating it to existence in a dark and hidden realm. This is why, of course, their relatives are not at first aware of the nature of their true selves. The family members are responding to the characters' personas and do not recognize the existence of the secret shadow selves. As Iaccino notes, "man's unconscious requires suitable expression to prevent his shadow from taking complete control." When the shadow is not consciously acknowledged, when it is not expressed as part of self, the human being becomes "more egocentric and repressive" (Iaccino, 112). Kingsley's and VJ's shadow selves have come to dominate their lives. Oblivious to anima (represented in the figures of the women who love them, Cassandra Kingsley and Marsha Frank), these characters use their personas to disguise their shadow selves. Vainglorious within their secret worlds, they can be seen to serve as examples of what Iaccino calls "unrepressed shadow abominations."

For a general introduction to myth criticism, see the concluding section of Chapter 4.

Mindbend
(1985) and
Harmful Intent
(1990)

Although Robin Cook is never at a loss when it comes time to concoct a chilling tale of nefarious deeds within the medical profession, in *Mindbend* (1985) and *Harmful Intent* (1990) he offers readers a different view of his favorite subject: the doctors, in his seventh and eleventh novels, are themselves the victims of malicious conspiracy plots. In *Mindbend*, Cook's institutional villain is a giant pharmaceutical conglomerate that plans nothing less than the "ultimate destruction of an independent medical profession" (*Mindbend*, 303; hereafter cited as *M*). Outlining the ways in which drug companies seek to court and influence the doctors who use and prescribe their wares, Cook imagines a scenario in which one of these companies takes a step beyond mere cajolery and attempts to gain control of doctors' minds. In *Harmful Intent* the enemy is yet another large institution; sued and found guilty of malpractice, and then convicted on charges of second-degree murder, Dr. Jeffrey Rhodes, in his efforts to vindicate himself, ultimately discovers unsuspected evildoing within the legal establishment. A law firm that specializes in multi-million dollar malpractice suits has found a murderous way to guarantee that it will have plenty of business. As one character remarks when the vile plot is finally exposed, "I've heard of ambulance chasers, but these guys are making their own accidents" (*Harmful Intent*, 347; hereafter cited as *HI*). Thus, in both novels greedy institutions set out to prey upon the medical profession.

SUSPENSE FICTION AND THE CONSPIRACY MOTIF

One of Robin Cook's great strengths lies in his ability to fashion plot. Even though his novels frequently propose quite unlikely eventualities (indeed, their unlikeliness is a good measure of their fun), he is generally masterful at luring readers into an ever deepening plot in which seemingly unrelated episodes are all expertly woven together. Drawing upon the variety of conventions offered by the thriller genre, Cook is able, as reviewer William A. Nolen puts it, to create "a plot with enough twists and turns to satisfy any reader." Nolen comments about the plot of *Brain*: "Shall I say, 'I couldn't put the book down'? Why not? It's true" (Nolen, 3:1). And Dr. Bernard H. Adelson, in his review of *Harmful Intent* for the prestigious *Journal of the American Medical Association*, notes: "The story is fast paced and compelling. . . . The plot becomes complicated, but it is never convoluted" (Adelson, 266). His facility in shaping plots that are intriguingly complicated without seeming convoluted or superficially contrived is one of the hallmarks of Cook's success. Because he is so adept at seamlessly unfolding the central action of his novels, he is usually able to convince his willing readers that the most improbable events are—just maybe—not that improbable at all.

Some critics have complained that the plots of *Mindbend* and *Harmful Intent* seriously strain their readers' credulity, but the counterargument could be made that these killjoys are not devoted connoisseurs of the thriller novel and have not permitted these books' deliciously demonic plots to fully sweep them up. Whether or not the events these novels depict could ever actually occur (and the hope is certainly that they could not), the engrossing tales *Mindbend* and *Harmful Intent* relate can nonetheless be usefully regarded as fables for the times. As always, Cook enlightens his readers about the inner workings of the medical profession while addressing some thought provoking social issues. Readers who enjoy these books are certain to have some second thoughts about the motives and interests of various familiar institutions.

Mixed critical response to Cook's medical thrillers could reflect some confusion about the nature of this slightly unusual—or even hybrid—genre. Cook is not the only fiction writer who centers his suspenseful action within a hospital setting, but the use he makes of this setting strikes most readers as eerily realistic. A doctor himself, and a writer who scrupulously researches the technical details pertinent to his plots, Cook grounds his fictive action in a disturbingly authentic world. All

medical details (including Cook's extensive use of professional terminology) lend credence to his work. Nevertheless, ever since the publication of his first novel—a semi-autobiographical and highly realistic
portrait of a doctor's internship—Cook has been unabashedly a suspense
writer. As he has said, "I decided early on that I would couch my stories
as thrillers. It was an opportunity to get the public interested in things
about medicine they didn't seem to know about" (*CA*, New Revision
Series, 77).

Convinced that readers enjoy the gripping entertainment of a truly
frightening story, Cook generally uses the medium of the conspiracy plot
to address the professional and ethical issues he hopes his reading audience will consider. The conspiracy itself thus serves to exaggerate or
highlight the particular social danger that Cook envisions within a novel
(and only the serial killer, who is really an independent conspirator,
seems to strike the kind of terror that conspiracy inspires). By no means
a heavy-handed moralist, Robin Cook finds that the conspiracy plot
dramatizes his concerns while providing readers with plenty of the
thrills and chills that they expect with suspense fiction. Clearly the conspiracy plot has enjoyed a certain vogue in recent years; in the wake of
the Communist scare of the fifties, the Kennedy assassination of the six-
ties, and the Watergate scandal of the seventies, fiction writers and movie
producers have found a ready audience for their assorted conspiracy
theories. However, his frequent use of the conspiracy plot apparently
troubles some of Cook's reviewers; admittedly, conspiracy plots by their
very nature stretch belief, but for those readers who are willing, at least
temporarily, to suspend their disbelief (or to acknowledge the conspiracy
plot as a standard convention of the thriller genre), Cook has many a
thrilling tale to tell.

PLOT DEVELOPMENT AND SUSPENSE IN *MINDBEND*

Mindbend's prologue provides readers with an initial clue as to what
is afoot at New York City's Julian Clinic, a strange new hospital housed
in an ultramodern skyscraper that occupies an entire city block. Although personnel at the clinic prefer the phrase "pregnancy termina-
tion," this is a place where many abortions are performed, and
Mindbend's opening pages offer a vivid description of this procedure.
When the operation conducted in the prologue is successfully completed,
the physician who performed it, Dr. Foley, carefully packs his "speci-

men" among the others stored in a large shipping crate containing dry ice. It is thus made clear early in the novel that the Julian Clinic has a great interest in gathering specimens for the purpose of conducting research on fetal tissue.

The prologue also establishes that such research has been banned by law in the United States since 1974, when a "moratorium on 'research . . . on a living human fetus, before or after induced abortion" (*M*, 8) was put into effect. As readers soon learn, the specimens gathered at the Julian Clinic are shipped to Puerto Rico, where the company that owns the hospital maintains a large research facility.

Cook's brief prologue serves both structural and thematic purposes. On the one hand, it prepares readers for their dawning recognition that something is odd at the Julian Clinic. Dr. Foley speaks to his patient in a "peculiarly inflectionless voice" (*M*, 14), a hint of further revelations soon to come. Readers will observe that members of Julian's staff as well as its doctors behave in a stilted, almost robotic manner. Eager to please, indeed overly solicitous in their treatment of all patients, the hospital personnel appear to run the clinic as though it were some extravagant hotel. Nevertheless, the clinical details of the abortion are presented with graphic realism (down to the snapping sound of the latex gloves Dr. Foley puts on), and Cook thus establishes the aura of authenticity that his depiction of medical procedures inevitably evokes. All in all, the prologue presents the Julian Clinic as a strangely sinister place. As to theme, readers are introduced to the controversy surrounding fetal research: they learn that even though the use of fetal tissue has proved efficacious in treatment of diabetes and spinal cord injury, the supply of tissue is severely limited, largely because medically induced aborted fetuses are its source. Fetal research in this country is thus ineluctably "tied to the highly emotional abortion issue" (*M*, 8).

Although readers only gradually become aware of the significance of its far-reaching activities, MTIC, the company that owns the Julian Clinic, is *Mindbend*'s villainous corporation. In addition to the Julian, MTIC also controls Arolen Pharmaceuticals, a subdivision that markets and distributes a new line of drugs. Originally formed by a small financial group wishing to invest in a variety of interests within the lucrative health care industry, MTIC has grown with amazing speed. Its Puerto Rican research laboratories specialize in experimentation with fetal tissue and psychotropic drugs. Its hospital steadily provides the supply of human fetuses required for the research, and its pharmaceutical division aggressively peddles its drugs, offering doctors free samples and encouraging them to participate in a series of medical conferences held aboard its luxury Caribbean cruise ship.

Chapter 1 introduces *Mindbend*'s protagonist, a young third-year medical student. When Adam Schonberg and his wife, Jennifer, discover early in the novel that they are faced with an unplanned pregnancy, their life is suddenly disrupted. Neither partner wants an abortion, but Schonberg's medical studies have already thrown them deeply into debt. The couple does decide to have their baby; unfortunately, however, Jennifer Schonberg, who earns their living as a dancer, must give up her work. Adam therefore approaches his father (an eminent doctor who occupies a high position in the Food and Drug Administration), but his entreaties in that quarter fall on deaf ears, for years earlier his family disowned him when he chose to marry outside his faith. Jennifer's family is quite willing to lend assistance, but Adam is too proud to move into their house.

These details established, the stage is thus set for Adam's decision to take a temporary leave of absence from his medical studies. Acting against Jennifer's strenuous protestations—she wants to seek a job in a department store—he applies for a position as a sales representative for Arolen Pharmaceuticals. (Adam happens to remember the company's name because Arolen had presented his entire medical class with complimentary doctor's satchels made of handsome leather.) Arolen immediately hires Adam Schonberg; with his medical training, and with his family connection to an important FDA official, Schonberg appears to be an ideal candidate for a management position within the firm.

As he is laying the groundwork for an unfolding of the horrendous discoveries Adam Schonberg will make while in the employ of Arolen Pharmaceuticals, Robin Cook gives ominous hints of what is to come. One such foreshadowing occurs when Schonberg informs the dean of his medical school about his decision to withdraw from his studies. After Adam has announced his intention to join Arolen, "Dr. Markowitz flinched as if he'd been struck. 'That's where the money is,' he said, sighing. ' But I must say I feel as if you were deserting to the enemy. The pharmaceutical industry has been exerting more and more control over medical research recently, and I for one am legitimately concerned' '' (*M*, 69).

Arolen, of course, is interested in controlling more than just research, and one basis for the dean's concern becomes immediately apparent just after Adam Schonberg starts his job. As a sales representative, Schonberg is expected to possess background information on all the medical offices within his assigned district. Because his wife's doctor practices within his sales territory, Adam decides to call up Dr. Vandermer's name on his computer. Expecting to see notations on Vandermer's prescribing habits, Adam is both astonished and appalled when his computer prints out nearly fifty pages of data on this one doctor alone: "My God, thought Adam, this is Orwell's *1984*" (*M*, 137). The readout contains both professional and personal information, including details on Vandermer's parents, wife, and children. His financial investments are listed, and even his interests, hobbies, likes and dislikes are cited in the report. Noticing a category entitled "Personality Profile," Adam is bewildered, for "There was no reason for a drug firm like Arolen to have such a complete file on a doctor" (*M*, 137).

Having already studied his background, Schonberg decides to make Vandermer his first customer. Dr. Vandermer, however, has no time to waste on drug salesmen and, after lecturing Adam on the folly of leaving medical school, quickly dismisses him. He also warns him, however, not to suggest that Jennifer take Pregdolen, a product Arolen offers to treat morning sickness. Pregdolen, Dr. Vandermer sternly declares, is not a safe drug. As he is brusquely ushering Adam out the door, Dr. Vandermer happens to mention that he is scheduled to deliver a lecture on the next Arolen Conference Cruise.

Up to this point in the novel, *Mindbend*'s readers have been entertaining growing suspicions about the activities of the company for which Adam Schonberg works; now, however, all the elements are in place for Robin Cook to reveal the ways in which Arolen's designs are to impinge directly on the Schonbergs' personal lives. When Dr. Vandermer returns from his Caribbean cruise, he seems very different to the people who know him well. At Jennifer's monthly checkup he does suggest that she take Pregdolen to curb her morning sickness. He also informs her that he is transferring all his patients to the Julian Clinic, and that although he had earlier discouraged her from undergoing amniocentesis, he now recommends the procedure as a necessary precaution. When the amniocentesis indicates that Jennifer's fetus is abnormal, Dr. Vandermer, who previously refused to perform abortions, now encourages Jennifer to schedule one as soon as it can be arranged.

Certain that Dr. Vandermer was somehow brainwashed while he took the Arolen cruise, Adam tries to persuade Jennifer to see another doctor. When she refuses, and the couple has a serious falling out (Jennifer returns to her parents' house), Adam searches frantically for some means to convince his wife that the "new" Dr. Vandermer cannot now be trusted. In his desperation, he decides to try to find out exactly what happened to the doctor on Arolen's luxury liner. Masquerading as Dr. Smyth, one of Vandermer's office partners, Adam thus sets sail on a series of thrilling adventures.

Although the first half of *Mindbend* employs some of the plotting strategies conventional to suspense fiction (in one exciting scene, for example, Dr. Foley goes berserk and shoots his wife and then himself), in the novel's second half Robin Cook clearly pulls out all the stops. As more and more details of the book's conspiracy unfold, its suspenseful action becomes enthralling. There are numerous chases and narrow escapes: Schonberg, for instance, must eventually flee the Arolen cruise ship hidden in a refuse dumpster. There are also eerie scenes of science gone completely mad, for Schonberg quickly discovers that the doctors attending Arolen's conferences are indeed drugged, with pills and with substances implanted in their food. (Schonberg arranges to buy his food secretly from a member of the crew.) MTIC's Puerto Rican research center has developed a powerful psychotropic agent called, most appropriately, Conformin; when Conformin has produced its desired effects, and doctors' resistances are down, they are taken into the indoctrination room, a theatre with seats that look like "miniature electric chair[s] with a myriad of electrodes and straps" (*M*, 241). There, "Adam realized he was seeing the very latest in mind-control techniques involving adverse conditioning and positive reinforcing." Knowing that he has witnessed a "nightmare where the doctor has become the patient" (*M*, 242), Schonberg hastens back to New York to try to reason with his wife. Jennifer, who is still staying with her parents, and who is greatly annoyed by Adam's seemingly erratic behavior, remains convinced that the abortion is her only course.

In *Mindbend*'s hair-raising climax, Adam Schonberg visits Puerto Rico, the heart of the MTIC empire. Having secured a temporary restraining order to delay Jennifer's abortion, Adam now has three days to obtain the proof he needs to back up his incredible story. Racing against the clock, he requires the means to regain Jennifer's confidence and to convince his father that government intervention will be necessary to put an end to the company's nasty plot. To visit Puerto Rico, Schonberg must employ another ruse; this time he pretends that he is now ready to enter Arolen's management training program, and the company officials, happy to accommodate him, give him the grand tour of their extensive research facilities.

New horrors await Schonberg at MTIC's central plant. In addition to its state-of-the-art laboratories, the company maintains a hospital where patients "voluntarily" undergo experimental treatment. When he visits the psychiatric ward, where supposedly mentally ill patients are being treated with therapeutic psychotropic drugs, Adam recognizes one of the doctors he met on the Arolen cruise. He therefore inquires about this patient and is informed that microelectrodes have been implanted in the limbic system of his brain to cure his "epilepsy." Knowing that in reality the psychosurgery was performed to gain control of the doctor's mind, Adam understands the implications of what he sees before him: "An entire generation of doctors programmed to be unknowing representatives of a pharmaceutical house" (M, 297).

Deciding that the rescue of this doctor will provide him with the evidence he needs, Adam plans an escape from the heavily guarded Puerto Rican enclave. The final chase scene is undeniably a thrilling one, including a jaunt through shark-infested waters on a flimsy Hobie Cat. Cook obviously delights in producing whimsical variations on his genre's standard chase motif, and *Mindbend*'s chases are no exception. The flight from Puerto Rico becomes particularly harrowing when MTIC's researchers activate the electrodes implanted in their victim's head. Then, ironically, Adam Schonberg must fend off the very man he is trying to rescue. In the end, however, the two are finally able to make good their escape, and *Mindbend*'s epilogue brings the novel to a close. Readers learn that Adam returns to medical school, witnesses the birth of his healthy son, and at last enjoys a long awaited reconciliation with his father.

PLOT DEVELOPMENT AND SUSPENSE IN *HARMFUL INTENT*

Harmful Intent is plotted with some special turns and twists. The novel actually features both a plot within a plot and a villain who unexpectedly turns out to be a friend. Essentially a tale about entrapment, this version of Cook's characteristic medical thriller recounts an innocent doctor's desperate efforts to free himself from a terrible web of circumstance that has thoroughly ensnared him. In *Harmful Intent* Cook is interested in examining the pall that the constant threat of malpractice litigation casts over the entire medical profession; he uses the unfortunate plight of his protagonist, Dr. Jeffrey Rhodes, to dramatize his point.

The novel opens with a fully detailed and clinical account of the tragic events that lead up to Dr. Rhodes's murder trial. When Boston's "bright September sunlight" is suddenly "eclipsed by a dark cloud" (HI, 3), readers recognize that September 9, 1988, is destined to be a fateful day. A young pregnant woman, Patty Owen, begins experiencing regular contractions a week before her anticipated delivery date. Exceedingly nervous about giving birth to her first child, she requests epidural anesthesia. Dr. Rhodes is the anesthesiologist on call at Boston Memorial, and although he is suffering the early stages of the flu, the case promises to be routine: Patty Owen is in good health, and there are at first no apparent complications with the delivery.

The prologue carefully accounts for Dr. Rhodes's every movement as he prepares to handle the Owen case; the significance of these details becomes readily apparent in Chapter 1, where those who testify against him at his trial misinterpret some of his actions. Before meeting with Patty Owen, Dr. Rhodes stops by his locker to take a dose of paregoric, an old remedy for upset stomach. Then, as is his habit, he spends time with his patient, explaining his procedures and determining that she has no allergies to the drugs that he will use. Jeffrey Rhodes is clearly a conscientious doctor, but his intestinal cramps threaten to interfere with his work. In an effort to make it through the delivery, his last case for the day, he tries an old trick he recalls from his time as a medical resident. Hooking himself up to an IV, he runs a liter of Ringer's Lactate liquid into his system. (Ringer's Lactate is a preparation used to restore the body's fluids and electrolytes.) Dr. Rhodes does feel restored, but, unfortunately, a nurse who observes him doing this later draws some sinister conclusions.

Patty Owen's labor is prolonged, and when complications become evident, her obstetrician, Dr. Simarian, decides to perform a Caesarean section. Everything goes smoothly until Dr. Rhodes injects an additional dose of Marcaine (her anesthetic) taken from a fresh vial. Unbeknownst to the operating team, the new vial contains deadly batrachotoxin, an exotic substance extracted from the skin of South American frogs. As the toxin enters her system, Patty Owen instantly begins to fail, and the prologue graphically describes her doctors' valiant attempts to revive her. Throughout the ensuing crisis, Dr. Rhodes remains "the ultimate professional. He had been trained to deal with this type of emergency situation. His mind raced ahead, taking in all the information, making hypotheses, then ruling them out" (*HI*, 16). Sparing no effort, including internal cardiac massage, Rhodes and the emergency doctors futilely attempt to save Patty Owen's life. The terrible day's unexpected disaster is finally complete when it becomes apparent that the baby, deprived of oxygen, has suffered brain damage. Gazing one last time at the "sorry sight of Patty Owen with her abdomen and chest rudely sliced open," Rhodes knows that he has reached the "nadir of his professional life" (*HI*, 20).

The gripping hospital scene that introduces *Harmful Intent*'s suspenseful action is replaced in Chapter 1 by an equally dramatic courtroom scene. Eight months have passed since Patty Owen's horrible death, and Jeffrey Rhodes, charged with second degree murder, is about to hear the jury's verdict. As he waits to learn his fate, the memory of the earlier malpractice trial comes back into his mind. Robin Cook's strategically skillful use of this flashback technique allows him to superimpose the details of one trial upon the other. Although the original civil suit had named the hospital, the obstetrician, the cardiac surgeon, and the drug company that manufactured the Marcaine in addition to Dr. Rhodes, all defendants except Jeffrey Rhodes had been exonerated at that trial. Insinuating that Rhodes had administered morphine to himself before attending to Patty Owen, the malpractice attorney had been able to persuade the jury to find him guilty and to award $11 million to the Owen estate. The sensational nature of the trial subsequently led the district attorney to file criminal charges, and it now seems to Rhodes that the jury's decision hinges, as it did before, on whether or not its members believe he took morphine rather than Ringer's fluid. If they conclude that the IV held morphine, "then they would find he had acted with harmful intent" (*HI*, 33).

The jury does indeed return with a guilty verdict, and *Harmful Intent* maintains its deeply suspenseful tension when, at the end of the first chapter, Rhodes very nearly ends his life. The months leading up to the trial have been nerve-wracking ones, and the crushing finale to them is almost more than Rhodes can endure. When the verdict is read, "deep down he realized that for all his fears, he'd really never believed he'd be convicted—simply because he was not guilty. He'd never been involved in the legal system before, and he'd always trusted that 'truth would out' if he ever was wrongly accused. But that belief had been false. Now he'd be going to prison" (*HI*, 36). Released on bail while his attorney prepares to appeal, Rhodes now has little faith left in the justice system and seriously doubts that an appeal would be to any avail. The jury, after all, has pronounced him guilty on purely circumstantial evidence, and there is no reason to expect that another decision would be different.

Rhodes's bail is a huge sum, $500,000. The bail bondsman arranges a lien against Rhodes's real estate property, but his own fee is $45,000, and he requires a cash payment within twenty-four hours. This detail is important, because although Rhodes does secure the money, he fails to pay the bondsman; this action, of course, brings an unwanted complication to his life: Devlin O'Shea, former policeman and bounty hunter, begins a relentless pursuit of Dr. Rhodes.

After his near suicide, Jeffrey Rhodes decides that he must leave the country. Carrying with him his bondsman's fee, he actually boards a plane for South America before he vacillates once again. Realizing that his flight would signify an irreversible decision, and that in truth he has no plans and is merely reacting in despair, he asks the cabin attendant to let him leave the plane. In these early scenes Robin Cook effectively renders Rhodes's frantic desperation as his feeling of entrapment deepens. Unable to decide what he should do, friendless and with little hope, Rhodes sees no purpose to his life. Developing his entrapment theme, Cook vividly demonstrates the shattering effects of the malpractice suit on a doctor's life.

Taking stock of his grim emotional state, Rhodes recognizes that it would be a great comfort to talk with someone who might understand the experience he is going through. On the off-chance that she might be willing to meet with him, he calls Kelly Everson, the widow of a friend who did commit suicide when he too was charged with malpractice two years earlier. Kelly Everson welcomes a visit with Jeffrey Rhodes, and it is she who gives him his first glimmer of hope. When she mentions that her husband, who was also an anesthesiologist, wondered if there might have been a contaminant in the drugs he used, Rhodes, for the first time, lights upon this possibility. Everson provides him with the notes her husband made about his last case, and Rhodes is stunned by its similarity to the Patty Owen case: both patients received epidural anesthesia using Marcaine, and neither patient had a history of allergy to that drug. Furthermore, the symptoms leading to cardiac arrest were the same in both the cases. Could there possibly have been a contaminant in the vials of Marcaine?

Armed with fresh hope, possibly even a reason to live, Rhodes heads back to his house, only to confront a new source of trouble. Devlin O'Shea awaits him, and when Rhodes fails to hand over his briefcase full of money, the burly O'Shea roughs him up. Promising that he will turn over his bail fee in the morning, Rhodes manages to get rid of O'Shea, but now he is thoroughly panicked. O'Shea is exactly the sort of person he fears he will encounter while in prison, and this thought is more than he can bear. Determined, this time, to flee to Brazil, Rhodes

once again drives to Logan International Airport. On this occasion, however, Devlin is trailing him, and just as Rhodes reaches the X-ray machine, his nemesis apprehends him. Using his briefcase, Rhodes delivers
O'Shea a smashing blow and is thus able to make his escape. Now,
however, clearly guilty of attempting to jump his bail, Dr. Jeffrey Rhodes
is a fugitive from the law. (Cook himself has commented on the apparent
similarities between his story and the plot of a recent popular movie,
The Fugitive.)

Having employed the high drama of his opening scenes to engage his
readers' sympathies for the plight of Jeffrey Rhodes, Cook shifts *Harmful
Intent's* narrative movement to the episodic pattern so familiar to the
suspense genre. His protagonist is clearly in big trouble: caught up in
circumstances he can hope to control only if he can somehow find proof
that he is innocent of harmful intent in the death of Patty Owen, Dr.
Rhodes sets forth to see what he can discover. After going into hiding,
shaving off his moustache and dying his hair, he obtains employment in
the housekeeping department at Boston Memorial. (With his housekeeping keys he has full access to documents stored in the hospital.) With
help from Kelly Everson (who is a nurse at another Boston hospital), he
begins to gather records on cases similar to his own. Indeed, a grisly
pattern is beginning to emerge, and Rhodes becomes more convinced
than ever that someone has regularly been tampering with the Marcaine
used at several of the city's hospitals.

Meanwhile, readers are introduced to Trent Harding, the psychopathic
nurse who is responsible for creating all the havoc in other people's lives.
Because skilled nurses are greatly in demand, Harding is able to move
easily from one job to another, invariably leaving ruin in his wake. A
truly frightening character, Harding denies his own homosexual inclinations by tormenting others. In addition to the patients who are his
victims, he maliciously injects with his deadly frog toxin a nurse who
has chanced to notice him in the vicinity of the hospital's drug cabinet.
(Although the nurse did not directly observe him substituting one vial
of Marcaine for another, Harding clearly suffers from paranoia.)

Devlin O'Shea, angry at letting Rhodes slip out of his grasp, is determined to track him down. In addition to the satisfaction he will gain in
finally cornering his prey, he stands to collect a hefty reward for bringing
to justice someone who has forfeited his bail. As a former policeman, he
is exceedingly effective at his job. When he does find the doctor, at the
sleazy hotel room he has rented, Rhodes is forced to give him an injection
of succinylcholine (a drug that induces temporary paralysis) to effect an

escape. As soon as O'Shea's body has metabolized the drug, he once again sets off in hot pursuit of the elusive Dr. Rhodes.

Shifting scenes among the activities of Harding and Rhodes and O'Shea, Cook steadily builds *Harmful Intent*'s suspenseful action. When Rhodes obtains personnel records that indicate that Harding was employed at each of the hospitals that experienced one of the anesthesia deaths, he arranges a meeting with Harding. His ploy is to get Harding to confess while he uses Kelly Everson, hidden nearby, as a witness. By this time O'Shea has once again discovered Rhodes's whereabouts, and he follows as Rhodes and Everson head for their rendezvous. This time O'Shea's presence is most welcome, for the plot suddenly takes a completely surprising turn. Professional killers are present, and they assassinate Trent Harding. O'Shea, protecting his interest in Dr. Rhodes, manages to rescue both Rhodes and Everson.

As Cook's novel nears its climax, it has become apparent that Trent Harding was not acting alone when he tampered with the Marcaine. Someone clearly intervened to prevent the meeting between Rhodes and Harding from taking place. Near despair because he had hoped that Harding would provide proof of his innocence, Rhodes tries one last desperate measure to find the evidence he needs. He persuades a pathologist friend to prepare an exhumation permit for one of the batrachotoxin victims. Now that Rhodes and the pathologist know the nature of the toxin they are seeking, they expect to find its residue in the victim's organs. With a grisly graveyard scene, one where Rhodes, Everson, O'Shea, the hired hitmen, and various public officials all converge on a remote cemetery on Martha's Vineyard, Cook offers his readers their final thrill. The gunmen threaten the gravediggers, but Rhodes manages to distract them momentarily when he wallops the leader of the killers over the head with a bag of entrails. Once again, however, it is Devlin O'Shea who really saves the day. Curious about the appearance of the hired thugs, O'Shea has discovered through his underworld informants that the lawyer who filed the malpractice action against Dr. Rhodes was the same man who hired the hitmen. Rhodes is finally led off to jail (the wheels of justice do not turn quickly), but he now has a future he can look forward to: his hospital has agreed to reinstate him, and Kelly Everson has agreed to be his wife.

CHARACTER DEVELOPMENT

Character development in *Mindbend* and *Harmful Intent* is secondary to Cook's depiction of the desperate circumstances in which both his protagonists find themselves. In other words, Adam Schonberg and Jeffrey Rhodes primarily engage readers' sympathies through their responses to the predicaments they encounter. Both are victims of the seemingly impersonal workings of remote institutions, and both fight back, with the ingenuity and determination born of their desperation. Readers are thus likely to see Cook's two heroes as modern-day Davids confronting monstrous new Goliaths.

Although Cook's angle of focus is directed more toward what happens to his protagonists than to the characters themselves, certain personal details are obviously important within the context of his plots. Schonberg's alienation from his father, for example, drives him to seek employment with Arolen Drugs; appropriately, therefore, it is his subsequent heroic behavior that finally wins him his father's respect. As for Dr. Rhodes, Cook takes great pains in *Harmful Intent*'s prologue to detail this experienced anesthesiologist's meticulous preparations for his case (Rhodes actually showers and changes his surgical garb twice before attending to his patient). It is, of course, crucial to the unfolding of his plot that Cook convince his readers early on that Rhodes is, in fact, blameless, and he achieves this by emphasizing Rhodes's competence as a doctor. When, however, his marriage failed and his career seemingly over, it appears that Jeffrey Rhodes has nothing left to live for, he too is driven to find within himself the capacity to take heroic measures.

Presenting his novels' central characters as quite ordinary people, Cook uses dire circumstances to fully test their mettle. Obviously a devoted couple, the recently married Adam and Jennifer Schonberg nevertheless begin to suffer disagreements when their plans are disrupted by the unexpected pregnancy. A strong-willed and responsible young woman, Jennifer wishes to uphold her end of their bargain and find a job to support them while Adam completes his medical training. Adam, however, is a proud young man, too proud to consider Jennifer's plan to take a menial job, and too proud to accept assistance from her willing family. Adam's stubborness in this respect is a shortcoming, one that in fact leads to his many harrowing adventures. His act of breaking trust with his wife strains the marriage and almost costs him his baby son's life. Nevertheless, having set forth upon his impetuous course, Adam proves himself to be brave and resourceful in the face of great danger; indeed, in this context his stubborn persistence serves him well.

In his struggle to reclaim the life he has lost, Jeffrey Rhodes finds a courageous companion in the person of Kelly Everson. Everson is one of Cook's several strong female characters: perceptive and sympathetic, she has attained remarkable emotional maturity through the experience of suffering the loss of her husband. It is thus Everson, speaking from the wisdom of her own unhappy experience, who points out to a despairing Rhodes the cruel consequences of anybody's suicide. Acknowledging the truth of Everson's arguments, Rhodes vows to himself that his new goal must be the job of clearing his name. In this pursuit he and Everson turn out to be a well- matched team. Relying upon their intelligence and determination, the two set forth to unravel the plot that has wickedly ensnared more than one conscientious doctor.

Surprisingly, perhaps, *Harmful Intent*'s Devlin O'Shea is unquestionably the most colorful character within the pages of these two books. Although the burly bounty hunter is clearly a variation on one of the thriller genre's stock character types, Robin Cook enjoyed some sport when he invented Mr. O'Shea. Looking "more like a sixties-style biker than a former Boston policeman" (*HI*, 62), O'Shea wears a gold earring, a ponytail, and black cowboy boots. Six feet, five inches tall and weighing 268 pounds, he is distinctly an imposing figure. Nevertheless, it is his wonderfully robust temperament that really catches a reader's eye. Wryly aware of the image he presents and aware, too, of the ways that image serves him in his unusual line of work, O'Shea cheerfully imposes, bullies, and takes command. (And like a bad penny, he keeps turning up.) A rogue (O'Shea was removed from the police force after he was caught accepting bribes), he is unswervingly cynical about large institutions, and it is this, in part, that leads him to sympathize with Dr. Rhodes. Ever interested in food and drink, this finally comical figure appears to have a touch of Falstaff in him.

THEMATIC ISSUES

In the author's note that accompanies *Mindbend*, Robin Cook directly addresses his novel's central theme when he warns his readers: "What we are witnessing today is the gradual but quickening pace of the intrusion of business into medicine. It must be understood that the corporate mentality of the balance sheet is diametrically opposed to the traditional aspects of altruism that have formed the foundation of the practice of medicine, and this dichotomy augurs disaster for the moral and ethical foundations of the profession" (*M*, 347). Of course it is his worry about a loss of his profession's "moral and ethical foundations" that inspires him to portray the mindbent doctors of his novel as mere automatons. Robots in the hands of business, Vandermer and Foley and the other members of the Julian's staff have in effect been robbed of their doctor's souls. Readers who appreciate the unmistakably allegorical implications of Cook's plotting device will recognize its similarity to one he employs in *Acceptable Risk*: in that novel the researchers who lose sight of their moral purposes are transformed into beasts.

Cook's general concern with the current relationship between medicine and business (a concern he also expresses in such novels as *Mortal Fear*, *Terminal*, *Fatal Cure*, and *Contagion*), is particularized in *Mindbend* to focus on an enterprise that has obvious associations with the medical profession. As he further comments in his explanatory note, he chose in *Mindbend* to focus on the pharmaceutical industry not because it has necessarily "been any worse than any other group, but because it has been around longer than most businesses associated with medicine and it exerts a powerful and growing influence." Given this influence, it is important, he believes, to note that "drug firms are corporations which do not exist for the public weal, no matter how much they try to convince the public otherwise. Their goal is to provide a return on their investors' capital" (*M*, 349). The strength of the industry's profit motive is such, Cook goes on to say, that it spends even more each year on advertising and promotion than it spends on drug research. He further notes that very few doctors indeed have never received some gratuitous product or service provided by the drug industry. MTIC, of course, spends vast sums on both promotion and research, but in his depiction of Arolen's aggressive sales techniques, Cook affords his readers special insight into the promotion angle. Besides presenting medical students with doctor's bags, Arolen representatives freely distribute Cross pens and plentiful pharmaceutical samples. Before he goes into the field, Schonberg is schooled in the use of effective sales techniques. He learns how to flatter secretaries and receptionists as a means of gaining access to the doctors. For the doctors he has stacks of literature detailing company-sponsored studies of the efficacy of its drugs. And Arolen's coup de grâce, of course, is its series of conference cruises. Hoping to further expand its deadly sphere of influence, MTIC plans to increase the size of its fleet from one ship to five.

Although not as significant as its central theme, two other issues worth considering are raised in *Mindbend*. Robin Cook's work frequently comments on the nature and direction of medical research, and this novel too poses some questions for readers to ponder. One has to do with research involving fetal tissue. Although the Julian Clinic is undoubtedly engaging in unscrupulous practices, Cook does make clear that this special field of medical inquiry has offered some promising results. While this country's deeply emotional public debate over abortion continues to rage, however, fetal tissue research will most certainly be caught up in the turmoil—with the result that politics will likely guide its course. After all, the Julian Clinic is responding to restrictive laws and attitudes as it employs its deceptions. The other related research question has to do with regulatory practices. As Cook illustrates in *Mortal Fear*, private research activity is difficult to govern. Although it produces drugs for the American marketplace, MTIC has purposefully established its research base outside of the United States and thus beyond its regulatory jurisdiction. Its products, of course, still require FDA approval, but its research is conducted in relative isolation. Although there is no apparent solution to the problem, Cook nonetheless wishes to draw it to his readers' attention.

In *Harmful Intent* Robin Cook looks at the way another specialized profession intersects with the practice of medicine. When doctors and lawyers meet, the issue is malpractice. Cook is not interested, in this particular novel, in exploring the possibility that legal remedy could serve an important public purpose. Rather, he is only concerned about the excessive or improper use of legal sanctions and duly alerts readers to this fact by using Shakespeare's familiar sentiment as his epigraph: "The first thing we do, let's kill all the lawyers."

Dr. Jeffrey Rhodes is the victim of a legal system that is more interested in who wins and who loses than in the pursuit of justice. A common enough complaint about the workings of the law, this point is driven home for Rhodes when he discovers that his faith that truth will out is completely unjustified. His disillusionment results in anger, and when he stops to think about it, he realizes that "what angered him was the legal system and the lawyers who ran it. How could lawyers like the district attorney or the plaintiff attorney live with themselves when they lied so much? From the depositions Jeffrey knew they did not believe their own prosecution ploys. Each of Jeffrey's trials had been an amoral process in which the opposing attorneys had allowed ends to justify dishonest means" (*HI*, 42). While neither Rhodes nor the reader is aware of the extent of these lawyers' monstrous dishonesty until the climax of the story, Rhodes's insight is clearly to the point: in each of the trials events were distorted and misconstrued until they pointed to conclusions far removed from actual fact.

Greed is usually a central motive in Cook's depictions of organized corruption. *Harmful Intent*'s legal partners in crime are taking advantage of the huge settlements that juries sometimes award plaintiffs who sue organizations or other groups of people. Called the "shotgun" approach, their strategy is to sue "everybody with 'deep pockets' whether or not there [is] any evidence of direct involvement in the alleged incident of malpractice" (*HI*, 25). Those with the "deep pockets," of course, are the doctors, hospitals, and drug companies covered by malpractice insurance. The plaintiff's attorney brutalizes Dr. Rhodes as a means of inflaming the jury members, but ironically, when the trial is over and the scapegoat has been sacrificed, he is "openly disappointed that he'd done such a good job destroying Jeffrey. Since the other defendants and their deep pockets had been exculpated, there was little chance of collecting much above and beyond Jeffrey's insurance coverage" (*HI*, 32). Naturally it is small comfort to Rhodes that the attorney has thus been hoist with his own petard, for his own life has been ruined in any case. The novel's "harmful intent" has been practiced by lawyers who ruthlessly exploit the legal system to enrich themselves at others' expense. Ironically, the justice system has thus been made the instrument of a terrible injustice.

ALTERNATIVE PERSPECTIVE: CULTURAL CRITICISM

Although a study of literature is one of the many interests of cultural criticism, this relatively new field of inquiry is more generally committed to a broad investigation of human social life. An interdisciplinary project, cultural criticism draws upon a variety of analytical methods to seek understanding of the multifaceted natures of different cultures and of their networks of interconnected institutions. As the editors of *Cultural Studies*, a 1992 anthology, explain in their introduction, "the major categories of current work in cultural studies" include inquiries into "the history of cultural studies, gender and sexuality, nationhood and national identity, colonialism and postcolonialism, race and ethnicity, popular culture and its audiences, science and ecology, identity politics, pedagogy, the politics of aesthetics, cultural institutions, the politics of disciplinarity, discourse and textuality, history, and global culture in a postmodern age'' (Nelson, Treichler, and Grossberg, 1).

This broad spectrum of interests offers several categories relevant to explorations of Robin Cook's work. An unquestionably successful writer of popular fiction, Cook plays a significant role in the contemporary cultural scene. His wide following suggests that his characteristically suspenseful treatment of the politics of medicine strikes a distinctly responsive chord in this society. His fascination with science and with the emerging trends in medical research addresses a growing awareness that developments within these fields generally carry with them far-reaching implications. In *Mindbend* and *Harmful Intent*, however, Cook presents his readers with an especially intriguing reading of the unmediated contradictions that vex two major cultural institutions.

When Cook declares in his author's note to *Mindbend* that corporations do not exist to serve ''the public weal,'' he is, without mincing words, merely pointing out that making money is the raison d'être of business. While business does indeed offer products or services that serve the public's needs, this fact is necessarily secondary to its central objective, for the company that does not make a profit is obviously unlikely to stay in business long. (Even the ''green'' enterprises that have recently sought to serve consumers who possess a public conscience need to make a profit. These companies, nevertheless, do make efforts to bridge the gap between self-interest and interest in the general welfare. Perhaps they signal a promising change within the institution of business itself.)

The traditional purposes of medicine and law, however, have been quite different from that of business, and it is for this reason that Cook notes that medicine has a ''foundation'' based on ''altruism.'' Cook purposefully chooses these terms to assert that medicine, while it unquestionably provides a living for its practitioners, nonetheless also demands of them dedication to an ideal of public service. And this is by no means Cook's private opinion; medicine's identity as a cultural institution has been shaped by a general agreement about its aims and goals: medicine exists to preserve and safeguard human life. Similarly, the practice of law is based on an assumption that it, too, rests upon a foundation, that of the ideal of justice. The society, therefore, identifies law as the cultural institution that exists to execute (as well as to preserve and safeguard) its principles of justice. Those who practice medicine and law therefore belong to socially sanctioned professions committed to the promotion of the general good.

Within contemporary society both medicine and law have formed strong partnerships with business. For-profit medical practices and law firms juggle traditionally defined social responsibilities and business interests. (As part of their social obligation, many hospitals treat a certain percentage of indigent patients, and most law firms provide some pro bono legal services.) Robin Cook, however, is exceedingly uneasy about the bonds between the medical and legal professions and the business world. Noting that the central business imperative of producing profit is "diametrically opposed" to the greater social purposes medicine and law both serve, he fears that profit motives threaten to compromise or displace the historical principles of altruism and justice. In *Mindbend* and *Harmful Intent*, therefore, he presents readers with scenarios wherein these professions have been stripped of their traditional cultural values.

Focusing in *Mindbend* on the institution of medicine, Cook demonstrates how health care, bereft of altruism, no longer serves its patients' needs. The ruthless company that has seized control of medical products and services manipulates its consumers, foisting on them its harmful drugs (Pregdolen), and using them for its own self-serving ends (medical experimentation and fetus collection). While the exaggeration Cook employs to dramatize his point encourages his readers to regard this story as a fable, the vision he proposes in *Harmful Intent* is much less farfetched. The legal profession's strong business interests in litigation are, after all, widely recognized. That entire law firms have devoted their practices to the pursuit of personal injury claims suggests that this special interest is a particularly lucrative one. More chilling, however, than the vision of lawyers capitalizing on the misfortune of others is *Harmful Intent*'s depiction of a legal system that has lost sight of justice. Dr. Rhodes's trials make a mockery of truth, and not only do the novel's malefactors violate the principles of their profession (as well as the laws they are sworn to uphold), but because the evidence against them is merely hearsay, they cannot themselves finally be brought to an account. Thus any justice the novel offers occurs outside the offices of the law.

When public service institutions are conjoined with big business, conflicting impulses emerge. Today many professionals within medicine and law find themselves balancing their traditional commitment to the general welfare of their society against the temptations of the profit motive. Cook's novels offer grim warning about the future of medicine and law should the business impulse finally prevail.

For additional discussion of the interests of the cultural critic, see the concluding sections of Chapters 3 and 8.

7

Outbreak
(1987) and
Vital Signs
(1991)

Outbreak (1987) and *Vital Signs* (1991), Robin Cook's eighth and twelfth novels, are the only books to date that share a central character. The protagonist in these thrillers, Dr. Marissa Blumenthal, is beyond doubt the most widely traveled of Cook's several adventuresome heroines. She is, as well, the survivor of more nasty scrapes and harrowing escapades than any of Cook's other characters. This is testimony both to the action-packed plots of these novels and to the feisty nature of their protagonist. Both books feature elaborate conspiracies, and in them Dr. Blumenthal is called upon to unravel the inventive entanglements of two of Cook's most compelling suspense thrillers. Both books, too, invite their readers' serious contemplation of important ethical issues associated with the contemporary practice of medicine.

Although readers need not be familiar with *Outbreak*, Cook's first Blumenthal novel, to thoroughly enjoy *Vital Signs*, there are obviously some advantages to reading these books in the order in which they were published. *Vital Signs* makes occasional reference to Dr. Blumenthal's past history, and Cyrill Dubchek, a major figure in *Outbreak*, also plays a minor role in *Vital Signs*.

It should further be noted that although a movie released in the spring of 1995 bore the title *Outbreak*, this production was not a film version of Robin Cook's novel. Because book titles are not subject to copyright laws, Cook could not lay claim to his original title. Ironically, therefore, when a version of Cook's novel was aired on television shortly after the appearance of the movie, it required a new title. He elected to call the televison adaptation *Virus*, emphasizing the highly visible role played by its killer microbe.

MEDICAL ISSUES

As is his habit, Robin Cook has carefully researched the medical issues and themes upon which *Outbreak* and *Vital Signs* build their suspenseful tales. *Outbreak*, as its title suggests, introduces readers to the specialized medical field of epidemiology. Dr. Blumenthal, who is a field examiner for Atlanta's Centers for Disease Control (CDC), is on call to investigate cases of mysterious or undiagnosed illness at sites across the country. (Readers will recall that over its history the CDC has dispatched teams to investigate such outbreaks as those of Legionnaires' disease in 1976 and, more recently, the Hanta virus.) In *Vital Signs*, which takes place a couple of years after Blumenthal has left the CDC, Cook leads readers into the controversial and as yet not fully regulated world of fertility clinics and their in vitro fertilization practices. This novel does much to enlighten readers about an intriguing medical field that has generally remained cloaked in mystery.

One of the villains Dr. Blumenthal encounters in *Outbreak* is none other than the deadly Ebola virus. In publishing *Outbreak* before the appearance of Richard Preston's *The Hot Zone* (1994) or Laurie Garrett's *The Coming Plague* (1994), Robin Cook anticipates the general interest in virology that has accompanied the spread of AIDS. *Outbreak*'s prologue acquaints readers with the details of the first known appearance of Ebola at a small mission hospital near the Ebola River in the Yambuku region of Zaire. At this time, in the autumn of 1976, samples of the new virus were sent for study to the Centers for Disease Control.

Cook uses the presence of the Ebola virus in the United States to concoct a wicked tale of conspiracy and intrigue. A vial of the virus, stolen from the maximum containment locker at the CDC, is turned into a terrible weapon. In imagining this scenario, Cook means not only to present his readers with a heart-stopping thriller, but also to suggest that *Outbreak* might be considered a cautionary tale. As he notes in respect to his plot, "In an age of terrorism, biological agents deserve the same level of concern and security as nuclear material. The adage 'an ounce of prevention is worth a pound of cure' could never be more apropos" ("Deadly Obsession," 24).

The conspiracy envisioned in *Outbreak* arises from a conflict of interests present today in the country's health care industry. In the novel, a political action committee composed of wealthy, ultraconservative doctors wishes to impede the growth of independent, low-cost clinics. Robin Cook's plots are notably inspired by actual circumstances or events, and about the scheme he depicts in *Outbreak* he has said, "In the '70s, investigators found evidence of collusion among fee-for-service doctors against the formation of HMOs. So I took that historical episode and used it" ("Doctor Fear," 84). Of course, in his use of the historical episode Cook elaborates on what actually occurred, but he does so to dramatize one of the recurring themes of his fiction: in *Outbreak* he illustrates once again the terrifying consequences of conscienceless self-interest and unbounded greed.

Vital Signs offers readers an unusual twist—in this novel the doctor becomes the patient. Marissa Blumenthal, now married and aware of the ticking of her biological clock, wants to begin raising a family. After her discovery that blocked fallopian tubes have rendered her infertile, she opts to undergo in vitro fertilization procedures. Doctors, it is said, make notoriously bad patients, but Marissa Blumenthal's excruciating experiences at the Boston Women's Clinic would prove trying for almost anyone. Strengthened by her obsession to become pregnant, she endures regular injections of mood-altering hormones as well as repeated cycles of egg extraction and implantation. This expensive, time-consuming, and emotionally exhausting effort takes its toll: Blumenthal's own medical practice suffers, and her marriage begins to deteriorate. A counselor she visits sums up her position well:

> "Basically, the problem is a Sophie's choice," Linda said halfway into the hour. "You have two equally unsatisfactory possibilities: you can accept your infertility without further treatment as your husband is suggesting and thereby live a life that is contrary to your expectations, or you can continue with the IVF, which will lead to continued stress on yourself and on your relationship, continued cost as your husband has pointed out, and continued stress for you both with no guarantee of success." (*Vital Signs*, 54; hereafter cited as *VS*)

Robin Cook has clearly studied the intricacies of the in vitro fertilization procedure and offers readers an exceedingly realistic understanding of the technicalities involved. As scenes between Marissa and her husband Robert Buchanan reveal, the process exacts an emotional toll on both members of the couple. Self-conscious about his repeated visits to the clinic to make sperm donations, Robert complains, "Part of the problem for me is that we have lost our private life. I feel like a fish in a fishbowl" (49). Marissa, caught in "a constant state of PMS" (16), fears that her whole life is about to spin out of control. Cook himself is greatly sympathetic to the courage and stamina required of those who choose this course and therefore dedicates *Vital Signs* to "the countless couples who have suffered the emotional and physical trials and tribulations of infertility and its modern treatments." He concludes the text with an annotated bibliography for readers who might wish to explore the subject further.

Like *Outbreak*, *Vital Signs* seeks to thrill readers with an account of devilish deeds that take place within the hallowed ranks of the medical profession. Greed is once again the motivating force for opportunistic scoundrels, and the conspiracy, which in this case successfully nets billions of dollars, takes place on a worldwide scale. Drawing upon an arcane set of medical practices, an international cartel of fertility clinics has found a means of cruelly capitalizing on the fears and hopes of infertile couples. Since each cycle of egg extraction, fertilization, and implantation costs up to $10,000, the clinics manipulate their success rates to guarantee that couples will undergo the process several times. (Marissa, for instance, is told that she should not give up hope of becoming pregnant before she has made eight attempts.) Even more horrendous, however, is the plot that lies beneath this scheme. Borrowing expertise from China, which has laws strictly limiting family size, the masterminds behind the clinics have found a way to create a steady market for the professional services they offer. Carefully choosing young, affluent couples as their victims, they themselves induce the damage that is likely to bring the couples back.

PLOT DEVELOPMENT

Robin Cook is indeed a master of the techniques of the suspense thriller, and in *Outbreak* and *Vital Signs* he pulls out all the stops. At heart, the action of each novel centers upon the protagonist's quest to get to the bottom of the very nasty suspicions circumstances have forced her to entertain. Since Marissa Blumenthal can say, "I've always been fascinated by stories of medical detective work" (*Outbreak*, 28; hereafter cited as *O*), she is the appropriate person for the job. In *Outbreak*, her investigations take her from coast to coast across the United States, and in *Vital Signs* she visits Australia, Hong Kong, and, eventually, China in pursuit of clues. Her travels provide Cook with a narrative structure suitable for the episodic adventures that characterize suspense fiction. Part of the thrill of this genre lies in the chase, and in this respect both books excel: Blumenthal chases her clues with an exotic assortment of villains trailing in hot pursuit. In *Outbreak* she must elude a wooden-armed assassin, and in *Vital Signs* a great white shark. Noting the exuberance of these surprising twists of plot, one reviewer has commented, "Robin Cook . . . is an original, one of those endearingly zany writers who give the lie to the notion that fact is stranger than fiction" (Queenan, 12).

In truth, Cook's plots depend upon his ingenious blending of fact and fiction. Cook is still the dominant figure within the genre he has done so much to shape, and his novels instruct or warn while they deliciously entertain. On the one hand, a reviewer has observed, "Cook's popular medical thrillers are designed, in part, to keep the public aware of both the technological possibilities of modern medicine and the ensuing ethical problems" (Steinberg, "*Vital Signs*," 55). On the other, Cook himself recognizes that his chosen genre has provided him with "plenty of mystery left to propel a good adventure yarn" ("Deadly Obsession," 24). The medical science out of which he spins his yarns belongs to the realm of fact. Eerily, in its way so too does human behavior. It thus remains for the reader to decide whether Cook's measure of humankind's capacity for greed falls into the realm of fiction.

Cook's strategies for building suspense in *Outbreak* work simultaneously on multiple levels of the story. Shaping a plot that mixes medical mystery with political intrigue and personal betrayal, he deftly incorporates ploys familiar to readers of the thriller genre: one exciting scene leads quickly to another, and readers who delight in narrow escapes have no reason to be disappointed. Like other suspense writers, Cook also plants clues intended for the reader. This tactic serves him well in guiding his readers' expectations. Because his design is to move seemingly improbable suspicions into the realm of terrifying possibility, the hints he provides work to draw readers ineluctably into his deepening plot.

Outbreak's first heart-stopping moment offers a frightening but distinctly plausible scene. As the narrative action unfolds, Dr. Blumenthal will become increasingly aware that she is confronting a great deal more than a medical puzzle, but her first case as an Epidemiology Intelligence Service Officer at the Centers for Disease Control seems straightforward enough. Summoned to Los Angeles because the State Epidemiologist is busy handling an outbreak of hepatitis B in San Francisco, she finds seven acutely ill patients hospitalized at the Richter Clinic. The initial laboratory work on the patients, one of whom is the founder of the clinic, indicates an infectious viral problem, but the illness is as yet undiagnosed.

Readers of *The Hot Zone* will appreciate the care with which Robin Cook accurately details the emergency action undertaken by Dr. Blumenthal as a representative of the CDC. In a flurry of organized activity, an isolation ward is hastily set up. Complete barrier nursing is initiated, patients' recent histories are assembled, and samples of their body fluids are flown to the CDC. Because Blumenthal quickly realizes that the mysterious disease is indeed an infectious one, she immediately begins a search for the index case (that is, the original victim) as well as the reservoir (the source or transmitter) of the infectious agent. When the diagnosis of viral hemorrhagic fever—specifically caused by the Ebola virus—arrives, a complete quarantine of the Richter Clinic is hurriedly imposed. The fatality rate for Ebola hemorrhagic fever is about 90 percent, and patients at the Richter Clinic soon begin to die. Naturally enough, Dr. Blumenthal is worried—did she contract the deadly disease before all her emergency precautions were put into effect?

The thrilling pursuit of the identity and source of the killer virus provides his first suspenseful action, but Cook quickly adds complications to his evolving plot. One such development takes the form of an unfortunate personal misunderstanding, one that illustrates the delicacy of relations between the sexes in a contemporary workplace. Marissa Blumenthal is a single woman, but the early pages of the novel make clear that at the time the action opens, she has been slowly recovering from the depression she has suffered in the aftermath of a failed relationship. She has been casually dating two men, Dr. Ralph Hempston, a highly successful Atlanta ophthalmologist, and Tad Schockley, a laboratory research assistant at the CDC. When Dr. Cyrill Dubchek (her immediate supervisor in the Special Pathogens Branch of the CDC's virology department) also expresses an interest in taking her out, Marissa is clumsy in her response: "She knew she was being mean, that Dubchek certainly had not been harassing her, but she felt . . . awkward and was unwilling to say something to ease over the incident" (*O*, 76). Dubchek, a reserved man whose beloved wife died tragically in an automobile accident, is both hurt and embarrassed by the exchange.

This brief scene turns out to be instrumental to plot development in crucial ways. First of all, there are significant ramifications for Blumenthal in her work at the CDC. Although Dubchek certainly admired her handling of the emergency at the Richter Clinic, he clearly loses interest in supporting her follow-up investigations after relations between them have cooled. He does not, for instance, grant her authority to use the maximum containment laboratory necessary to study the virus, and she must therefore resort to trickery to gain entrance to the lab. (She somewhat unscrupulously cajoles her friend Tad Schockley to admit her with his pass.) Although the task at hand is an important one, Blumenthal's working conditions are difficult, and she experiences increasing isolation within the CDC. Feeling like a mere "errand girl," she ends up wondering "if she would ever regain Dubchek's respect" (*O*, 111).

As a further consequence of her troubled relationship with her boss, Blumenthal has no authority to whom she can turn when she begins to form theories about the origin of the virus. Because additional outbreaks of Ebola hemorrhagic fever soon appear in St. Louis, Phoenix, and Philadelphia, Blumenthal can see certain emerging patterns among the cases. All of the outbreaks occur at private clinics and, in each instance, the index case is a person who was mugged shortly before falling ill. Furthermore, all of the outbreaks feature the same unmutated strain of Ebola as that housed at the CDC. These suspicious circumstances clearly call for investigation, but, lacking a sympathetic ear, Dr. Blumenthal finds that she must pursue her inquiries alone.

Her independent snooping leads Blumenthal to Washington, D.C., Chicago, and other sites around the country. These journeys unquestionably provide Cook the opportunity for much suspenseful action. His heroine is relentlessly tracked by those who fear what it is she might discover. (In one particularly nightmarish scene, she struggles with a killer armed with an injection gun loaded with Ebola.) The chase is on, and yet Robin Cook has one more surprise to add to the plot of his engrossing thriller. Because the villains always seem to know what Blumenthal's next destination will be, readers recognize that there is an inside source of information. Unbeknownst to her, someone close to Marissa Blumenthal is a party to the conspiracy she is attempting to uncover. The likely candidates, of course, are the three men most central in her life—is her secret antagonist Cyrill Dubchek? Or Tad Shockley? Or is it Ralph Hempston? *Outbreak*'s action leaves room for readers to suspect any one of these three.

By the time readers reach *Outbreak*'s heart-stopping climax, Blumenthal has succeeded in locating the names of doctors who belong to the political action committee's governing board. Having confronted several of these doctors with her knowledge of their involvement in the Ebola outbreaks, she can only hope that one of them will agree to turn state's evidence and thus implicate the others. Because she is in trouble with the law herself (an all points bulletin was issued for her arrest after an unauthorized visit to the CDC's maximum security lab), it is time for Blumenthal to meet with the lawyer Ralph Hempston has recommended.

Blumenthal's last visit to Hempston's house offers readers a scene of utter terror. There is no lawyer present and, overhearing a telephone call that Hempston makes, Blumenthal realizes too late that she is trapped in the lair of the villain. Pretending to swallow the tranquilizer that Hempston has given her, she looks for an opportunity to make her escape. Here Cook pulls out all the chestnuts of the thriller genre. Blumenthal cannot get the telephone to work, and it is only after pretending to seduce Hempston (and secretly fishing the car keys from his pocket) that she is able to clamber out a second-story window, locate the fire escape, and finally make her desperate dash for freedom.

When the action of *Vital Signs* opens, Marissa Blumenthal has left the CDC to join a partnership in pediatrics, the field in which she originally served her residency. Pleased with her new job, happily married and resettled in Boston, she assumes that the adventures of her earlier years are now safely in her past. It does not, of course, take long before the plot of *Vital Signs* reveals that this is most assuredly not the case.

Although her futile attempts to become pregnant have left her frustrated and emotionally exhausted, and her experiences at the Women's Clinic have thus been far from satisfactory, Blumenthal does not fully recognize that something is amiss in her treatment until she joins a self-help group. She then chances to discover that several other women have also suffered from the exceedingly rare disorder that has blocked her fallopian tubes. As it happens, one of these women is Wendy Wilson, an old friend from medical school. Their suspicions aroused by the unusual coincidence, the two doctors decide to conduct some research into the facts relevant to their condition. They quickly find that the Women's Clinic is unwilling to release any medical records (including their own), but they do turn up one promising clue: a Dr. Tristan Williams, pathologist at an experimental fertility clinic in Australia, has published an intriguing paper detailing his study of the very medical puzzle that interests them. Deciding to combine a much needed vacation with further investigation, Blumenthal and Wilson fly to Brisbane to seek out Dr. Williams.

Thrillingly for readers, the trip to Australia turns out to be just the first leg in another series of hair-raising adventures for protagonist Blumenthal. Once again Robin Cook implements the chase motif so central to the suspense genre. Not satisfied, however, with a standard car chase or an ordinary set of hired thugs, he plays out fantastic variations on these regular thriller conventions. Within the action of *Vital Signs*, the humdrum car is replaced by the gaping jaws of a great white shark, and the thugs turn out to be members of the exotic Wing Sin sect, a powerful international crime cartel. When Cook adds to these astonishing episodes an account of Blumenthal's completely unauthorized visit to China, it is clear indeed that he has found some fresh ways to spin a good yarn.

Marissa Blumenthal is interested in meeting with Dr. Tristan Williams because he has published a scholarly paper reporting an unusual number of cases of TB salpingitis in infertile women. (TB salpingitis has been diagnosed as the source of Blumenthal's own problem.) When she seeks him out at Female Care Australia, she discovers that he is no longer on the staff there, for the clinic has both discredited his research and fired him. Now a bush doctor, flying into Australia's remote regions, Williams proves to be quite difficult to track.

When the two finally get together and pool their information, they realize that Female Care Australia has some deadly secret it wishes to hide. From time to time, Chinese-speaking doctors mysteriously visit the clinic and then quickly disappear. Hoping to discover what purpose these doctors serve, Blumenthal and Williams decide to visit China. Authorities at the clinic are naturally determined to put a stop to these investigations, and the two are therefore dogged by Wing Sin assassins every step of the way.

As *Vital Signs* reaches its climax, all the pieces of its puzzle fall neatly into place. In China, Blumenthal and Williams discover that Female Care Australia has learned from rural Chinese doctors how to sterilize women without the use of anesthesia. Using this technique, and then inoculating the women with a vaccine that produces symptoms resembling TB, the clinic is able to achieve its desired ends without leaving traces of the sterilization procedure it has used. Having successfully eluded the persistent hitmen, the two doctors finally make their way to the United

States—where the FBI uses its secret witness program to offer them protection in the distant wilds of Montana.

Although both books are successful suspense thrillers, there are differences between the effects the plots of *Outbreak* and *Vital Signs* register. In *Outbreak*, readers cannot help but be mesmerized by the destructive power of the killer virus. That this natural enemy might be purposefully unleashed by evildoers violates readers' sense of fair play. Dr. Blumenthal, whom *Time* has quite appropriately called "a composite of Nancy Drew and Wonder Woman" ("Outbreak," 73), succeeds, through persistence and ingenuity, in righting the terrible wrong. In *Vital Signs*, however, the outrage is deeply personal, for in this instance readers actually know the victim. Within this plot, therefore, Marissa Blumenthal's quest for understanding becomes a means for her to find redemption for the great injury she has suffered. This, along with the poignancy of the novel's subject matter, especially invites the sympathy of readers.

CHARACTER DEVELOPMENT

As *Outbreak*'s protagonist, Marissa Blumenthal is the most fully developed character in the novel. Generally speaking, suspense writers (whose main interest is understandably development of plot) use techniques of characterization to establish conflict, explain motivation, enhance credibility, invite readers' sympathies, and other such practical ends. Robin Cook's common practice is to provide useful insights into the backgrounds and personalities of his most important characters and then to use stock, one-dimensional figures for his supporting cast. His characterization of significant figures is usually relevant to the needs of his plot, and this is particularly true of his portrayals of central characters, upon whose actions plot depends. Because it is important to Cook that his protagonists be regarded as both interesting and believable, he most fully develops the psychology of these characters, providing a rational context for their choices and behavior. Other relatively important characters are often portrayed primarily in terms of their relation to the protagonists.

In the opening pages of *Outbreak* Marissa Blumenthal, at the age of thirty-one, is presented as suffering a "crisis of confidence" (18) in both the professional and personal dimensions of her life. Her plans for career and marriage have recently been disrupted. Having completed her training in pediatrics, she had intended to join her husband-to-be while he finished his medical education, but instead he has unexpectedly ended their relationship. Stunned by shock and disappointment, Blumenthal now seeks a new direction for her life. She applies for a position with the Centers for Disease Control and is assigned to the prestigious department of virology after being ranked the top student from the introductory training class. Although her achievements demonstrate that she is both intelligent and conscientious, she is nevertheless apprehensive about the demands of her new job; she recognizes that when she is called into the field she will need to respond quickly and confidently to any unusual situation.

With this background introduction, Robin Cook sets the stage to test the mettle of his protagonist. The ordeals she experiences in *Outbreak* will indeed prove a trial by fire. As it happens, her life has never been an easy one. Cook provides some psychological insight in noting that Marissa was "the baby in the family, with three older brothers and a cold and dominating neurosurgeon for a father" (21). Much like Laurie Montgomery of *Blindsight*, Blumenthal feels a compulsion to please her father: "She knew that part of the reason she had gone into medicine was to enable her to compete with her brothers in their relationships with their father" (28). All of this experience competing with men does stand her in good stead when she takes charge at the Richter Clinic and, of course, later, when she commits herself to her dangerous quest. Independent, strong-willed, and resourceful, Marissa Blumenthal is also a heroine who dares to take risks.

Because developments in *Outbreak*'s plot hinge on relationships among its characters, it is useful to consider Cook's portrayals of three additional figures, Ralph Hempston, Cyrill Dubchek, and Tad Schockley. That these other important characters are all men serves to remind readers of the degree to which the medical world in which Marissa Blumenthal moves is still dominated by males. Significantly, these three men are all personally attracted to Marissa.

Dr. Ralph Hempston, a well-to-do ophthalmologist, is fifty-three years old, significantly older than Blumenthal. Distinguished, urbane, and solicitous, he enjoys taking Marissa "to dinner, the theater, a concert without pressuring her to go to bed" (22). When Marissa dines at his elegant house, she finds herself in the company of the "cream of Atlanta's medical community" (29). Although Marissa regards Hempston as a concerned friend (and values the opportunity to confide in him), the two usually try to avoid discussing political issues: Cook makes it clear that Hempston, unlike Blumenthal, is a deeply conservative person. A supporter of the old school of medical practice, he belongs to Atlanta's wealthy establishment and does not welcome change. Readers grow suspicious of his motives when he seems altogether too interested in Blumenthal's investigation of the Ebola crisis.

Cyrill Dubchek, like Marissa herself, has experienced personal loss. He is, in fact, attracted to Marissa because in certain respects she reminds him of his wife. One resemblance he finds is in Marissa's tremendous enthusiasm for her work. He says of his wife to Marissa: "She was a musician, and when she played well, she had the same excited expression I've seen you get" (76). Widely respected among his colleagues, he has a reputation for dedication and thoroughness in his work at the CDC. As a supervisor, however, he can seem somewhat brusque. He is unquestionably a deeply private man, and his contretemps with Blumenthal suggests that he is perhaps overly sensitive; certainly his subsequent treatment of her shows that he can be unforgiving. Readers recognize that Dubchek's presence serves an important function within the plot: it is, after all, his attitude toward her that forces Blumenthal to work alone. After the Ebola conspiracy has finally been disclosed, Dubchek and Blumenthal become fast friends. (Indeed, when Blumenthal encounters a new medical mystery in *Vital Signs*, it is Dubchek she calls on to seek advice.)

Marissa Blumenthal's third admirer is a young (four years younger than Marissa) microbiologist who works in the maximum containment facilities of the CDC. Tad Schockley, in fact, is the person who conducts the analysis of the Ebola virus when samples are sent in from the field. Smitten with Marissa, Tad values her intelligence and spunk. He is, therefore, willing to help her when she wants to sneak into the lab. (Initially, at least. Later in the novel Marissa takes "advantage of Tad's friendship" (213) when she makes off with his identity card.) Tad Schockley is actually presented as something of a type: painfully shy, devoted to his work, he is the image of the kind of scientist who feels most at home in his lab. It is obvious that Schockley's helpfulness to Marissa serves to advance the novel's plot.

Although *Outbreak's* other characters (an assortment of doctors, Ebola patients, and thugs) can generally be seen as stock characters, one of the villains does indeed make a memorable impression. Marissa Blumenthal is stalked by several evil figures, but the most terrifying of these is a man "whose pale blue eyes were as cold as a winter sky" (257). Like a flashback from a nightmare, an image of this man recurs in *Vital Signs*. Gazing up at her gynecologist from her position on the examination table, Marissa briefly envisions him again. Later she wonders "what Dr. Carpenter would have said if she told him that during her biopsy his blue eyes had reminded her of the man who had tried to kill her" (*VS*, 13).

The flashback image from *Outbreak* is an appropriate one, for the clinic's doctors in *Vital Signs* are a particularly evil lot. They, however, are presented as stock characters, living embodiments of maliciousness and greed. In addition to its protagonist, therefore, only two other characters are central to this plot. These, once again, are the men in Marissa Blumenthal's life—Robert Buchanan, her first husband, and Tristan Williams, who, at the end of the novel, becomes her second.

Although Marissa Blumenthal is perceptive in many ways, the plot of *Outbreak* has already revealed that she is not always a good judge of men. Robert Buchanan, who is doubtless a delightful companion in happy circumstances, is shown to be less than ideal when the going gets rough. Admittedly, the couple's exasperating attempts to have a child have left them both on edge, but Cook makes clear that Robert's patience with Marissa is quickly running out. With her marriage in trouble, Marissa grows ever more desperate to understand what has happened to her. It is for this reason that she travels to Australia. Later, when Robert attempts to meet her in Hong Kong, he falls victim to the Wing Sin assassins who are waiting for Marissa. Cook's use of *deus ex machina* thus removes Robert from the scene,[1] but his death presents readers with a striking irony: Robert, who has been a health care entrepreneur, has invested significantly in the very organization that has brought about his murder.

Dr. Tristan Williams is a good match for Marissa. Brave, and game for adventure, he readily joins her when she travels to Hong Kong and Communist China. (Marissa lost her friend Wendy Wilson to the hungry shark.) As it happens, Tristan too has a personal interest in solving the mystery of the clinics—those who guard their monstrous secrets are also responsible for the murder of his wife. Together the two doctors search for the missing pieces of their puzzle, and when they have found them, they decide to embark on a new life together. Williams has a six-year-old son who has been staying with his grandparents in Berkeley, California. Marissa plans to add to her ready-made new family by adopting a Chinese baby.

THEMATIC ISSUES

Because greed motivates the antagonists of both *Outbreak* and *Vital Signs*, Robin Cook reveals in these novels a danger inherent in the practice of medicine for profit. This is, of course, a timely theme, and one that serves as a subtext in much of Cook's fiction. Health care today is undeniably part of a capitalist economy and therefore, generally speaking, must produce a profit. Of late, shifting circumstances within the practice of medicine have raised new questions about who it is that profits and how large those profits will be. Not necessarily concerned with doctors' desires for reasonable profit from their highly professional work, Cook nevertheless sees in the transformation of medicine into big business a possibility for terrible temptation.

Published in 1987, *Outbreak* dramatizes the turbulence that accompanied the emergence and growth of HMOs. For-profit hospitals or clinics, the new health maintenance organizations promised to lower medical costs for patients and insurers by providing prepaid, comprehensive care for large groups of people. By spreading out costs and keeping profits low, these independent businesses began to mount an economic challenge to doctors in private practice. (Of course, greed for inordinate profit or spiraling costs of care can undermine the reasonable scheme behind the HMOs. Robin Cook examines this problem in both *Mortal Fear* and *Fatal Cure*.)

Outbreak's private doctors have formed a political action committee called Physicians' Action Congress in their attempts to "rescue American medicine from the economic forces that are trying to destroy it" (281). In its proclamation of this goal, the committee means of course to establish its opposition to all arrangements that might challenge its own proprietary interest in controlling the practice of medicine. When its efforts to legislate restraints on HMOs prove too slow a process, the PAC finds more drastic means to put them out of business. The diabolical plot to plant the outbreaks is an effective one. The first victim, the Richter Clinic, closes quickly when it develops "as bad a reputation because of Ebola as the San Francisco bathhouses have because of AIDS" (91).

In exposing competitive struggles between factions that want to stake their claims to health care dollars, Robin Cook aims both to demystify some of the complexities that enshroud the business of medicine and to diminish the mystique of doctors themselves. The conservative, established physicians of *Outbreak* are a very wealthy and powerful group. Accustomed to living well and to the great prestige that comes with their profession, those in private practice have much to lose if their profits are reduced or their images are threatened. That their conspiracy to destroy any competition is a measure of both their arrogance and their greed is a realization that strikes Marissa Blumenthal forcefully when she finally realizes that Ralph Hempston is indeed one of their number: "Looking at Ralph's expensive silk shirt, the heavy gold cuff links, the tasseled

Gucci loafers, everything about him suddenly seemed a ridiculous affectation, as did the whole elaborately furnished house. It all represented the conspicuous consumption of a wealthy doctor, now fearful of the new medical competition, of changing times, of medicine no longer being a seller's market" (318). Hempston, who seemed in so many ways "the quintessential physician" (25), skilled and successful, is here shown to be merely a selfish man.

One additional question about the economy of health care greatly interests Robin Cook in *Outbreak*. The CDC, the organization for which the novel's protagonist works, is a federally supported health agency and therefore "forced to scrounge for funding in an atmosphere of budget cutting" (16). Because so much of the public's attention is ordinarily focused on the profitable sectors of the health care industry, this very important branch of public service medicine is often overlooked. In depicting the CDC's response to the public health emergencies described in *Outbreak*, Cook hopes to educate readers about the valuable services it renders. He would no doubt agree with the author of *The Hot Zone*, Richard Preston, who has warned: "They have terrible funding problems and are spread really thin. And they don't have any political constituency. There's no political-action group there hammering away at Congress to give them the money they need to do their job. . . . If Congress cuts the budget of the CDC, Congress is going to cut the throat of the American people" (Preston).

Outbreak's scenario of doctors' ugly competition to claim the health care market offers a frightening example of the force of human greed. In *Vital Signs*, where doctors create their own market for specialized services, Cook takes his conspiracy plot one step further to illustrate here the evil ingenuity of greed. In this novel the practice of medicine is presented as big business full-blown. Operating fertility clinics in Australia, the United States, Europe, and Asia, the successful cartel threatens to corner the world market. As to how the cartel has achieved its amazing growth and has also been able to enter the American market, Dr. Blumenthal explains: "The whole infertility industry is totally unregulated and unsupervised. It's grown up in a no-man's land between medicine and business. And the government has just looked the other way. Anything to do with reproduction is politically dangerous" (328).

The operation of the fertility clinics in *Vital Signs* presents an example of medicine for profit, pure and simple. When Blumenthal visits Female Care Australia, she is astonished by the lavish facilities she sees. The clinic's public relations man explains to her: "It's a tribute to capitalism.

Private initiative and private investment. It's the only way to get things done in the modern world" (152). The financial success of this business strategy is readily apparent when Blumenthal sees the suite of offices occupied by the clinic's director: its splendid trappings make her feel as though she were entering the "office of the CEO of a major Fortune 500 company" (154). Obviously, this impression aptly reinforces the strong ties to the world of business that the clinic represents.

There is an irony behind Female Care Australia's money-making scheme that raises important questions about the funding and support of scientific and technological research. Experimenters at this clinic have, in fact, developed techniques for in vitro fertilization that produce an extremely high level of success. Paradoxically, this technological break-through guarantees that the clinic's revenue will be lowered; patients, obviously, will require fewer visits. Directors of the clinic make their heinous decision to create and control their own market, in part, because income is needed to support additional research (which will then pro-vide opportunity for new sources of profit). Without question, at Female Care Australia, the business and medical science have formed an unholy alliance.

ALTERNATIVE PERSPECTIVE: FEMINIST CRITICISM

Feminist criticism in literature is part of a larger and more general social movement whose central goal is to improve the conditions of women's lives. Feminist critics participate in this project in a variety of useful ways. Recognizing that both language and literature have tradi-tionally been dominated by men, some feminist critics practice a cultural criticism that exposes the male agenda implicit in forms of linguistic or literary expression. Others, wishing to draw attention to women's voices, study the work of overlooked or undervalued women writers. Both of these angles of focus heighten understanding of women's social positions and of their experiences in the world.

Literature provides a particularly useful means to examine cultural experience, for, as Mary Anne Ferguson suggests, "Literary images do not exist in a vacuum. . . . Literature both reflects and helps create our views of reality; it is through their preservation in works of art that we know what the stereotypes and archetypes have been and are. Literature conserves traditional images" (Ferguson, 3). Studies of literary depictions of women have revealed much about society's perceptions of their public and private circumstances through the ages. The analysis of literary images has allowed scholars to speculate about women's changing roles in social and family life. It has afforded them opportunities to consider the ways in which women have slowly realized increased access to political power. Significantly, it has disclosed insights into men's visions of women—both how men have regarded women, and what men have desired women to be.

In studying what women themselves have written, feminist critics have addressed the question of what it means (and what it has traditionally meant) to be a woman. Focusing upon women's literary expression of a variety of images of themselves, critics learn how women have responded to the social and political circumstances of their lives. They explore what women's goals and fears and choices have been and how it is that women have struggled to define new identities for themselves. By listening to women's voices and calling attention to women's concerns, feminist theorists promote a social movement whose ultimate goal is to improve the lives of both women and men.

In addition to their obvious concern with literature written by women, feminist critics and theorists are distinctly interested in studying the ways male writers depict women characters, or the ways they portray relations between the sexes. *Outbreak* and *Vital Signs* are clearly worth exploring in both of these respects, and *Vital Signs* in particular offers another provocative feature: its subject matter treats issues that directly touch upon the lives and experiences of women.

Like *Coma's* Susan Wheeler or *Blindsight's* Laurie Montgomery, Marissa Blumenthal presents readers with an image of a strong female character. Although the very fact of her womanhood suits the design of plot development in both novels (in *Outbreak* her sex provokes the disagreement that forces her to work alone, and in *Vital Signs* she undergoes the treatment that she will later come to investigate), this does not diminish Cook's portrait of his protagonist. Like the heroes of many suspense thrillers, Blumenthal takes the initiative when other characters fail to recognize that bold action is needed. Persistent and clever, dedicated to discovering the solutions to her mysteries, Marissa Blumenthal proves that female protagonists can claim their rightful place in thriller fiction.

As to Cook's depiction of relationships between the sexes, *Outbreak's* action clearly introduces the possibility of an instance of sexual discrimination. Although Blumenthal acknowledges to herself, after her unpleasant encounter with her boss, that he has not in fact harassed her, Dubchek's treatment of her following this incident might well be understood to be gender discrimination. Certainly he does not provide her with the support she needs to perform her job reasonably, and he dismisses her grim suspicions as paranoid delusions. The ways in which these circumstances serve plot development have already been noted, but it is also true that Cook illustrates here a situation that is not uncommon in the workplace. Critic Gayle Greene, for example, envisions something very close to Blumenthal's predicament when she describes many contemporary working women "struggling in the professions, isolated in male-defined hierarchies and environments that convince them, when they approach a decision differently from their male colleagues, that they are crazy and alone" (Greene and Kahn, 14). In *Outbreak*, it turns out to be very fortunate indeed that Blumenthal does approach decisions differently from her male colleagues. With this heroine, Cook dramatically demonstrates the value of a woman's contribution to the workplace.

At the end of *Vital Signs*, when Marissa Blumenthal is explaining the fertility clinic conspiracy to an astonished friend, she has occasion to ask, "Is it just too hard for you men to believe that women could be victimized to this extent?" (328). It is, of course, particularly appropriate that the central character of this novel (wherein women—women's bodies— are violated) is herself a woman and, as well, a victim. With Blumenthal, Cook uses a woman's voice to protest the grievous outrage and a woman's strength to strike back in her role as heroine.

Recent studies of research practices have revealed the extent to which medicine for women has been a neglected field. Interestingly, another of Cook's novels, *Brain*, also features a medical conspiracy that centers upon the violation of women's bodies. Because Cook is, in both *Brain* and *Vital Signs*, deeply sympathetic to the personal indignities women often suffer at the hands of medical science, these novels draw needed attention to problems that are all too often overlooked. The inside view of the practices and technology of fertility medicine that Cook offers in *Vital Signs* provides readers with a useful perspective on this important branch of women's health care.

NOTE

1. *Deus ex machina*, from the Latin "god from a machine," denotes the unexpected or artificial use of a plotting device to resolve circumstances within fiction.

Mortal Fear
(1988)

Mortal Fear (1988), the ninth of Robin Cook's seventeen novels to date, is a medical thriller that features a conspiracy plot as well as a futuristic scenario drawn from the mysterious realm of genetic research. Like other Cook novels, this one offers readers a view of recent activity within one of medical science's many specialized branches of inquiry, in this case the field of highly sophisticated experimentation with DNA. A brilliant scientist investigating growth hormones makes an astonishing discovery: he locates the mechanism that controls the natural aging process, the process that in all living organisms inevitably leads to death. Working in deep secrecy, Dr. Alvin Hayes hopes to find a means to switch off this aging mechanism in human beings, but before he is able to begin to fully pursue this alluring possibility, he realizes, to his horror, that the secret of his "death hormone" has, in fact, been stolen. Unhappily for a goodly number of middle-aged patients enrolled in Boston's Good Health Plan, whoever absconded with the results of Dr. Hayes's research is more interested in death than life.

The conspiracy Cook depicts in *Mortal Fear* anticipates the somewhat similar plot he later devises in *Fatal Cure* (1993; see discussion of this novel in Chapter 2). Both books call attention to the problems rising medical costs have caused for health maintenance organizations. In both books the administrators of HMOs, desperate to slash their spiraling expenses, concoct wicked schemes designed to eliminate those patients they fear might eventually "use more than their fair share of medical services" (*Mortal Fear*, 364). *Fatal Cure*'s victims, as the title indicates, are people who suffer chronic illnesses (cystic fibrosis, for example). For them, death is the final cure. *Mortal Fear*'s administrators choose to target patients with "high-risk" social habits, people who drink too much or smoke or fail to exercise enough, for example. Thus, engaging in a kind of administrative Darwinism, the culprits in these books attempt to re-serve health care services for the healthy. (This policy is obviously more cost-effective than is that of administering services for the seriously ill.)

Mortal Fear is both fast-paced and action-packed, and it is full of quirky characters. (Among others, these include a deadly female villain, an un-flappable medical examiner, a psychopathic hitman, a Columbo-like de-tective, and a topless dancer who is completing her Ph.D. in psychology at Harvard.) For these reasons, the novel is one that readily lends itself to film adaptation, and a successful television movie based on the book was indeed aired in the autumn of 1994. Not altogether true to the print version of *Mortal Fear*, the movie exchanged the novel's male protagonist for a female lead character. (Thus Dr. Jason Howard became Dr. Jennifer Howard and, correspondingly, the identity of certain of the novel's vil-lains was also altered.) The changes notwithstanding, Cook, who "is not an author who expects absolute adherence to his print vision on the screen" (Heldenfels, D1), was quite satisfied with the production. He felt that it expressed the ethical issues raised by his plot and that its portrayal of his central character was appropriately sympathetic to his own inten-tions.

Mortal Fear's protagonist is a particularly important character, but not only because he commits himself to unraveling the novel's mysteries. In a world of medicine that Robin Cook regards as becoming disturbingly impersonal, Jason Howard is a physician who makes extra time for his patients, who worries about them after hours, and who mourns for them when they are gone. In many respects he therefore embodies the old-fashioned image of the family doctor. Early in the novel he is presented as a man who is still deeply grieving his own wife's untimely death (two years earlier she was killed in an automobile accident), but he is also haunted by other images of death. His patients are inexplicably dying at what seems to him an astonishing rate, and when he meets Dr. Hayes, his colleague, at a restaurant one evening, Hayes too suddenly drops dead, right before his eyes. Indeed, in *Mortal Fear* death seems omni-present, and because "death had always been Dr. Jason Howard's en-emy" (18), he feels compelled to do all he can to understand why it seems now to have entered his life in such strangely vicious ways. (Readers who see in *Mortal Fear*'s death imagery a somewhat uncharacteristically dark vision may have noted the acknowledgments, in which Cook offers his thanks to friends who have helped him through a "difficult" time in his life.)

PLOT DEVELOPMENT

Mortal Fear dramatically opens with a one-page prologue that serves to introduce the monstrous effects of Dr. Hayes's death hormone. For Jason Howard's patient, Cedric Harring, it is a "death sentence with no chance of reprieve." Coursing through Harring's bloodstream, the hormone registers its hideous effects on every cell in his body. Suddenly beginning to age at an incredible rate, the hapless Mr. Harring is, readers are grimly told, "about to disintegrate into his stellar elements" (11).

Chapter 1 builds upon the immediate suspense created in the prologue. In the throes of a massive heart attack, Cedric Harring nevertheless manages to drive himself to the Good Health Plan Clinic. There he crashes violently into a concrete abutment and falls on his horn, gasping for breath. Harring is undeniably dying, and the death is a horribly painful one: "Despite the morphine, Cedric felt a sudden stab of white-hot, crushing pain" (18). Dr. Howard certainly recognizes that his patient is suffering excruciating physical pain, but he also sees in his face the horrendous reflection of his mortal terror. Harring's obvious fear deepens his doctor's sense of hopelessness. A fifty-six-year-old man who only three weeks earlier had in fact passed an exceptionally thorough physical exam simply cannot now be saved.

Although all Dr. Howard's patients are important to him, Cedric Harring, as it happens, is a rather special case, for Harring had been Howard's patient years earlier when he had been in private practice with his wife. Deciding after her death to leave his old life behind him, Howard had sold his house and practice and taken a salaried job at the Good Health Plan. Harring had then changed his own insurance arrangements so that he could stay with the doctor he had learned to trust. Besides losing a patient, therefore, Dr. Howard is losing an old acquaintance, someone who is a link to his earlier life.

The dramatic events of the first few pages of *Mortal Fear* unquestionably excite readers' curiosity about where Cook's plot will lead them, but the graphic depiction of Cedric Harring's death serves additional purposes as well. Harring is not the first of Jason Howard's patients to age and die quite suddenly, and, as readers soon see, he will not be the last. His death, then, can be recognized as part of an emerging pattern, one that greatly puzzles Dr. Howard. Fearing that he might be witnessing a "non-AIDS-related epidemic involving the autoimmune system" (122), he begins to ask that autopsies be conducted on all similar patients. Strangely, in all the cases, the medical examiner finds internal organs that appear to be more than one hundred years old. (Like Cedric Harring, all the patients have also recently undergone thorough checkups, and, in the two or three weeks following those checkups, all have begun to experience skin drying and hair loss; several have developed cataracts.)

Besides introducing one of the central mysteries of his novel, this early scene affords Cook an opportunity to acquaint readers with Jason Howard's compassionate nature. Although the doctor takes every possible measure to try to save his failing patient, his task is finally an impossible one, for it soon becomes apparent that Harring's heart has ruptured. Meeting with the patient's distraught wife, Howard gently voices the lie he knows will provide her with some small comfort: "At least he didn't suffer" (22), he tries to reassure her.

Readers, who have seen just how much Harring and his family did suffer when his life was unexpectedly cut short, will be appalled when the hospital administrators, their scheme at last uncovered, try to justify their actions by claiming that the process they used was a natural one, that they simply hurried the inevitable along. Indeed, one of the administrators dispassionately argues, "If aging and death have an evolutionary value, perhaps they have a social one as well" (341). In *Mortal Fear* Cook uses the quite particular and personal suffering of the Harrings (and their deeply concerned doctor) as a means to take a measure of the grossly impersonal stance toward patients that is here adopted by the coldly calculating representatives of corporate medicine. He fears that in diminishing the value of an individual life, marketplace health care threatens to pervert the very purpose of the medical profession.

In addition to Jason Howard, readers are introduced to two other significant characters before *Mortal Fear*'s thrilling first chapter reaches its conclusion. Dr. Alvin Hayes, who is employed exclusively as a researcher by Good Health Plan, stops by Dr. Howard's office to explain that he needs to meet with him as soon as possible. Hayes looks disheveled and appears to be unwell; because he claims that his business with

Howard is extremely urgent, the two quickly agree to meet later that evening.

Dr. Howard's other visitor is none other than Shirley Montgomery, Chief Executive Officer of Good Health Plan. Attractive, intelligent, and exceedingly personable, Montgomery enjoys good relations with everyone at the hospital. In fact, readers are told that it is Shirley Montgomery who deserves "personal credit for providing . . . the glue that held GHP together and made it work so smoothly" (42). Although readers do not realize it yet, one of the reasons Montgomery is able to make GHP work so smoothly is that she is one of the conspirators, one of the administrators determined to hold costs down at the expense of unprofitable patients. Interested in Dr. Howard (or at least interested in keeping track of his activities), Montgomery frequently seeks him out. Although Howard is not yet ready to make another emotional commitment, he, too, is interested in Montgomery, and they have developed a "relationship that hovered somewhere between friendship and romance" (43). Because he admires and trusts Montgomery, this friendship will prove to be a very dangerous one for Jason Howard.

Mortal Fear's exciting action is maintained in Chapter 2. When Alvin Hayes reaches the restaurant where Jason Howard already awaits him, he keeps glancing furtively over his shoulder. He believes that he is being followed, he explains, and then goes on to declare that he is certain that his life and the life of his young son are both in danger. Mystified, Howard encourages him to tell his story. Hayes readily reveals that he has been studying the ways genes turn off and on and that he has made an "ironic" discovery, one that could lead to a major scientific breakthrough. "Believe me," he says; "it is Nobel material" (52). He fears, however, that his recent discovery has been taken from his lab and that someone is, in fact, already using it. Just as Hayes is about to describe the nature of his secret work, he too becomes a victim of the devastating effects of his own research. In a death scene that is even more gruesome than Cedric Harring's, Hayes spews his lifeblood across the table. For a moment, in the ensuing commotion, Howard thinks he recognizes the man Hayes had described as following him, but he quickly dismisses this thought: it seems apparent to him that Hayes, who was unquestionably behaving very strangely, was probably delusional.

With the dramatic deaths depicted in the first two chapters, Cook sets up the central mysteries of his thriller: Why are so many of Good Health Plan's middle-aged patients dying shortly after taking medical exams, and did Dr. Hayes indeed make a medical breakthrough—and, if so, what was it? Although Jason Howard does not yet know that the two mysteries are, in fact, connected, his patients continue to die and the memory of Hayes's last words continues to trouble him. With "the shadow of death" hanging "over him like a noxious cloud" (93), he briefly considers trying to find a new occupation. Then, in an effort to at least satisfy his own curiosity, he decides to see if he can discover what Hayes had hoped to tell him on the night he died.

Howard's investigations lead him to Alvin Hayes's lab, and there he views a scene of "science gone mad: rabbits with several heads and mice with supernumerary extremities and extra sets of eyes" (151). Although Howard does not find there the answer to his question, he does begin to suspect that Hayes might actually have made his breakthrough when this lab is ransacked and all of the animal experiments are destroyed. Soon thereafter Helene Brennquivist, Hayes's laboratory assistant, is discovered brutally murdered, and all evidence suggests that a professional hitman carried out the job. By this time Howard is fully convinced that Hayes must have been telling the truth. Someone, it seems, is greatly interested in destroying all traces of his work.

Now thoroughly obsessed with discovering the nature of Alvin Hayes's breakthrough, Dr. Howard begins to read accounts of genetic research in his evening hours. He also decides to follow another promising lead in the case: perhaps Carol Donner, the woman with whom Hayes was living before he died, could somehow be helpful. Carol Donner turns out to be a breathtakingly beautiful young woman who dances in a topless bar in Boston's raunchy Combat Zone. (Although Dr. Hayes does not realize it until the climax of the novel, Carol is dancing to finance her doctoral studies at Harvard.) The hit of a show that features "Topless College Girls," Carol is exceedingly difficult to approach—a burly bodyguard named Bruno is always at her side.

When Howard and Donner finally meet, and quickly develop a friendship, Howard learns that Hayes took several trips associated with his research. Carol Donner was not privy to Hayes's breakthrough, but she did, in fact, accompany him when he traveled to the Pacific Northwest on one of these scientific expeditions. Deciding to retrace Hayes's steps, Howard persuades Donner to join him in a flight to Seattle. After following some false leads, the two end up at a rustic fishing lodge where Hayes and Donner had once stayed. The old caretaker there tells Howard that although Hayes did not fish for salmon, he did request that heads from twenty-five salmon that had recently spawned and died be gathered and packed in ice for him. So Hayes had been in quest of salmon heads—how very odd. But as Howard watches dying salmon flopping and then expiring near the shore, their significance suddenly dawns on him. The salmon are somehow programmed to die soon after they have finished their spawning; indeed, this is when they reach the natural end of their lifespan. Recognizing the use Hayes must have made of their heads, Howard now has his answer to the mystery of the breakthrough, and now he knows why his patients are dying, very much like the salmon. As *Mortal Fear* moves toward its climax, Howard and Donner successfully elude the hitman who has recently been assigned to follow them.

Back in Boston, Howard thinks of a way he might confirm his newly formed theory. Remembering that Hayes had claimed that his son was also in danger, he breaks into the institution (owned by Good Health Plan) where the young boy, who is severely retarded, has been living. There a truly hideous spectacle awaits him. He finds the children lying in their beds in a huge dormitory, but, horribly, these youngsters do not look like children at all; rather, "they all looked like miniature senile centenarians with beady eyes, wrinkled dry skin, and thinned white hair, showing scaly patches of scalp" (319). His worst suspicions thereby confirmed, Jason Howard immediately calls Shirley Montgomery—he quite naturally believes that Good Health Plan's CEO needs to know what has been happening within the hospital she heads.

In *Mortal Fear*'s heart-stopping climax Shirley Montgomery pretends to summon the police. Then, revealing her own complicity, she and her hired killer lock Jason Howard in her basement. Knowing that Montgomery intends to use the death hormone on him, Howard desperately searches for a means of escape. When he locates the house's circuit breakers, he knows that he might have a slim chance of saving his life. Plunging the house into darkness, he hides until Montgomery and the hitman open the basement door. Howard is shot and wounded as he makes his mad dash for freedom, but just as the hitman is about to finish him off, to his great good fortune, Bruno the bodyguard suddenly appears. (Howard's unlikely rescuer is, of course, accompanied by Carol Donner. Worried about him, she has arranged to have him followed.)

Mortal Fear's epilogue reveals that Jason Howard and Carol Donner plan to go into private practice together when Donner completes her degree in clinical psychology. Howard, for obvious reasons, is no longer interested in practicing corporate medicine. Good Health Plan, named in numerous malpractice suits, has declared bankruptcy, and six of its ad-

ministrators, including Shirley Montgomery, have been charged with
murder.

STRATEGIES FOR DEVELOPING SUSPENSE IN
MORTAL FEAR

Part thriller and part mystery, *Mortal Fear* is designed to provide readers with uninterrupted spine-tingling entertainment. The many chase
scenes, the descriptions of the grisly deaths, the presence of a hitman,
the chilling moments of discovery—all of these standard thriller conventions work to keep excitement high while suspense builds aound the
central puzzles upon which the plot is based. Readers, who suspect that
the novel's mysteries will turn out to be linked, must wait until they
near the conclusion to fully discover how this is true. Robin Cook, of
course, meanwhile plants his provocative clues; he characteristically uses
his prologue to present readers with their first clue, and this is indeed
the case in *Mortal Fear*, where an oblique reference to a death hormone
first occurs. The full significance of this reference, however, becomes apparent only later in the novel, when its context has been developed.

Like the action of other thrillers, *Mortal Fear*'s is episodic. Jason Howard has several exciting run-ins with the loyal and protective Bruno, as
he attempts to meet with Carol Donner. He also keeps bumping into
Detective Curran, a stocky and gruff investigator who is looking into the
Hayes affair. (To discredit Dr. Hayes, the conspirators planted drugs in
his apartment.) Curran, who finally grows impatient with Howard's amateur sleuthing, beseeches him, "Please, doctor—would you get back to
your doctoring?" (133). Although Howard's several minor escapades
serve to keep the novel's action moving, he gets into more serious
scrapes as well.

Among the several episodes designed to keep readers on the edge of
their seats is the thrilling chase scene that takes place at the old fishing
lodge. Howard and Donner are eating dinner in the dining hall when
Howard spots a man who looks very much like the person he fleetingly
glimpsed on the night Alvin Hayes died. When the man's eyes meet his,
and Howard sees in them a sign of recognition, he instantly knows what
this man's deadly purpose most likely must be. Frozen for a moment,
he wonders what he should do. The man, whose hand is ominously held
inside his pocket, begins to move toward the table. Suddenly Howard
seizes the tablecloth, upending all the dinnerware. Taking advantage of

the commotion he has created, he grabs Donner's hand, and the two run to the end of the dock and leap into one of the boats they find moored there. A river chase ensues, the hitman firing his silenced revolver at Howard's rubber raft. When Howard is finally able to start his boat's motor, he and Donner quickly outdistance the canoe that bears their pursuer. What they do not know, however, is that they are heading straight for a series of white-water rapids called, appropriately enough, Devil's Chute. Informed at the end of their nearly catastrophic adventure that they are the first people ever to have navigated Devil's Chute successfully in the dark, Howard and Donner are drenched, but deeply thankful to be alive. Donner, who is at all times a good sport, wryly comments, "You sure know how to entertain a girl" (305).

While exciting chase scenes are stock in trade for the thriller novel, this genre also delights in presenting its readers with spooky effects. *Mortal Fear* offers its fair share of these, including the vivid descriptions of Alvin Hayes's "mad scientist's" lab. The novel's eeriest scene, however, takes place when Jason Howard visits the Hartford School, the institution for retarded children. Having been denied admittance at the gate, he sneaks into the building to search for its dormitory, where the children are all fast asleep. When Howard switches on a light so that he can look for Hayes's son, several of the children "began getting out of their beds, balancing precariously on wasted limbs. Then, to Jason's horror, they began to move toward him. One of them began to say feebly the word *'please'* over and over in a high-pitched, grating voice. Soon the others joined in a terrifying, unearthly chorus" (320). Waving their arms, pushing and clutching, the children mill and swarm like images from some unspeakable nightmare. As Howard makes his way down the fire escape, he can still hear the "monotonous chorus of *please*" (321).

The suspense surrounding *Mortal Fear*'s central mystery, that of the conspiracy plot, builds up to the personal betrayal that occurs with the novel's climax. Alone with Shirley Montgomery, a woman with whom he has seriously "considered the possibility of a real relationship" (73), Howard is oblivious to his danger until he hears her say, "If aging were speeded up in certain circumstances, it might be best for both the patients and the hospitals" (342). This moment of enlightenment is quite similar to those that occur in both *Coma* and *Outbreak*, where the protagonists also confide in someone who seems trustworthy—only to discover, too late, that the "friend" is in truth no friend at all.

Thus, Cook draws upon a variety of strategic devices to tell his thrilling tale. Using the dramatic death scenes early in the novel to first establish *Mortal Fear*'s suspense, he later turns to other conventions of the thriller genre: the chase, the eerie scene, the unmasking of the villain, and, finally, the entrapment of the hero. All of these devices work to shape the surprising twists of plot that drive the book's suspenseful action.

CHARACTER DEVELOPMENT

Like many other suspense novelists, Robin Cook focuses his readers' attention on the character of his protagonist. The book's other characters, useful insofar as they play roles within the plot, are generally presented in brief sketches or are described as clearly recognizable types. *Mortal Fear*'s professional hitman, psychopathically malicious and inordinately proud of his deadly efficiency, is, for example, a type of character who frequently appears in both thriller fiction and drama. (This particular hitman is one of the Cuban criminals sent to the United States from Mariel.) The police officer, Detective Curran, is another familiar type: both intelligent and observant, he is, like television's Lieutenant Columbo, far shrewder than he generally likes to let on. It is not at all unusual for writers of suspense fiction to take advantage of the fact that stereotypical characters (like Bruno, for instance) are common within the genre. Establishing the identity of figures like these with a few clearly defined characteristics allows the thriller writer to concentrate on the fast-moving action of the plot.

Although Carol Donner turns out to be a fairly important character, her background is not fully revealed until near the conclusion of the book. Because Jason Howard has assumed that Donner, who is, after all, an exotic dancer, also works as a prostitute, he is greatly surprised to finally learn all about her Harvard studies. Donner, as it happens, is the niece of the man who owns the topless bar. Bruno, of course, is not her pimp, but rather an employee of her uncle. (Interestingly, it was the nature of her doctoral thesis, a study of the psychology of grief, that first drew Donner to Jason Howard, for Hayes had earlier informed her about how Howard had suffered after the loss of his wife.)

By the end of *Mortal Fear*, Jason Howard comes to see Carol Donner differently. Donner, however, is not the only character about whom Howard must completely revise his opinion. Shirley Montgomery is yet another figure who serves as proof that within the thriller novel appearances can often be deceiving. Although Montgomery's solicitous attitude toward Jason Howard often seems quite genuine (she is particularly sympathetic because she too has lost a spouse, in her case to cancer), alert readers will note that she is consistently portrayed as an exceedingly ambitious woman, one determined to ensure the continuing success of Good Health Plan. That Montgomery cares about the medical business there is no doubt. Her father was a doctor, and she once thought about studying medicine too. Her father, however, talked her out of that plan, for, as she says, "He told me that it would be taken over by big business and that someone who cared about the profession should go into management" (170). From her position in management, Montgomery has clearly become one of the administrators who has lost sight of the life-preserving principles intrinsic to the actual practice of medicine. Looking at the profession from the business angle, she is convinced that certain patients represent an unreasonable burden to be borne by the rest of society. She therefore turns out to be a zealot in the cause of employing Hayes's death hormone, and whatever her personal feelings for Jason Howard might actually be, they are clearly secondary to her business interests.

In sharp contrast to Shirley Montgomery, Dr. Howard is devoted to the sanctity of the individual life. He always takes the extra step to help a patient, even when, as with Cedric Harring, the cause appears to be a hopeless one. Readers see Howard primarily in his role as doctor, and it is really in this capacity that he acts on his curiosity about Hayes's breakthrough. Thinking about the scientist's last words, he comes increasingly to believe that if Hayes really did discover something that could prove beneficial to medical science, then every effort should be made to find out what it was. As to Montgomery's attempts to persuade him that the use of the death hormone could serve a worthy purpose, Howard can only respond in complete outrage to a proposition that violates all of his professional (and private) principles. As he bitterly remarks, "Some excuse for murder—we're all going to die anyway" (364).

Within his medical practice, Dr. Howard's reputation is that of a skilled as well as an especially sensitive internist. He himself acknowledges that he has been, since his wife's death, acutely aware of the pain of others. Although he is clearly attempting to find ways to leave his past behind him, his own sorrow, and that of others, is often on his mind. (In the movie version, Dr. Jennifer Howard's memories of her husband are visually expressed through poignant flashback scenes.) Somewhat ironically, perhaps, it is through his involvement in Hayes's mystery that he comes eventually to find a new direction for his life. As doctor, and as human being, Howard represents the antithesis of Good Health Plan's cold-blooded administration.

It is because Jason Howard is so obviously an appealing character, indeed a sensitive and gentle man, that readers take great interest in the possibility that he might discover a new romance within the pages of *Mortal Fear*. The misjudgments he has made about Shirley Montgomery, whom he is in fact considering as a romantic partner, and about Carol Donner, whose personality seems so much more attractive than Montgomery's, contribute to the intrigue of the novel. In making false assumptions about Carol Donner, Howard overlooks an important dimension of her life. He fails to appreciate her dedication to her chosen career, a commitment the two clearly have in common. He also underestimates her resourcefulness, for it is Donner who arranges for his rescue at the climax of the book. Finally, not the least of Donner's charms is her ready and good-natured humor, a quality noticeably absent in Shirley Montgomery. Spirited, independent-minded, and as thoughtful as Howard himself, Carol Donner promises to be a good match for Cook's protagonist.

THEMATIC ISSUES

The "noxious cloud" of death that hangs over *Mortal Fear* is finally lifted in its last scene, where Jason Howard and Carol Donner agree to begin a new life together. Recovering in the hospital from his gunshot wound, Howard appears to be recovering from his emotional wounds as well, from his lingering grief over his wife's tragic death, and from the horror he has experienced in witnessing so many other needless deaths. Cook's novel, in many ways a meditation upon death, thus ends with the reassurance of renewal.

In its concern with medical science's role in the natural (but often costly) processes of aging and dying, Cook's novel takes up a question pertinent to today's ongoing debate about the "rationing" of medicine. When the availability of health care services is limited, either by cost or by supply, who will have access to these services, and who, then, might not? A troubling social problem that has been exacerbated by medicine's transformation into big business, this issue is one that Cook clearly believes should be openly aired, and one that should by no means be left to the discretion of medical business interests. In fact, *Mortal Fear* issues an unmistakable warning about the direction in which those special interests might well lie. Envisioning a scenario in which business attempts to engage in social engineering, Cook highlights the disparity between its money-making motives and the far more personal concerns of Dr. Howard and his individual patients. In abusing the results of Dr. Hayes's medical research, Montgomery and her cohorts also abuse the medical profession. Much of Robin Cook's fiction has been devoted to exposing the ways in which the defining goals of medicine and business are distinctly at cross-purposes. Indeed, this is one of his most common themes, and, as he so frequently does, Cook here uses the dramatic possibilities of the thriller genre to summon readers' attention to this unresolved dilemma.

Although Good Health Plan's administrators are motivated by their economic concerns, they rationalize their conspiracy by making an appeal to the common good. Their claim is that by eliminating those patients who are likely to drain their resources, they will be better positioned to serve other kinds of patients. In effect they have, then, decided who deserves medical care. Because the medical profession has traditionally honored the value of an individual life, the practice of choosing patients by desert is anathema to committed physicians like Dr. Howard. Howard would not consider weighing the welfare of a patient against a possible benefit to society, but Cook clearly fears that such a possibility is not beyond imagination. When medical resources are scarce, as indeed they already are for those patients who await organ transplants (an issue Cook addresses in *Coma*), how are crucial decisions made? Medicine has historically practiced an economy of need. Will this be possible in the future? Or will health care services be available only to those who can afford them, or those who are deemed worthy in some special way? In *Mortal Fear* Cook invites readers to ponder the implications for the medical profession should it continue to be increasingly driven by market forces.

While his interest in alerting readers to the dangerous links between health care and big business is of central importance to Robin Cook, *Mortal Fear* takes up another issue of grave concern to medical science. As in *Terminal* and *Acceptable Risk*, Cook here addresses the vexing problem of secrecy in medical research. It is, of course, because Dr. Hayes's work has been so deeply cloaked in mystery that the conspirators are able to take such ready advantage of his unsuspected discovery. When Detective Curran asks if there are not "watchdogs" who are supposed to oversee the kind of experimentation in which Hayes had been engaged, Dr. Howard explains that it is practically impossible for government agencies to monitor the activities of independent researchers. Because there is always the chance that significant money could be made with a scientific breakthrough, independent research companies generally keep close guard over the secrets of their work. Although there is no doubt that medical science research would generally benefit from an open exchange of ideas and information, most unfortunately, here too the pressure of market forces once again comes into play. As Cook emphasizes in *Terminal*, this problem is one that recently has been exacerbated through a series of severe cutbacks in public funding of science projects. More and more, medical research is finding itself under the sway of big business interests.

Mortal Fear raises yet one more question about the practice of scientific research, that of the use of animals in genetic experimentation. Jason Howard is aghast when he views the distorted creatures housed in Alvin Hayes's laboratory. Although he admits that he is not squeamish about the genetic manipulation of bacteria, he is horrified by Hayes's cruel use of mammals as a means to test his growth hormone. An issue that has been well debated in many public forums, the indiscriminate use of animal subjects in scientific experiments has been sharply curtailed in recent years. Dr. Howard's sensitivity to the monstrous spectacle presented by Hayes's obscene zoo serves to further reflect his own deep regard for the sanctity of life.

ALTERNATIVE PERSPECTIVE: CULTURAL CRITICISM

When U.S. Senator Orrin Hatch requested that copies of Robin Cook's novel *Fatal Cure*, be sent to all members of Congress as well as President Clinton, his gesture spoke to the relevance of popular literature as a mode of cultural expression within contemporary society. Cook's work of fiction, written to entertain its readers, presented a vision of current social affairs that Hatch obviously deemed pertinent to the concerns of his fellow politicians. Cook's novels have also been assigned reading in medical ethics classes, a fact that further suggests that the critical movement known as "cultural studies" has begun to attract wide-spread interest in this country.

An interdisciplinary critical movement that originated in Europe, particularly in Britain and France, cultural criticism encourages the analysis and interpretation of diverse cultural objects, products, and forms. Cultural critics assume that how people live, what people believe, and what a society produces are all interrelated issues, and that the conscious act of defining and interpreting these networks of relationship can lead to an understanding of the nature and problems of particular societies. Early cultural critics, those working during the 1920s, were primarily interested in analyses of modern industrial societies, but since that time cultural criticism's interests have expanded to include all kinds of social artifacts, those from the past as well as the present. In the diversity of its range of studies, cultural criticism clearly challenges the assumption that there is within any society a monolithic culture. Acknowledging the intricate complexities of social life, cultural critics see societies as composed of multiple, interactive, and constantly changing elements, and "Cultural studies is thus committed to the study of an entire range of a society's arts, beliefs, institutions, and communicative practices" (Nelson, Treichler, and Grossberg, 4).

Robin Cook's popular fiction is of interest to cultural studies in several respects, not the least of which is the simple fact that he, too, is engaging in cultural criticism. In consistently using a major social, political, and economic institution, the health care industry, as the setting for his plots, Cook has occasion to provide his readers with an insider's view of the workings of that institution. Neglecting neither the social, the political, nor the economic character of the medical profession, Cook analyzes trends and changes, often hypothesizing about their possible implications. His characters embody the conflicting principles or interests that contend for power within the medical establishment, and readers know which side Cook favors when the "good guys" always win. His novels, furthermore, offer insights into the technological developments that are constantly reshaping the traditional practice of medicine, and they also scrutinize the motives of those who control the uses of those technologies. Informative as well as entertaining, his books address important and complex institutional problems in a highly public forum.

Cultural critics, fascinated by the ways popular literature both reflects and interrogates the society from which it is produced, are greatly interested in the reception Robin Cook enjoys. An immensely well-read writer, and one whose books have risen to the best-seller charts numerous times, Cook is a suspense novelist who supplies his large following with provocative critiques of a tremendously powerful institution. As Senator Hatch's interest implies, popular fiction can give voice to important societal concerns. Indeed, Jonathan Swift chose the fiction genre when he addressed the plight of Ireland's poor in his widely familiar piece, "A Modest Proposal." Cook, who also appreciates popular fiction's effectiveness in confronting social problems, has noted that "not only can fiction gain you a much larger audience than, say, if you wrote a serious essay about these problems, but you also get people to experience the emotional aspects of the problems and reach an understanding which they couldn't have otherwise, short of actually participating themselves" (*CA*, 120). Literature, of course, does offer readers a special form of participation, and the success of Cook's fifteen medical thrillers to date attests to contemporary society's preoccupation with the issues that these novels raise. Readers who experience "the emotional aspects of the problems" can clearly see Cook's vision of what is at stake within the society he depicts.

In *Mortal Fear* (and also in *Fatal Cure*), Cook identifies a problem that exists within the structure of health maintenance organizations. HMOs have fully emerged on the medical scene during the last twenty years or so, and their creation was inspired by the profession's growing awareness of an imperative to devise ways to control rising medical costs. By offering large groups of prepaid subscribers the opportunity to share medical expenses, the organizers of HMOs hope to contain costs for all participants. (The original appearance of HMOs signaled a significant change in medicine's ways of doing business, and this change caused a great stir within the profession at the time. Robin Cook writes about this development in his novel *Outbreak*.)

The problem Good Health Plan faces in *Mortal Fear* is simply one of demographics. When it was founded twenty years earlier, the HMO's clientele had consisted largely of young and healthy subscribers. This population has aged, however, and the administrators anticipate that medical costs for treating the ailments of these older patients will balloon. The solution presented in the thriller novel is, of course, farfetched, but Cook is interested in drawing attention to the authority that HMO management exercises over policies affecting patients. Those who manage HMOs are essentially running a business, and although the very special business of providing medical care obviously demands close attention to the needs of clientele, Cook wonders about the instances in which business imperatives might override the best interests of a patient. Recent reports of the deaths of infants whose hospital stays after birth were limited by business management policies do suggest that these regulations do not always serve the needs of patients.

Mortal Fear is not the only novel in which Cook expresses concern about the relationship between medicine and business. By persistently dramatizing the dangers he sees in this relationship, he demonstrates one of the ways popular literature can voice significant social issues. When, in fact, the book was chosen for adaptation to the television screen, the questions it posed were addressed to a national audience.

For additional discusssion of the perspective of cultural criticism, see the concluding sections of Chapters 3 and 6.

Blindsight
(1992)

As an old and oft-quoted adage goes, "None so blind as those that will not see." The aptly chosen title of Robin Cook's thirteenth suspense thriller hints at its own ironies, for in *Blindsight* (1992) Cook weaves together multiple themes of vision and blindness. At its most explicit level, *Blindsight*'s plot recounts the unfolding of a murderous scheme that originates in New York City's underworld: a mob lieutenant, blinded by acid burns, attempts to acquire through brutal and unnatural means the cornea transplants he needs to restore his vision. Unquestionably this grisly action provides all the ingredients necessary for an ordinary pot-boiling thriller, but the true terror of Cook's tale lurks elsewhere, in blindness of a very different kind. Drawing its readers into a world darkened by political conflict and intrigue, *Blindsight* exposes a moral blindness endemic in the law-abiding world of social institutions.

This novel employs many of the suspense strategies described in Chapter 2. As is characteristic of Robin Cook's medical thrillers, *Blindsight* probes a contemporary social issue, that of the imbalance of supply and demand in the use of organ transplants. The novel also features a medical setting, introducing readers in this case to the specialized branch of medicine known as forensic pathology. Laurie Montgomery, the main character in *Blindsight* (and a significant figure, as well, in Cook's latest novel, *Contagion*), is a public servant who works in the New York City morgue. As an associate medical examiner, Dr. Montgomery is, in effect, a medical detective, someone who inquires into the mysteries of death. It is part of her job to perform autopsies in cases of unnatural or unexplained deaths among New York's citizenry. When an unnatural death is determined to be an instance of murder, Dr. Montgomery's office works closely with homicide detectives from the police department to document the evidence required for a criminal investigation.

But when is unnatural death indeed murder? Establishing the cause of a death is not necessarily a straightforward proposition, as events in *Blindsight* dramatically reveal. Within the coroner's office, an argument for cause of death must rest upon evidence; however, what might constitute evidence is not always readily recognizable. Furthermore, the significance of evidence, even so-called hard evidence, is itself subject to interpretation.

Thus it is that Dr. Montgomery, from her perspective in the morgue, becomes increasingly suspicious about the coincidental nature of a series of deaths apparently caused by cocaine overdoses. Seeing a pattern in these deaths, she attempts to interpret its significance. *Blindsight* offers a study of the frustrating ways in which Montgomery is thwarted in her persistent endeavors to perform her job. Reading the "evidence" through the distorted lenses of their own political and personal interests, other public officials first discount and then attempt to silence Dr. Montgomery's interpretations. In this fashion, the suspense in *Blindsight* centers around the question, "Who can see?"

THE WORLD OF THE NOVEL

Blindsight's action moves between two quite different social orders, that of the secret underworld of the mob on the one hand, and that of the bureaucratic world of public and business institutions on the other. The very presence of mobsters within the novel's urban landscape provides Cook with one of the stock elements of the thriller genre, but his depictions of mob conspiracies serve additional purposes as well. The mob, after all, is a kind of business enterprise, and in *Blindsight* Cook is deeply interested in exploring the protocols and ethics of work. Using the underworld's macabre business practices as a point of departure, Cook is able to frame provocative questions about the actions of characters who work within the law. Moreover, one of *Blindsight*'s themes is that of class distinctions. As a closed society, one that exists apart from the mainstream's class structures, the underground plays an interesting role in Cook's representation of a cross-section of American social organization.

Although the designs and purposes of the mob are indisputably antisocial, particularly in the context of an ideal of civic good, these associations nevertheless take the form of quite elaborate social entities, as books such as *The Godfather* (Mario Puzo) have revealed. Their organizational structures are hierarchical, and their membership observes codified rules of behavior. Their internal regulations serve to preserve their status as competitive operations. In other words, when they are regarded as management systems, mob dynasties function much as legal institutions do. In setting the activities of one world beside those of the other, Robin Cook implicitly invites comparisons between the two.

Within both worlds, for example, a sense of professionalism is a point of pride. In a grotesque caricature of work well done, two mob hitmen congratulate themselves after spending a night engaged in a successful murder spree. Standards for professionalism, in this kind of work, require that the two carry out their orders, act as team players, and ask no questions about their job. Surprisingly, perhaps, Dr. Montgomery is expected to observe a similar code of conduct in her place of work. Reprimanded by her supervisors for independently pursuing her investigation of the puzzling cocaine deaths, she is told that the questions she has been asking are not part of her job. Her unrelenting interest in finding a satisfactory explanation for these deaths is considered unprofessional, and when she embarrasses her department by speaking to a reporter it becomes clear to those in charge that she is not playing by their rules. In effect, she has violated the standard of professionalism that demands the sort of institutional loyalty practiced in *Blindsight*'s underworld.

Of course Laurie Montgomery has her own carefully considered understanding of the professional requirements of her work. She naturally wonders why it is that the overdose victims she has seen are all young, professional people who have no history of drug use. If it is true, however, as her colleagues have concluded, that these people have indeed taken cocaine in secret, she suspects that the drug has been contaminated in some way. Her sense of civic duty therefore compels her to warn the general public that a killer drug is being circulated in New York. It is here that she most certainly runs afoul of the political interests of her department, for there has been "a lot of pressure from the involved families to sign the case[s] out as natural." As her supervisor states, "With upscale overdose deaths like these the families will certainly want to keep the whole episode low profile. I think we should cooperate in this regard. Politically we cannot afford to alienate this constituency" (167). To Dr. Montgomery, keeping the deaths "low profile" is an obvious disservice to the public. Secrecy, the hallmark of the underworld, is out of place in public life.

Demonstrating the ways in which the ethics of the workplace can be twisted by institutional politics, Robin Cook raises troubling questions about the values of an essentially competitive society. As is the case in the underworld, too often in the lawful realm the ends are used to justify the means. Locked by self-interest within their closed definitions of professional behavior, most of *Blindsight*'s characters remain blind to questions of the common good. Certainly the greed and arrogance that motivate mob gangsters can also fuel the ambitions of those who compete within the law. In this respect, the novel's most telling example is that of Dr. Jordan Scheffield, eye surgeon extraordinaire.

Although he is a member of a profession dedicated to the well-being of others, this fact is a mere irony in Dr. Scheffield's case. An expert at the top of his field, the doctor works long hours to enjoy the luxuries of life. His values are defined by the competitive code of business, for he regards his work as a form of investment. His magnificently equipped office (it contains five revolving examination rooms) is the center of an enterprise that, as he explains to Laurie Montgomery, "pays off handsomely. Currently I'm grossing between one point five and two million dollars a year" (121).

With the rewards of his labor, Dr. Scheffield surrounds himself in extravagant opulence. On the walls of his waiting room hang original Picassos. He escorts Montgomery to New York's fanciest restaurants in a chauffeured limousine. Although she is flattered to be the recipient of the attentions of this successful man, Montgomery cannot help but reflect upon the values of the economy he represents. When she compares Scheffield's private practice with "the shoestring budget the medical examiner's office ran under" (121), she must conclude that "the idea of such ostentation in a medical setting seemed obscene, especially given the runaway cost of medical care" (118).

Within all levels of *Blindsight*'s societies, rules of competition define its world of institutions. One mob faction struggles against another for control of local turf. In the realm of private business, Dr. Scheffield enjoys success because he offers an expert service that is greatly in demand. Even its status as a public service agency does not protect the medical examiner's office from the pressure of competition. Administrators there worry about unfavorable publicity because of the ways "reduced city funding was affecting operations. Every other week one service or supply was being curtailed or eliminated" (166). It is hardly surprising, then, in this dog-eat-dog setting, to find that characters are tempted to set aside their scruples. On one hand, the scramble to get ahead promotes small acts of dishonesty, as when two low-paid police officers take money from the scene of one of the overdose deaths. On the other hand, however, temptation beckons on a larger scale: when Dr. Scheffield discovers that his cooperation with the mob has increased demand for his professional services, he quickly proves that there is no limit to his greed.

In the murky world of business that Robin Cook portrays, acts of personal and political expediency are commonplace. Protagonist Montgomery soon learns that her professional integrity is threatened by the very standards of professionalism that her supervisors ask her to observe. This is deeply ironic, for "one of the attractions for Laurie of pathology in general and forensics in particular was that they tried to deal with the truth. The idea of compromise for whatever reason disturbed her. She hoped she would never have to choose between her scruples and the politicking" (45). Of course, in her refusal to close her eyes to the suspicions that continue to trouble her, this is the very choice that Montgomery is forced to make.

PLOT DEVELOPMENT AND SUSPENSE

Following a formula he uses frequently, Robin Cook opens *Blindsight* with a brief scene of vivid drama: inside a human body, violent chemical warfare rages. Molecules of cocaine, carried by the bloodstream, assault a heart and brain. The body summons its defenses, but the invasion is too great. Printed in italics, Cook's technical portrait of a drug overdose is a staging device, designed to haunt the imagination with its microscopic detail. The neurological battle it describes reaches a crescendo in a fleeting thrill of pleasure, as "circuits of nerve cells divinely wired to ensure the survival of the species rang with excitement and filled afferent pathways running up to the cortex with ecstatic messages" (2). The messages, however, are deceitful, for they are but harbingers of death. The ghastly fate of *Blindsight*'s first overdose victim thus presents an image of horror that will recur throughout the novel as other deaths take place.

Robin Cook's suspense thrillers are built upon fast-paced, page-turning action. After the shocking scenario presented in the prologue, therefore, the reader is quickly introduced to protagonist Montgomery and her place of work. As the first chapter opens, tension is running high in the medical examiner's office. In fact, "trouble" is the first word Montgomery hears when she arrives at work on Monday morning. A young girl has been strangled by her boyfriend, and news reporters, remembering the sensational "preppy murder" from a couple years before, have swarmed into the coroner's office. The case is a delicate one—there is some question of the mishandling of evidence—and Dr. Harold Bingham, Chief Medical Officer, is in a foul temper. Although Laurie Montgomery is not directly involved with this case, it serves to introduce readers to the stressful atmosphere in which she works. Clearly Bingham is already experiencing political pressures when Montgomery's troublesome overdose cases first begin to appear.

Blindsight's action takes place over the course of one week. The plot is developed in an episodic fashion that features alternating scenes of underworld activity and scenes that take place in the mainstream social world. This back-and-forth arrangement allows readers to witness events as they unfold on two levels of the plot. Naturally the two social spheres in which the action occurs remain, for the most part, worlds apart. Cook withholds his final revelations until the closing pages of the book, and one review of *Blindsight* has complained that "readers . . . will guess the ending long before any of the characters has a clue" ("*Blindsight*," 62). Yet Robin Cook's technique for building suspense in the novel depends precisely upon this effect. Evaluating the evidence as it mounts, readers quickly come to share Laurie Montgomery's suspicions as well as her frustrations. Along with Montgomery, readers perceive clues that other characters fail to see.

Readers, however, also have an advantage over Montgomery. Because they directly observe the ruthless machinations that take place within the underworld, their angle of vision is actually broader than Montgomery's. If *Blindsight's* protagonist is curious about the strange pattern of deaths she is seeing, readers have even more cause to suspect that ultimately the novel's two spheres of action will somehow intersect. Seeing more than any character sees (and recognizing the significance of what cannot be seen), heightens the effects of suspense for the readers.

One element of suspense in Cook's fiction is his use of the Cassandra motif (described in Chapter 2). Cassandra, of course, is able to see into the future; the curse that accompanies her gift of foresight is simply that no one pays heed to the predictions she makes. Like Cassandra, Laurie Montgomery attempts to alert others to the dangers that she foresees. Certain that the unusual deaths will continue if some explanation for them is not found, Montgomery warns her colleagues, her supervisors, and the police officer with whom she works. Her predicament, however, is very much like Cassandra's, for those to whom she appeals do not, for a variety of reasons, pay attention to her fears. Dr. Bingham, preoccupied with the possibility of further political damage to his office, hastily dismisses Montgomery's concerns. Detective Lieutenant Lou Soldano, who is more sympathetic than Dr. Montgomery's immediate colleagues, nevertheless does not see how he can help.

Laurie Montgomery possesses no magical powers of prophecy, but she has a strong, inquiring mind. Acting upon her moral convictions, she continues, as the number of cocaine deaths does indeed increase, to give voice to her alarm. In doing this, she falls completely into the trap that is Cassandra's fate. Her associates come to view her as a nuisance, even a troublemaker, and Dr. Bingham decides to put an end to her investigations by reassigning her to cases that have nothing to do with the overdose deaths. He goes even further, in fact, instructing other staff members to withhold information about the cases from her should she inquire about them. Dr. Montgomery thus finds that she is the only person in the coroner's office who has recognized that the deaths of a group of young, promising people might well be linked in some horrendous way. She is effectively silenced by those who have the power to act upon what she fears, and the simple fact that she can clearly see the peril to the public changes nothing. Bodies continue to arrive at the morgue.

With his use of the Cassandra motif, Cook gives shape to a plot that calls for heroic action. If the mystery surrounding the peculiar deaths is to be solved, it becomes clear that the novel's protagonist must work alone. What Dr. Montgomery needs is the direct evidence that will prove the truth of her suspicions. Her search for this evidence is a hero's task, and *Blindsight*'s suspense deepens as Montgomery sets out to find her proof. Like other heroes who search for truth, Laurie Montgomery encounters risk. She risks her job, and she loses that. Because her quest eventually leads her into the realm of the underworld, she risks her life as well.

Having observed the activities taking place among *Blindsight*'s gangsters, readers are well primed to anticipate the suspenseful excitement with which the novel ends. There have been numerous chase scenes and many murders as the mob forces led by Paul Cerino battle those headed by Vinnie Dominick. Cerino, the victim of the acid attack, exacts his nasty revenge upon those of Dominick's men who carried out the deed. (In the most monstrous of these murders, the victim is prepared for the embalming process before he has even died.) Readers also know that Cerino's hitmen, Tony and Angelo, have set out to work each night. Carrying with them lists of victims, they have followed a plan laid out for them by their blind leader. It is into this world of terrible carnage and blood revenge that Dr. Montgomery finds herself drawn when she decides to see her mystery to its end.

Even though she is no longer officially employed by the coroner's office, Montgomery continues to be haunted by images of the grisly cocaine deaths. (Several of the victims were found stuffed into their refrigerators.) Because one of the victims had an organ donor card in her possession, she decides to make inquiries at the Manhattan Organ Repository. When she finds that this establishment has recently suffered a break-in, the pattern behind the deaths is suddenly made clear. Not victims of accidental overdoses at all, the young professionals have been murdered for their eyes—and put into their refrigerators in the hope that their corneas will be preserved until their bodies are discovered.

In *Blindsight*'s thrilling climax, Laurie Montgomery is pursued and captured by Cerino's hitmen. Attempting to rescue her, Lou Soldano is caught as well. In an ironic twist that serves to underscore Cook's theme of ruthless competition, Vinnie Dominick and his men make a last-minute appearance at Cerino's hideout. Knowing that he now has a chance to put his mob rival out of business for good, out of selfish interest Dominick invites Soldano to call in the police. His own selfish motives finally exposed, Cerino wails, "What was I supposed to do? . . . In my business, every day I couldn't see I risked death. Is it my fault the hospitals don't have enough corneas?" (334).

CHARACTER DEVELOPMENT

In suspense thrillers, plot is commonly afforded greater emphasis than characterization. Engrossing action is central to this popular genre, and for this reason both readers and writers are generally most interested in what it is that happens in novels of this type. Focusing on why and how events occur, writers often use their characters to advance their plots. In other words, rather than developing complex characters and elaborating upon their individual histories, suspense writers are likely to regard characters as secondary to the field of action in which they exist. It follows, then, that stock characters (undeveloped figures of the sort seen in television or movie dramas) frequently appear in thriller fiction. With a handful of exceptions, *Blindsight*'s characters fit this type.

If characters in suspense novels are used by writers to enact the drama of their plots, they can also be used to give voice to the political or social positions significant to the world in which the alarming events of the thriller take place. Several of *Blindsight*'s characters serve as representatives of the ethical or political questions that the novel poses. Dr. Bingham and his associates, for example, speak for the authority of those of society's conservative, controlling administrations that believe they must keep a defensive eye on all political ramifications. Short-sightedness, rather than evil intent, is Dr. Bingham's fault. Thus *Blindsight*'s plot involves much more than the simple scenario of good guys versus bad guys, or law-abiding citizens contending with the extralegal mob. Robin Cook is highly aware that law itself cannot contain the many forms of corruption, or blindness, that social competition fosters.

In point of fact, the extraordinary force of heartless competition is the source of *Blindsight*'s vision of evil, and Cook draws his characters to illustrate this insight. The actions of his characters demonstrate a range of competitive strategies for life in today's workaday world. For instance, the highly stereotypical portraits of gangsters (all of whom have Italian names and some of whom listen to Italian operas or wear Brioni clothes) show that these figures comprise a group. It is likely that these mobsters, if they had elected to become part of mainstream society, would be members of the working class. (Indeed, Vinnie Amendola, whose family knows Cerino, holds a low-paying job at the city morgue; there he is in charge of making coffee for the staff.) Refusing, however, to enter into the competitive circles of the general social order, mobsters seek a competitive edge outside the society that seems to have offered them limited opportunities within its bounds. Worldly success, in the form of power or material goods, is available beyond the law. Presented as stereotyped members of an alienated social group, the gangsters have no stake in a belief in some common social good. Because blatant self-interest is its single concern, *Blindsight*'s mob represents the evil embodiment of a grossly selfish blindness within the business world.

In sharp contrast to the sociopathic members of the mob, Cook's novel offers another set of characters that also form a group. The overdose victims, although they are not acquainted with one another, have much in common. Bankers, editors, business executives, they are all successful professional people, rising stars in the mainstream social world. In addition to being productive members of the business sphere, they all pursue other interests as well. As the boyfriend of one of the victims explains to Montgomery, "She was so gifted . . . so strong-willed, so committed. She cared about people. . . . And she was involved in everything, like pro choice, the homeless, AIDS, you name it" (218). These characters are linked together not only in their successful working lives, but in a spirit of altruism that each of them expresses.

Cook's characterization of Dr. Jordan Scheffield offers a view of the successful businessman who has no social conscience. Educated at the finest schools, Scheffield is worldly, urbane, and utterly self-centered. Successful corporations are in the habit of endowing worthy organizations or donating funds to charity, but there are no indications whatsoever that Scheffield shares this inclination. In fact, he exhibits little interest in the welfare of others, including that of his own secretary when she mysteriously disappears. His efforts are all directed toward enhancing his own position, and his general practice is to schedule as many patients as he can each day as a means of increasing his personal productivity.

Unquestionably Dr. Scheffield enjoys his work. His occupation not only brings him financial reward, but, as he exercises his surgical expertise, it also provides him with the deep satisfaction that comes from mastery of his art. (The psychological power that a surgeon commands is a subject that greatly interests Robin Cook, who explores it fully in *Godplayer*.) Dr. Scheffield's immense arrogance arises from his professional pride in his role as surgeon. In truth, Jordan Scheffield is best described in terms of pride: he is exceedingly proud of who he is, and he is equally proud of what he owns.

One Italian American who resents the association between that ethnic group and the underworld is Detective Lieutenant Lou Soldano. Before his promotion and reassignment to the homicide division, Lieutenant Soldano spent years tracking the mob as a member of the police department's organized crime unit. Now that he is in homicide, he hopes to find evidence linking Paul Cerino to various murders in New York.

Soldano, who is frequently described as resembling television's Columbo, first meets Dr. Montgomery in the morgue. Soldano watches Montgomery's work, as she performs an autopsy on the victim of what is obviously a gangland killing. The two quickly become friends, and Cook uses their lively conversations to illustrate features of their personalities and beliefs. Soldano and Montgomery debate a variety of ethical issues, among them the overdose cases that worry Montgomery. Soldano, whose burning passion is to indict members of the mob, argues strongly that his mission is more immediate than Montgomery's. After all, he points out, if rich yuppies choose to poison themselves with drugs, they knowingly embrace the risks they take. Although Lieutenant Soldano is a compassionate man, his single-minded purpose obscures his larger view; he too remains blind to Laurie Montgomery's interpretations of the evidence she finds.

Lou Soldano and Jordan Scheffield are contrasting figures in *Blindsight*'s plot. Vying for Laurie Montgomery's attention, the two prove that moral character is not always obvious at first sight. Outward appearances, of course, weigh greatly in Scheffield's favor. Tall, attractive, well-educated, Scheffield has caught the eye of Montgomery's matchmaking mother. Soldano, who often looks as though he had slept in his clothes (and sometimes has), most certainly lacks Scheffield's polish. Self-conscious about his community college education, he recognizes that Montgomery's social background is more like Scheffield's than his own. Nevertheless, he is quick to discover that Scheffield's charm is superficial, and in this respect he sees more clearly than Montgomery, who is finally forced to admit, "The embarrassment for me is that I was . . . blind to Jordan. . . . I was bowled over by the rush he gave me . . ." (339).

Laurie Montgomery is at the heart of the story *Blindsight* tells. Accordingly, she is its central consciousness, the character with whom readers' sympathies are most engaged. Because she is the moral compass within the conflicted circumstances of the plot, Robin Cook provides readers with special insights into her background, experiences, and state of mind. Indeed, these insights extend beyond attention to her working life to include information about her relations with her family; hence Laurie Montgomery is the most fully developed character in the book.

Although Lou Soldano is at first greatly surprised to meet someone like Montgomery employed at the morgue, it is quite clear that she is deeply satisfied with her job. Her occupation is intellectually stimulating to her; she finds meaningful challenge in confronting the varied puzzles she regularly encounters. One such puzzle is presented early in the novel to afford readers a glimpse of the kind of work she does. An autopsy on a young, healthy woman has turned up no abnormalities at all. Yet, the woman's heart was not beating when her roommate discovered her lying in the hallway of their apartment. Dr. Montgomery conducts tests on electrical appliances found in the apartment and soon discovers that the woman possessed a faulty curling iron. The mystery of the death is solved when Montgomery realizes that the woman must have suffered arrhythmia shortly after receiving a low voltage shock.

Dr. Montgomery's expertise is focused on the dead, but she nonetheless thinks of her work as beneficial to the living. She knows that family and friends need to understand what has happened when an unexpected death occurs. Furthermore, as in the case of the malfunctioning hair curler, determining the cause of one death might well prevent another. It is this strong conviction—this need fully to comprehend the circumstances surrounding death—that Montgomery acts upon when she persists in asking questions about her overdose cases.

Laurie Montgomery is particularly sensitive to the deaths of the young cocaine victims because several years earlier her only brother suffered a similar fate. This tragic event occurred when Montgomery was quite young, but she is haunted by a lingering guilt. Her brother, a beginning college student at the time, was experimenting with drugs, and Laurie happened to discover what was taking place. In their grief and anger, her parents later blamed her for failing to inform them about the secret she knew.

Although her own youthful rebellion did not take the course her brother's took, the novel makes clear that Laurie Montgomery's decision to specialize in pathology did not please her parents. Her father, an accomplished cardiac surgeon, is especially disappointed in the choice that she has made. And her mother has disapproved of Laurie's boyfriends and wonders when her daughter, now age thirty-two, will find a suitable young man. Montgomery herself is a little surprised that she has not yet married, and this is a concern that is on her mind. One of the many reasons she settled on pathology was that its predictable working hours would allow her to pursue her interest in medicine while enjoying family life. Cook's portrayal of the private dimension of Laurie Montgomery's world has the effect of strengthening the bonds of sympathy readers feel toward *Blindsight*'s protagonist. The kind of pressure she experiences in her office also exists in her private life. However, Montgomery is obviously a heroine who knows her own mind. Readers can certainly see why her stubborn adherence to her strong principles will earn her the respect of her family in the end.

THEMATIC ISSUES

If Robin Cook's novel establishes the truth of the old maxim that hindsight is the clearest sight, its author is nevertheless committed to exploring the various social conditions that cloud people's vision in the choices that they make. Cook's titles often announce his themes, and *Blindsight* is no exception. Recognizing the possibility of building suspenseful action around the terrifying implications of characters' inability to see, Cook uses the concept of blindness as his central theme. His dramatic use of the Cassandra motif (wherein one character sees what cannot be seen by others) works well in this respect. Of course, blindness can take many forms, and finally all of the novel's characters are shortsighted or see falsely in some way.

In *Blindsight* Robin Cook shows that what can be seen, and how that which is seen is then interpreted, are matters that are largely determined by the position or perspective of the viewer. Blindness consists of what cannot be seen from the position occupied by a particular character. In some cases, characters wear blinders by dint of who they are. It is thus through his use of metaphors of blindness that Cook is able to weave together the many sociological issues that his novel probes. Characters' views of the differences of class and gender or their responses to the powerful forces of competition and politics are understood in terms of what they can or cannot see—or sometimes what they will not see.

One kind of failure of vision presented in the novel might well be described as "occupational blindness." When people are accustomed to seeing the problems of the workplace through the lenses of their professional experiences, it is frequently difficult for them to envision solutions that might exist beyond the terms of their own expertise. A simple anecdote has often been used to illustrate this point: a truck enters a tunnel where there is not sufficient clearance and becomes thoroughly wedged in place. A team of engineers ponders strategies for jacking up the tunnel until someone who does not see the dilemma as an engineering problem suggests that if the air is let out of its tires it should then be fairly easy to remove the offending truck. Occupational blindness is thus a problem of angle of vision, of people making interpretations from within the boundaries of established contexts.

In like manner, both Lou Soldano and the administrators at Laurie Montgomery's office are deeply committed to those interpretations of events that square with their own professional understandings of the world. As a policeman, Soldano looks for evidence and for motive to determine when a murder has taken place. In the absence of these conditions, he is unlikely to suspect that wrongful death has indeed occurred. Dr. Bingham and the other officials at the morgue are besieged by political problems. As administrators, they define their jobs in terms of their efforts to control or contain the sources of their troubles. Preoccupied with these concerns, they too fail to see the larger vision. When it appears to them that Dr. Montgomery is herself becoming something of a problem, they move quickly in an attempt to control the new threat they have now perceived.

In addition to its examples of professional blindness, the novel offers Laurie Montgomery's misjudgment of Jordan Scheffield as an instance of personal blindness. This category of failed vision is nicely exemplified in the old folktale about the emperor's new clothes. Like the citizens in that tale, Montgomery sees in Scheffield what she wishes to see rather than what is quite obviously there. (This is not a matter of misunderstanding an ambiguous character: Cook makes a point of consistently emphasizing Jordan Scheffield's shallow nature throughout the book.) Eventually Lou Soldano dismisses Montgomery's short-sightedness about Scheffield, claiming that she is less "cynical" (339) than he; readers, however, recognize that the heroine who has otherwise seen with such great clarity has been mistaken in this case.

The third type of blindness explored in the novel is relevant to characters' visions of society. Generally speaking, "social blindness" occurs when people fail to recognize the ways in which other people count. This quite basic understanding that some kind of social contract binds people together is necessary to all forms of community life. Laws establishing common rules of fair play set certain limits to social conduct, but many other conventions, beliefs, and behavioral codes play important roles in dictating people's relations to one another. While *salus populis*, the traditional concept of the general good, is an active force in contemporary life, it can be countered by the imperative of the individual good, as exemplified in the competitive struggles that *Blindsight* depicts. Characters seeking to enhance their own positions are all too often blind to their obligations to others.

For the novel's two mob factions, community loyalty is centered upon family relations. Acting on their determination to compete outside the law, the gangsters have defined a social world that admits no possibility of kindness to strangers. This denial of the humanity of others is characteristic of the mentality of the sociopath and accounts for the mobsters' willingness to commit murder with impunity. Of course Robin Cook's gangsters do think of themselves as "civilized people" within the confines of their family and business associations. Vinnie Dominick uses this very expression in a meeting of the mob lieutenants, and after the meeting Cerino assures his henchmen that "Vinnie wouldn't lie about family" (124). Interestingly, an implicit rule among competing mob factions requires that "civilized" businessmen refrain from engaging in activities that might draw unusual attention from law enforcement officers, and observation of this code generally works in such a way that Cerino's and Dominick's gangs keep one another in check. Gangsters' greatest loyalties, however, extend only to immediate family and to the members of their individual mob groups. When the activities of one mob faction prove threatening to the other, all sense of "honor among thieves" quickly fades away.

The social blindness from which Jordan Scheffield suffers is not far removed from that of the gangsters, and it is perhaps for this reason that he is able to turn a blind eye to the brutal activities of the mob. Most people are of little consequence to Dr. Scheffield, whose superficial judgments about others appear to be based upon their background or class. As Lou Soldano reveals to Laurie Montgomery late in the novel, "He [Scheffield] always made me feel like a second-class citizen" (338). Because she is the daughter of a highly respected cardiac surgeon, Montgomery's own credentials are seemingly sufficient to have engaged Scheffield's attention, but readers attentive to the dialogue between them will note that Scheffield never seems to express genuine interest in Laurie herself—rather, he enjoys the company of someone who will listen appreciatively to his talk about himself.

Certainly Scheffield delights in an awareness of his own importance, and the very design of his revolving examination rooms reflects his sense of power over his patients. Instead of coming to meet his patients, he manipulates the examination rooms so that patients appear before him, while he is magisterially seated at his desk. This exercise in authority, as he explains it to Montgomery, encourages the confidence of patients. If such a gesture encourages confidence, it clearly does not express respect; the elaborate revolving rooms are but a manifestation of Scheffield's arrogant indifference to the humanity of others. Not only does this character fail to acknowledge his general responsibilities to his community, he is unable to extend to others the common courtesies that might afford them dignity. In his portraits of Scheffield and the mobsters, Robin Cook locates social blindness in both of the worlds his novel depicts.

ALTERNATIVE PERSPECTIVE: FEMINIST CRITICISM

Within the practice of literary criticism, feminist approaches seek to draw particular attention to questions associated with the social/political positions or roles and life experiences of women. Feminist critics are interested in how women express themselves in their own writing and in how they are represented in the writing of men. In studying and discussing literary representations of women, feminist critics actively participate in today's general women's movement. The cultural critiques offered by feminist critics help advance the goals of the women's movement by addressing many of the ways in which women's social, political, and economic conditions have been or can yet be improved.

Although the roots of the modern women's movement reach at least a couple of hundred years into the past, it has been during the last thirty years or so that an amazing assortment of feminist projects has enlivened the field of literary studies. Critics and theorists have avidly discussed the work of women writers and have examined anew the ways in which men have portrayed women in literature throughout the ages. Of course, the work of academic feminists can be seen in the larger context of the significant cultural changes that have taken place in Western societies over the course of the twentieth century. Writing in Elaine Showalter's 1985 anthology of feminist essays, Sandra M. Gilbert summarizes the implications of this recent cultural change for contemporary literature:

> To be quite plain, I am saying that we live the way we live now, and think the way we think now, because what was once a wholly masculinist, patriarchal culture has begun fragmentarily, haltingly, sometimes even convulsively, but, I suspect, irreversibly, to evolve into a masculinist-feminist culture, a culture whose styles and structures will no longer be patriarchal in the old way, even if they remain patrilineal. I am therefore saying as well that the way we read and write now, the way we imagine literary texts and traditions now must inevitably and irrevocably change under the pressure of the sociocultural changes we are experiencing. (Gilbert, 43)

Robin Cook's career as writer of popular fiction spans the very period of immense sociocultural changes described by Gilbert, and it is thus instructive to note the ways in which his work indeed belongs to a contemporary "masculinist-feminist culture." For one thing, Cook has never been averse to centering his plots upon the adventures of female protagonists. Beginning with his second and third novels, *Sphinx* and the bestseller *Coma*, Cook has introduced with his fiction a series of intelligent, introspective, and strong-willed women characters. Like Laurie Montgomery, these characters have been professional women who have encountered overt or subtle instances of sexism in their public or personal lives. Obviously, Cook himself is highly conscious of the changed roles of women in the workplace (particularly the increased presence of women in the upper echelons of the medical profession), and he does not fail to acknowledge the social implications of these changes. When Marissa Blumenthal, the protagonist of *Outbreak*, proves to be overly sensitive to the possibility of sexual harassment by her boss, she finds that the resulting misunderstanding brings with it severe complications within her working life. Cook portrays his female protagonists as strong and resourceful women, but he is also quite candid in his recognition of the ways they experience today's cultural changes—all of these characters are highly aware of their positions in a society where new gender roles are still being negotiated.

Blindsight and its protagonist are of particular interest to feminist readers in two related respects. On the one hand, Laurie Montgomery is a heroic figure, a character whose brave adherence to principle is not swayed by the repressive politics of her bosses, by her own fear of failure, or even by the personal dangers she encounters. She is thus a character from popular fiction who can represent for readers the image of woman as hero. On the other hand, *Blindsight*'s plot clearly casts Montgomery in the role of the silenced woman, the possessor of the unwelcome and disregarded voice. This is a position that women have often occupied, throughout history and in the annals of literature as well. Cook's protagonist, however, is a contemporary woman, one who will insist somehow that her voice be heard. Thus Laurie Montgomery's unlooked for heroism actually comes about because she refuses to be history's silenced woman.

As a deeply reluctant hero, one forced by circumstances to take up her own quest for truth, Laurie Montgomery does not fit the mold of the classic hero, the commanding figure who emerges from traditions of epic literature. She is no leader born to her destiny, and she speaks from no position of extraordinary power or strength. Rather, she is an example of what Nadya Aisenberg has recently called the "ordinary heroine." In her 1994 study of the appearance of a new kind of female hero within contemporary literature, Aisenberg explores such genres as mystery and crime fiction, romance, and science fiction to locate a vision of heroic action that might serve modern social needs. The heroine she discovers is "an ordinary woman endeavoring, nevertheless, to tackle extraordinary problems" (Aisenberg, 13). Montgomery, who attempts in *Blindsight* to fulfill the moral obligation that she understands to be essential to her job, is confronted with the extraordinary problems that arise from the fierce territorial and competitive struggles surrounding her. Not ambitious for personal power, never engaged in these struggles herself—"Laurie realized . . . that she had no desire to be chief" (30)—she is, like Aisenberg's ordinary heroine, "deeply committed to a more humane society" (Aisenberg, 13). A public servant, she is determined to serve the public well.

For Laurie Montgomery to become an example of the emerging new heroine, the ordinary woman who can make a difference in the lives around her, she must find a means to make her voice heard—she must break free from the role of the silenced woman. As widely recognized instances from literature illustrate, the silenced woman is often a character who has a message that other characters do not wish to hear. Cassandra, who speaks with foresight, is one example, and the witches in *Macbeth* are another. *Lear*'s Cordelia, silenced, banished, has spoken unwanted words of truth.

In the context of *Blindsight*'s action, Montgomery's voice represents that of a social conscience, expressing the will to do the proper thing. Those who place self-interest above moral principle are quite clearly not interested in hearing what she has to say. It would, of course, be easy for Montgomery to defer to the wisdom of her superiors, to accept their judgments about the circumstances of the cocaine deaths. She could turn to her new assignments and, as so many do, quietly serve as a small cog in the machinery of the system. But Dr. Montgomery greatly fears that human lives might be at stake. Trusting her instincts, she must refuse to accede to the silence imposed upon her. Ostracized by her colleagues and hunted by the mob, she pays a high price for speaking.

For additional discussion of a feminist approach to literature, see the concluding section of Chapter 7.

Acceptable Risk
(1994)

In *Acceptable Risk*, Robin Cook's sixteenth novel, revisiting an old medical mystery provides occasion for thoughtful speculation about the direction of a new trend in medical technology: cosmetic psychopharmacology.[1] Cook's old mystery takes place in 1692 when the Puritans of Salem Town came to fear that there were witches and devils in their midst. In *Acceptable Risk*, Cook suggests that the frenzies suffered by people assumed to have been possessed by demons were actually hallucinogenic responses to fungi or molds that grew on the food they ate. This interesting theory about people's unintentional use of mind-altering agents leads quite logically to Cook's entry into the current debate about the intentional use of Prozac or Prozac-like drugs for the express purpose of enhancing personality traits. Edward Armstrong, the brilliant neuroscientist in Cook's novel, aspires to design the ultimate antidepressant. He believes that his drug, which he has pointedly named Ultra, promises to "combat fatigue, increase contentment, sharpen the senses, and encourage clear thinking by enhancing long-term memory" (189). Perhaps, he claims, it can even enhance sexual experience. Although Cook has read *Listening to Prozac*, Peter Kramer's popular and provocative book, *Acceptable Risk* makes clear that he remains skeptical about the wisdom of this course. Borrowed from *Hamlet*, the epigraph for his novel suggests that there might well be new demons in the land:

the Devil hath power
to assume a pleasing shape. (*Hamlet* II, ii 600)

Departing somewhat from techniques he characteristically employs in his medical thrillers, Cook presents *Acceptable Risk*'s readers with a detailed study of the growth and maturation of his central character, whose quest for self-realization is central to the novel's theme. There is no doubt, however, that this novel also provides Cook's usual allotment of suspense, for here he situates his protagonist in a truly gothic setting. Kimberly Stewart has inherited a moldering ancestral castle, and it holds clues to a tale of witchcraft that has marked her family's past. Three hundred years earlier Kimberly's ancestor, Elizabeth Stewart, was condemned to die because of "incontrovertible evidence" (207) that she was one of Salem's witches. In her search for knowledge of the mysterious evidence that was used to convict Elizabeth, Kim indeed uncovers one of the monsters from Salem's past. This ancient horror, however, cannot be compared to the terrors that she experiences when she finds that quite modern ghouls have come to occupy her castle.

As he frequently does, Robin Cook has included an annotated bibliography at the conclusion of his text; there he cites reference works that might prove useful to readers interested in investigating further the subjects that inspired his plot. In addition to Peter Kramer's book, he lists several studies of the Salem witchcraft trials and Richard Restak's *Receptors*, which offers a thorough discussion of contemporary understandings of brain function. In its exploration of the dangers of the current drift toward entrepreneurialism within the practice of medicine, Barry Werth's *The Billion-Dollar Molecule* takes up a subject that greatly preoccupies Cook himself.

PLOT DEVELOPMENT

Acceptable Risk is a tale of two obsessions. Indeed, the novel features a double plot wherein the quests of two of its characters are ironically counterpoised. Kim Stewart's search for an understanding of her ancestor Elizabeth's fate quickly turns into a quite private quest for a deeper knowledge of herself. As it happens, her exploration of the past leads eventually to the discovery of what an unexpectedly bright and promising future might hold for her. Edward Armstrong's quest, on the other hand, is directed toward the future. He hopes, with his discovery of a drug that produces effects similar to those of Soma, the drug used in Huxley's *Brave New World*, to ease the pain of people's lives. Of course, along the way he plans as well to secure fame and fortune. Ultra, he suspects, could quite possibly be his very own billion-dollar molecule. The path he chooses, however, does not lead to the glorious future he has envisioned. Ironically, it takes him on a strange journey back into the past, to a region of the mind dominated by the reptilian brain. Horribly, in the course of his quest, Edward Armstrong transforms himself into a brute.

In the prologue to *Acceptable Risk* Robin Cook briefly transports readers back to the New England of 1692. There a young wife and mother, Elizabeth Stewart, maintains her household while her husband Ronald, who owns a shipping firm, is off in Europe on company business. Cook takes pains, in his brief sketch of Elizabeth, to portray her (even in her rigid Puritan setting) as a vibrant and engaging woman. His purpose in so doing is made clear when readers quickly recognize that, as Kim Stewart gradually learns more and more about her unfortunate ancestor, Elizabeth becomes for her an attractive alter ego. As she comes to fully understand what Elizabeth suffered so many years ago, Kim is able to "feel the force and character of Elizabeth's personality through her anguish: caring, empathetic, generous, assertive, and courageous; all the traits Kim wished she had herself" (231).

Elizabeth Stewart generally has a house full of children, for in addition to her own three, she regularly takes in refugees from Indian raids that have occurred in the vicinity. She bakes a great deal of rye bread, for, as she explains to Mercy Griggs, the doctor's wife, "I have in mind to encourage the whole village to utilize rye to conserve the wheat supplies" (4). It is quite likely, as readers soon learn, that the rye bread is the cause of her undoing. The children who have visited her household begin to suffer fits, and when Ronald Stewart finally sails into Salem's harbor, he finds his wife in shackles and awaiting execution. Although he makes appeals to such colonial luminaries as Samuel Sewall and both Cotton and Increase Mather, Ronald Stewart can do nothing to forestall Elizabeth's scheduled hanging. The Reverend Cotton Mather explains to him that the special court of Oyer and Terminer has convicted Elizabeth on evidence that it considers to be "material proof of the existence of the invisible world" (21).

In its allusions to the mysterious evidence used to convict Elizabeth Stewart, the prologue introduces the puzzle destined to preoccupy her descendant. Ronald Stewart, who is a witness to his wife's public hanging, cannot but wonder in his grief, "Why Elizabeth?" But he too has seen the evidence, and "clearly it was the devil's work" (30).

Readers meet Kim Stewart and Edward Armstrong in Chapter 1. Knowing that Kim has recently broken off her relationship with her boyfriend, her cousin, Stanton Lewis, arranges a blind date for the two painfully shy people. An entrepreneur in medical technology, Lewis does, of course, have an ulterior motive in arranging his little dinner party. He hopes that Armstrong, who enjoys a brilliant reputation as a neurochemist at Harvard, will agree to join the advisory board of a new company he is forming. Arguing that famous athletes and movie stars frequently endorse products, Lewis does not see why scientists should not do the same. Armstrong, however, is a man with scruples (at least in the opening pages of *Acceptable Risk*). Devoted to his teaching and research, he has no interest in selling his name to a company in whose products he has no stake. Committed to "knowledge for knowledge's sake," he explains: "In some respects academia and industry are at odds with each other, especially in regard to industry's imperative of secrecy. Free communication is the lifeblood of science; secrecy is its bane" (42). These are words that Armstrong would do well to live by, but when true temptation comes, readers quickly discover that there is indeed a higher price at which his principles can be bought.

Kim and Edward are drawn toward one another by the social handicaps they share—both are hesitant, awkward, and overly apologetic— and a relationship soon blossoms into romance and a decision to share the cottage on her estate that Kim has arranged to have renovated. The cottage itself once belonged to Elizabeth Stewart; in addition to it, Kim's property includes the castle that the Stewart family built a generation or two after Elizabeth's time as well as a large, empty stable. All of these facilities are destined to be put to practical use by the new couple, for when Armstrong does decide to set up his own research company, he asks Stewart for the use of her stable. (He believes that its isolation will guarantee the secrecy he now requires to protect his work.) The old castle becomes a second home to the five elite scientists invited by Armstrong to join his company. Working together at maximum speed, the six researchers hope to perfect their drug in record time.

Edward Armstrong begins to violate all of his own moral guidelines for the practice of scientific inquiry when he discovers that a sample of fungus taken from the food-storage cellar of Kim's cottage possesses as yet undiscovered psychotropic properties. Ironically, his original purpose in testing the sample arose from a desire to be helpful to Kim.

Because the Stewart family has been deeply ashamed of the "witch" in its history, Edward thought that suggesting that Elizabeth might have been the victim of hallucinations would serve to assuage the sense of disgrace the Stewarts have long felt. Having read that *Claviceps purpurea*, a fungus that grows on rye, can cause hallucinogenic responses similar to those produced by LSD, Edward had assumed his analysis would offer proof that the people of Salem might have been victims of ergotism. Instead, he isolates another fungus, one whose three new alkaloids excite his curiosity.

In the first of the several changes that Edward Armstrong's character undergoes over the course of *Acceptable Risk*, he suddenly abandons his Harvard duties and reverses his position on the issue of secrecy in research. He successfully persuades Stanton Lewis that his discovery has the potential to lead to the production of a truly remarkable new drug, and financing for Omni Pharmaceuticals is hastily arranged. If readers are a little surprised by the alacrity with which Armstrong's impetuous change of heart occurs, his own words in fact express his deepest inclinations. "When it comes to science, I'm a man of action" (105), he readily declares. Completely absorbed by his new tasks, he commits his days and nights to his recently acquired but burning passion: here is an opportunity to make a name, to reap incalculable reward, to improve the lives of others. What more could a scientist hope to achieve? Perhaps there even could be, as Stanton Lewis has suggested, a Nobel Prize in the offing. Lured by all this promise, Edward Armstrong is not a person to refuse the gift that chance has thrown his way. As he says, "It's amazing how often serendipity plays a role in drug discovery" (132). His change of direction is complete when Stanton Lewis finally notes, "The good doctor has become so greedy he will not sacrifice any equity [in the company]. He's metamorphosed overnight from an avowed ascetic academician to an insatiable capitalist" (319).

While Edward is busy installing his new state-of-the-art equipment and then initiating his experiments, Kim Stewart oversees the renovation of her cottage and begins the task of sorting through voluminous family documents stored in several rooms of the old castle. A surgical intensive-care nurse at Massachusetts General Hospital, she decides to take a leave of absence to allow herself time to pursue these projects. The family documents do contain letters and diaries relevant to the mystery of Elizabeth's sad fate, but these are randomly mixed in with shipping orders, company records, and other accounts of family affairs. The job of sifting through boxes and trunks proves to be a slow and painstaking one, but

Kim feels deeply rewarded whenever she finds a reference to Elizabeth or to the circumstances of her trial. Among her most provocative finds are several letters that clearly indicate that Ronald Stewart took great pains to attempt to recover the compelling evidence presented against Elizabeth. Kim wonders what this evidence, frequently mentioned but never explained, could possibly have been—a doll, or book? Or something else Elizabeth made?

In the course of overseeing the renovation of the old cottage, Kim experiences some revelations about herself. Determined to retain the integrity of its original design, she delights in finding ways to make her new home comfortable while still preserving its distinctly colonial charms. Amazed at the great pleasure she takes in selecting appropriate furnishings, in choosing colors and designs for her decor, she recognizes that she has long been fascinated by architecture and interior decoration. Thinking back on her career choice, she becomes aware that in truth she chose nursing primarily to please her father, a man with whom she rarely gets along.

In the very early days of their relationship, Kim and Edward freely discuss their mutual social problems. Edward, who actually begins to stutter when he becomes emotionally excited, admits to being too self-conscious, "even," he says, "a little nerdy" (41). Strongly believing that both behavior and mood can be understood as essentially biochemical in nature, he recommends the use of Prozac. Kim, who reveals that she has in the past taken Xanax for anxiety attacks, nevertheless does not subscribe to a belief that drugs can provide a panacea. As she explains, "I'm not in favor of using drugs for minor personality flaws like shyness. I think drugs should be reserved for serious problems, not mere everyday difficulties" (51). With this exchange, readers can readily see that Kim's philosophical position places her in direct opposition to the goal of Edward's research; it is therefore hardly a surprise when the two quite soon begin to drift apart. Explaining that he feels a strange restlessness at night, Edward suggests that they take separate bedrooms when they actually move into Kim's cottage. Thus, sharing only the roof over their heads, Kim and Edward spend the late summer months individually engrossed in their different kinds of research.

Suspense in *Acceptable Risk* largely depends upon readers' growing curiosity about where the quests Kim Stewart and Edward Armstrong have taken up will lead them. However, Cook also uses details of setting and subtle nuances that hint of the mysterious to create an atmosphere charged with apprehension. Spending long hours alone in the castle, Kim is haunted by the "spookiness of the huge, empty house." Sometimes too she feels the "guilt of trespassing into a forbidden and troubled past" (91). Old letters and documents, with their unfamiliar syntax and old-fashioned orthography, certainly invoke the ghostly specters of that past. And as she uncovers Elizabeth's history, unusual coincidences strike her. She notes that the days of the week for 1692 correspond to those of the present year (1994) and that, eerily, she and Elizabeth have birthdays that fall only a few days apart. Furthermore, Kim herself is twenty-seven years old, exactly Elizabeth's age when she died so long ago. Interestingly, a dramatic portrait of Elizabeth, showing her remarkable green eyes, looks very much like Kim herself. A gloomy castle, a haunting portrait, diaries that bring to light figures from the past—all of these gothic elements serve to heighten suspense in *Acceptable Risk*.

Quite obviously, Cook also incorporates gothic strains in his presentation of the scientists and their work. The frenetic activity of the researchers more than hints of the sinister compulsions characteristic of fiction's long tradition of "mad scientists," and in a scene reminiscent of some old horror movie where graves are robbed for body parts, Armstrong violates Elizabeth's last resting place. Not buried with other family members in the Stewart cemetery, Elizabeth's remains are mistakenly discovered by workmen who are digging a trench for new sewer lines. Armstrong, of course, wants to see the mummified body and so opens up the coffin. In most macabre fashion, Elizabeth's head comes off in his hands (her neck had been broken when she was hanged); with the head so handily in his possession, Armstrong decides he must collect a sample of Elizabeth's brain. (Indeed, he does find there traces of his new alkaloids.)

When Edward Armstrong begins to undergo yet another personality change, readers know that this time the change is drug-induced. In their efforts to move quickly through the necessary experimental stages of their work, Armstrong and the five researchers on his staff have all agreed to use themselves as guinea pigs. Although they take Ultra in varying doses, all the researchers claim enhanced performance of their jobs. Once a collection of snapping and bickering prima donnas, the scientists are completely transformed into efficient and harmonious members of a team. They also seem to possess more energy than they once had, and therefore work both day and night. When, in the early morning hours, they finally collapse into exhausted sleep, they cannot be reawakened. But in fact they do not sleep peacefully. When police officers arrive to investigate reports of strange goings-on at night (small animals mangled and garbage cans overturned), it becomes clear that the researchers now suffer from somnambulism. Perfectly cognizant of their surroundings when they are awake, they are not conscious of their actions while they are asleep. Indeed, they have all become modern incarnations of Dr. Jekyll and Mr. Hyde.

As *Acceptable Risk* reaches its climax, Kim Stewart makes two discoveries that she knows will be relevant to Edward Armstrong's work. On the one hand, she finds references in letters to episodes of violence experienced by those who were thought to be under the spell of Salem's witches. The researchers, already subject to such episodes themselves, have by now stopped taking Ultra. Kim's other discovery, which might indicate an additional effect of the drug, has to do with the evidence used against Elizabeth at her trial. Following leads that suggest the evidence was in fact preserved by Increase Mather, she finally locates it in the basement of Harvard Medical School's Warren Anatomical Museum. Elizabeth, it seems, had prematurely given birth to a seriously malformed fetus. Anencephalic and possessing a cleft palate as well as a fishlike tail, the little creature preserved in a jar looks very much like a tiny demon. This, then, was the material proof of Elizabeth's connection to the "invisible world," and Kim can well imagine how Elizabeth herself might have feared that "she was guilty of some horrid transgression against God" (373). Realizing that Edward's drug might be teratogenic (that is, capable of causing damage to fetuses), Kim decides that the time has come to confront the overly ambitious scientists.

Kim Stewart's newly found knowledge of the way the circumstances of 1692 had cruelly conspired to entrap a young woman inspires her immediate resolution to change her own life. Taking stock of her present situation, she admits to herself that Armstrong and the other researchers are merely taking advantage of her. She thus finally recognizes that the Omni lab should never have been installed on her property and that the researchers should never have been permitted to move into her family's ancestral house. Although she is determined to insist that the scientists make new arrangements for themselves, the opportunity to speak with Armstrong never comes. In a final night of terror, the researchers all revert to their primitive, bestial states. This time they stalk Kim, and pursuing her into the castle, they form a ring around her and begin to close in. Seizing a blowtorch left by the workmen, Kim temporarily manages to hold them at bay. When the creatures become emboldened and begin to move in again, Kim loses control of the torch, and within moments the castle goes up in flames. In the mighty conflagration with which *Acceptable Risk* ends, the mysteries of the Stewart castle are all transformed to ash. Only Kim, Edward Armstrong, and one of the five researchers survive the dreadful night.

CHARACTER DEVELOPMENT

Kim Stewart's relationship with her parents is not a happy one, and she believes that her lack of confidence and general reserve can be attributed to this fact. She finds her father, an assertive and dominating man, extremely hard to please. Moreover, she knows (as do all the family members) that he regularly sees mistresses, and this knowledge disturbs and disappoints her. Overwhelmed, perhaps, by the force of her husband's personality, Kim's mother leads a listless and reclusive life. Lacking social activities or work to do, she remains at home—usually wearing her robe to suggest that she really has no good reason to get dressed. Although Kim feels sympathy for her mother's position, she is also frustrated by the way she leads her life. All in all, Kim Stewart's parents do not serve as models of what she would like to be.

Robin Cook provides details of Stewart's family background to mark the point from which she begins her ascent to self-knowledge and acceptance. He leaves no doubt that her social problems have caused many difficulties in her life; in fact, her relationship with Kinnard Monihan, the boyfriend with whom she eventually makes up, is presented early in the novel as a casualty of her insecurity and excessive sensitivity. That she generally has trouble with relationships is further indicated when she is readily drawn to Edward Armstrong, who shares her lack of confidence. Although Kim early on interprets Edward's hesitant manner as a mark of his sensitivity, readers, who quickly discern that Armstrong's true commitment is to his work, may suspect that he is a manipulative man. Indeed, when Kim herself finally perceives this fact, she acknowledges that her relationship with Edward has come to bear a strong resemblance to the one she has with her father.

Although Kim Stewart's desire to lead a happy and productive life is not an unusual one, Robin Cook is interested in the ways features of her own personality have become obstacles to this goal; characteristics of her nature have indeed entrapped her or seemingly worked to limit her choices. This, of course, is where the use of psychotherapeutic drugs becomes an important theme in *Acceptable Risk*. Because Kim decides to confront her problems in the "old-fashioned way with introspection, a little pain, and effort" (288), Edward accuses her of a "pharmacological Puritanism" (97). As Cook's characters debate this issue back and forth, and Edward, in fact, presents many convincing arguments to support the use of Prozac, Cook implicitly invites his readers to ponder the question for themselves. There is no doubt, however, that he offers in his protagonist a study of a character who struggles to attain personal maturation without the help of drugs.

It is by initially looking outward, by becoming deeply involved in the life of another human being (no matter that Elizabeth is no longer alive), that Kim Stewart finds the occasion to turn inward, to thoughtfully weigh her own experiences and actions. Moved by what Elizabeth endured, she sees in her history a useful image of women's strength. When she compares her understanding of Elizabeth's personality with her own (in a letter, Elizabeth's father described his daughter as a "high spirited gyrl"), she ruefully wonders if each would not have done better living in the other's world. But in the end, Elizabeth's story is for Kim an extraordinary source of inspiration; when she gazes at the portrait, she can finally begin to see something of herself smiling back through her ancestor.

Using Elizabeth Stewart as her model, Kim takes several steps to turn her life around. She knows that "it's not easy breaking old patterns" (398), but she is determined to try. Although she does not have the chance to dislodge (as she had intended) the ghoulish research team, she does confront her father. To her amazement, her relationship with him is thereafter much improved. And happily, her relationship with Kinnard Monihan is also much improved. As he comments, "I feel less like I'm walking on eggshells when we're together" (398). In *Acceptable Risk*'s epilogue, the two decide to move back to Kim's cottage together. Kim has decided to turn her stable into a studio, for she believes it is time to pursue a career that is truly of interest to her. She also believes that it is time her family contributed something to the community. Before the flames consumed them, Kim had found the business documents of over three hundred years stored within the castle. Three hundred years of Stewarts had run the shipping business, and during all that time the family had produced no artists or public servants. As Kim acknowledges, "For all their money, they'd developed no art collections, philharmonic endowments, or libraries. In fact, they'd made no contribution to culture unless entrepreneurialism was a culture in and of itself" (380). Certainly Kim has seen enough of entrepreneurialism to last her a lifetime.

In *Acceptable Risk*, Cook's depiction of Kim Stewart's personal growth is contrasted with Edward Armstrong's steady descent into compromise and self-deceit. As Kim finds her identity, Edward increasingly loses his. He squanders his brilliant reputation at Harvard, forcing the university to consider bringing action against him. Telling himself that his decision to take Ultra before it has been fully tested is an acceptable risk, he allows his strong ambitions to overwhelm his common sense. Readers will readily recognize that his eventual transformation into a creature with only brute appetites serves as a metaphor for the gradual dehumanization he brings on himself. If Armstrong's drive to acquire fame and fortune through science is the means he finds to finally assert himself, then his is a Faustian bargain, for there are terrible consequences to pay. After the fire, Armstrong and the colleague who also survived continue their study of Ultra. (They now understand that the drug has the effect of blocking cerebral control of the brain's limbic system.) Greatly disfigured, hairless and missing fingers, the two work in a lab designed to accommodate their handicaps. Although all traces of Ultra have been flushed from their systems, they are still subject to hideous flashback attacks. This time, in their analysis of Ultra, their goal is to find a way to reverse its effects.

Two other characters are of particular interest in *Acceptable Risk*, primarily because they act as foils to Kim and Edward. Stanton Lewis, always ebullient, joking, glad-handing, is shown to be perfectly at ease in any situation. The model, perhaps, of the successful entrepreneur, Lewis is readily able to cajole and persuade, to flatter and entice; his very living, after all, depends upon his skills in working smoothly with other people. Years earlier, he and Edward Armstrong were classmates together, and since that time Edward has greatly admired Lewis's ability to assert his personality. In fact, Edward is delighted when he finds that under the influence of Ultra he is able to keep pace with Lewis, confidently exchanging jovial witticism for friendly barb. In interesting ways, Stanton Lewis serves to represent the high value contemporary society places on such attributes as social ease and the ability to make small talk.

Acceptable Risk's other significant character is, of course, Elizabeth Stewart, of whom readers actually see very little, but whose presence looms large throughout the book. Just as Robin Cook's novel relates a story about Kim, it also tells the story of Elizabeth's life. Using the letters and diary entries to piece together the details of her story, Kim manages to learn a great deal about Elizabeth's nature and about the conditions of the time when she was alive. Kim, for example, is somewhat shocked to discover that Elizabeth's marriage, which took place when she was seventeen years old, was arranged by her father. Elizabeth's diary indicates that she was interested in a young man who lived in her village. Nevertheless, when Ronald Stewart, widower and prominent citizen of Salem, approached her father, Elizabeth cheerfully agreed to accede to her family's wishes. In return for his daughter's hand, James Flanagan struck a bargain with Ronald Stewart: he demanded that Stewart provide him employment and arrange to move his whole family to Salem Town. Kim can see that Elizabeth, then, had been regarded as chattel, available to be bargained away in a business deal.

Kim's documents reveal that Elizabeth was a devoted mother and a woman who possessed a great deal of community spirit. In addition to taking orphans into her home, she clearly spent a great deal of time working with children, teaching them the art of doll-making and providing games for them to play. When readers briefly encounter Elizabeth in the prologue, they learn that her bread-baking too served a civic purpose. Because Salem had suffered bad weather and poor harvests, Elizabeth used her rye in an attempt to conserve community stores of grain. She regularly sent loaves home with children who had come to visit, and this, of course, was the unfortunate means by which the rye mold was spread. (That Elizabeth's active participation in community concerns was seen as unbefitting a woman's role is established in the prologue when Mercy Griggs reminds her that all civic matters should be discussed by the men at their town meetings.)

Robin Cook's portrait of Elizabeth serves important functions within the novel. It is quite obviously through her haunting presence and through the mystery that surrounds her that Cook first establishes the gothic elements he uses throughout *Acceptable Risk* to create an atmosphere of suspense. Elizabeth, after all, was hanged as a witch, and Kim notices that three hundred years of Stewarts have subsequently avoided naming their daughters Elizabeth. Centering his plot upon Kim's efforts to reclaim Elizabeth's good name, Cook is able to link the two women's stories. In this way Kim, who often feels that Elizabeth is trying to communicate with her over the years that separate them, uses a voice from the past to learn to listen to her own voice.

THEMATIC ISSUES

In addition to reinforcing one of Robin Cook's most common themes, that of alerting readers to the dangers of entrepreneurial greed within the fields of medicine and science, *Acceptable Risk* implicitly poses questions about the nature of personality and the role of emotional pain in human experience. Suggesting through his protagonist that some of life's inevitable pain and disappointment can lead to maturation, Cook offers arguments to counter a recent tendency of doctors to prescribe Prozac for people who merely wish to feel better about themselves. *Acceptable Risk* does make perfectly clear that Cook is in no way opposed to the use of psychotherapeutic drugs in cases of emotionally crippling disorders. (Kim herself speaks of using a drug whenever she experiences severe anxiety attacks, and she also meets with a therapist when she feels the need.) Rather, Cook's objection is to the so-called cosmetic use of these agents by people who are not suffering deeply.

In the debates conducted by his characters, Cook offers his readers a glimpse of several of his reservations about the practice of cosmetic psychopharmacology. One fear, of course, is that people who use such drugs might actually avoid the occasion to confront their problems in a more satisfactory way. Kim Stewart, especially when she is compared with Edward Armstrong, can serve as an example of someone who is able to make a permanent change in her life. (When he stops taking Ultra, Edward stutters and generally reverts to his old behavior.) Another possible problem with psychotropic drugs is that the effects of their long-term use are, as yet, unknown. Although Ultra is merely a fictional drug, Cook sounds a cautionary note in his depiction of Edward's flashbacks. (Too, for some people, psychotropic drugs can produce fairly serious side effects.) Yet a third concern might well be called the "Soma effect." Cook worries that widespread use of Prozac or similar drugs could result, across society, in the general loss of what is understood to be individual character and personality. In other words, the acceptable norms for human conduct might be narrowed. Would it really be desirable for everyone to behave like Stanton Lewis? What about the wonderful ways in which people can be different from one another? Kim certainly ponders this consideration, thinking particularly about the creative impulses that are often understood to arise from people's special ways of working out their problems. She wonders what the world be if Beethoven or Mozart had taken these drugs.

While offering his readers the opportunity to consider all these provocative questions, Robin Cook once again issues a strong warning about
the dangers of the relationship between medicine and money. Even
though the researchers do hope, at least in theory, to produce a drug
that will serve the needs of people, their decisions to work in absolute
secrecy and to take ill-considered shortcuts in their research are clearly
motivated by greed. These researchers, in fact, are a particularly greedy
lot, and when Cook's plot vividly exposes their base motives by actually
reducing them to a pack of sniffing, grunting, and grubbing beasts, little
more need be said about how their natures and actions are meant to be
regarded by the readers of *Acceptable Risk*.

ALTERNATIVE PERSPECTIVE: GENRE THEORY

Borrowed from French, the word *genre* means "type" or "kind," and
literary critics who are interested in genre studies are committed to identifying relationships among literary works that possess similar characteristics. Literature, for example, can be classified by type: epic, tragic,
comic, satiric, and so on. It can also be classified by form: the novel, the
drama, the poem, the sonnet, and so on. Although some of these categories can be seen to overlap within individual works of literature, and
type and form are by no means the only ways literary works can be
grouped together, the genre critic's goal is to determine those ways in
which classification can lead to heightened understanding of the nature
of literary art. In classifying literary works into groups with common
elements, genre critics are able to describe the purposes or functions of
different types of literature. They are, as well, able to identify the various
categories of literary conventions or codes that work to shape the effects
individual literary works achieve.

Although genre studies of one kind or another are at least as old as
Aristotle, and traditional categories for classifying literature have come
and gone over the years, contemporary theorists, drawing upon the work
of structuralists, have now begun to see writers' uses of particular literary forms, conventions, and codes as constituting a kind of contract
with readers. On the one hand, using a clearly identifiable literary convention or form allows the writer to work within a certain literary category (the thriller, for example). On the other hand, the writer's use of
a conventional category allows the reader to expect to see a certain type
of work. Indeed, many fiction readers today have developed quite spe-

cific tastes and interests and often enjoy reading a variety of books within a given genre. While drawing upon the basic characteristics of a particular category of literary work, writers, of course, are free to experiment with form or to play out variations on standard conventions, and writers working in many of the popular fiction genres will frequently do so, in part to avoid producing work that is merely formulaic.

Popular fiction today offers readers a wide variety of genres from which to choose books written primarily to entertain. (Of course, books written to entertain can and do serve other purposes as well.) The popular genres, or, as they are also called, the formula fictions, are often classified by type in libraries, bookstores, or even grocery stores. The most common categories are mystery, suspense, science fiction, fantasy, the western, romance, and historical romance. (Other popular genres directed toward readers' specialized interests might include such categories as sports literature or, in recent years, vampire literature, a distinct subgenre of the romance.)

Although, once again, novels that fall into these generic categories might possess features that overlap with those of books in different categories (many romances, for example, make use of the gothic elements that also characterize novels written about the lives of vampires, and books from both fantasy and science fiction can often be classified as examples of utopian literature), such structuralist critics as Tzvetan Todorov have attempted to explain the distinct generic contracts implicit within the categories. Distinguishing in *The Poetics of Prose* the significant differences between mysteries and novels of suspense, Todorov points out that within these two genres, readers' expectations of the course of plot development are, in fact, reversed. While mystery's classic form, the whodunit, is centered upon finding a solution to a crime, the thriller offers an action-packed account of the unfolding of the crime itself. In the mystery, in other words, the movement of action is from effect (crime) to cause (solution). In the suspense thriller, "the movement is from cause to effect: we are first shown the causes . . . and our interest is sustained by the expectation of what will happen, that is, certain effects (corpses, crimes, fights)" (Todorov, 47).

Robin Cook's characteristic genre is the suspense thriller, for, by Todorov's definition, his novels focus on the suspense created as readers directly observe malevolence taking shape. His special contribution to this category of popular fiction is, of course, his use of a medical setting to introduce the *frisson*—the thrill of excitement—readers experience when evil occurs where it is generally unexpected. Several of Cook's suspense thrillers do, however, include elements of mystery, for, in some cases, he withholds the identity of villains until the climax of the book. (*Mortal Fear* and *Outbreak* are examples.) A few of Cook's suspense thrillers have also been classified as science fiction. In such novels as *Mutation* or *Brain*, Cook's depiction of hypothetical scientific discoveries fulfills the special expectations of science fiction readers. As is obvious, then, this writer of suspense fiction is not averse to borrowing useful features from other popular genres.

Acceptable Risk provides yet another example of an interesting mix of genres, for here Robin Cook blends the medical thriller with both the historical romance and the gothic novel. (Because Ultra is a scientifically plausible but undiscovered agent, readers could even argue that Cook has also included a touch of science fiction.)

As medical thriller, *Acceptable Risk* familiarizes readers with the frightening implications of current developments in the field of drug research. Focusing particularly on the widespread practice of secrecy among researchers, Cook shows how difficult it is to control the protocols and test procedures employed by independent labs. When there is secrecy, and when the opportunity for great reward presents itself, Cook knows that he has the ingredients he needs to shape a suspenseful tale. Dropping hints about his scientists' gradually changing natures, he prepares readers to expect the thrilling climax that they find. As is true of Cook's other medical thrillers, readers are strongly reminded that the world of science should never be viewed as sacrosanct.

It is from the historical romance that Cook borrows the strategies he uses to tell Elizabeth's tale. The historical romance, a work of fiction grounded in an actual historical event or time, or that presents characters who once were actual historical personages, has long been a popular literary genre. Sir Walter Scott, with books like *Ivanhoe* and *Rob Roy*, was the first widely successful writer of historical romance, but Nathaniel Hawthorne, James Fenimore Cooper, and Robert Louis Stevenson all helped to popularize the genre. Perhaps the most widely read American historical romance is Margaret Mitchell's Civil War novel, *Gone with the Wind*. In more recent years, Alex Haley's *Roots* has also enjoyed an immense popular following.

Although Elizabeth Stewart is herself a fictional character, Robin Cook has carefully researched the Salem witchcraft scare and populates Elizabeth's "history" with figures who actually took part in the ensuing trials. Readers, of course, will readily recognize the names of Samuel Sewall and Increase and Cotton Mather; in imitating locutions these men actually used in their writing, Cook makes every attempt to capture the authentic sound of their voices in the letters Kim finds in her castle. Offering numerous details of Elizabeth's experiences, Cook invites readers to join Kim Stewart in imagining what life might have been like in colonial New England. Cleverly, he even leaves open the possibility that an Elizabeth Stewart might have existed. He suggests that her family members went to great lengths to excise her name from the historical records of the Salem trials, and that her son Jonathan, who eventually went to Harvard, succeeded in changing the name on Elizabeth's evidence to read "Rachel Bingham."

Finally, Cook's *Acceptable Risk* is also indebted to the traditions of the gothic novel. A popular literary genre that flourished during the late eighteenth and early nineteenth centuries, it derived its name from Horace Walpole's *The Castle of Otranto: A Gothic Story* (1764). Using the word *gothic* to denote the Middle Ages, Walpole's story introduced many of the conventions that became more or less standard to the gothic genre. Often set in the past, these novels featured gloomy castles, hidden passageways, and occasional dungeons or ghosts. The stories they told related horrific or supernatural events, and in them a vulnerable young woman frequently found herself entrapped or otherwise at risk. In later variations on the gothic theme, novelists often dropped the use of a medieval setting but retained these novels' traditional atmosphere of gloom and horror and their fascination with the macabre or the grotesque. Certainly Mary Shelley's *Frankenstein* can be regarded as a classic of this later type of gothic novel. In recent years, elements of the gothic have reemerged in such popular forms as the romance novel or the horror film.

As noted earlier, Cook draws freely upon the stock conventions of the gothic genre to enhance the suspenseful effects of *Acceptable Risk*. The Stewart family castle does not possess a dungeon, but it does offer a moldy old wine cellar and even an artificial moat. Kim's sense of Elizabeth's constant presence suggests a troubled "ghost" from the past, and the nocturnal activities of the researchers are nothing if not grotesque. In fact, Edward Armstrong turns out to be something of a Victor Frankenstein himself, creating in his lab not one but several monsters over whom he can exercise no control. In addition to his use of these classic gothic motifs, Cook also draws inspiration from the traditional black-and-white horror film. In an episode that resembles a scene from *Night of the Living Dead*, the zombie-like researchers advance upon a parked car that contains a teenage boy and girl. Horribly, grasping hands reach through the windows, seizing hair and ripping skin. The frantic teen-agers are able to make their hurried escape, but the lesson they learn is one well known to all aficionados of gothic horror movies: it is always foolhardy indeed to pursue romantic adventures in a cemetery late at night. As one reviewer has aptly noted, *Acceptable Risk* "dabbles in witch-craft and delights in spooky effects" (Madrigal, 4). Cook's playful pas-tiche of the horror film well illustrates this observation.

NOTE

1. Cosmetic psychopharmacology is a phrase used to describe instances when people who are not suffering from debilitating mental disorders nonetheless use drugs to enhance features of personality or to put themselves at ease in social situations. In some cases, people use alcohol for this purpose, but the use of other psychotropic drugs (those that alter perception or behavior) is growing more commonplace.

Contagion
(1995)

Medicine as big business has fully come of age in Robin Cook's seventeenth novel, *Contagion* (1995). In this book, gigantic medical corporations that have succeeded in driving large numbers of private physicians from their independent practices ferociously compete with one another to attract new clientele. The field of battle for these megacorporations is the advertising industry, and if the profit stakes are high for the medical companies, they are equally important to the advertising firms that carry their accounts. Indeed, in the blunt words of one of the advertising executives depicted in *Contagion*, "these health-care giants are going to be the advertising cash cows of the next decade" (35). Convinced that advertising for medical corporations is "in the ascendancy," the powers within the advertising world hope, with marked irony, that these new accounts will "fill the hole vacated by cigarettes" (33).

Thus, Robin Cook's most recent book both continues to chart the seemingly ineluctable transformation of medicine into corporate industry and also introduces readers to yet another of the capitalist enterprises closely associated with the growth of the health care business. (Cook's medical thrillers have served to expose the activities of various ancillary industries in the past. In *Harmful Intent* he examined the economic relationships between medicine and law, in the form of malpractice litigation, and in *Mindbend* he focused upon the symbiotic links between medicine and the pharmaceutical industry.) In drawing striking parallels between the corporate structures of the medical companies and the advertising firms portrayed in *Contagion*, Cook once again emphasizes the fact that, for competitive businesses, economic considerations are of central importance. Furthermore, because it is medicine's recently acquired status as a competitive business that has drawn its executive officers to call upon the services of the advertising industry (and to spend there the millions of dollars that might have remained in health care), Cook sees this additional step in the commodification of medicine as a particularly unfortunate one. It is for this reason that he chooses for *Contagion's* epigraph the somber appeal made by Dr. Jerome P. Kassirer, writing in the *New England Journal of Medicine*: "Our leaders should reject market values as a framework for health care and the market-driven mess into which our health system is evolving" (52).

In *Harmful Intent* and *Mindbend*, Cook showed how greedy malefactors from businesses associated with contemporary health care practice might conspire to enrich themselves through manipulation of specific vulnerabilities within the current system. In both instances, the medical profession, as well as those it serves, were victimized by unscrupulous predators. Precisely this scenario is repeated in *Contagion*, where an ambitious executive from an "up-and-coming" (29) advertising firm, Willow and Heath, schemes to discredit a major health care company by arranging that patients housed within its facilities contract nosocomial infections (nosocomial diseases are those acquired within the hospital itself). In thus blackening AmeriCare's reputation, the novel's villain hopes to guarantee the success of her own advertising campaign on behalf of a competing corporation, National Health Care. In Robin Cook's view, an alliance such as this one between the worlds of medicine and advertising presents a new opportunity for those who would find means to prey upon a heritage of public trust in the offices of medicine. Indeed, it provides for him yet another timely example of the "market-driven mess" to which Dr. Kassirer has referred.

As its title hints, a hideous array of pestilences is unleashed upon hospital victims within *Contagion's* pages. In the book's focus upon the threat posed by the alarming possibility of patients contracting a nosocomial disease, Cook draws attention to another issue of timely significance. Recent reports, in fact, indicate that instances of hospital-based disease are increasing, particularly as virulent strains of bacteria become resistant to familiar antibiotics. Although the cases of pneumonic plague, tularemia, Rocky Mountain spotted fever, and influenza documented in *Contagion* are more or less successfully contained by hospital personnel, the book's plot clearly invites speculation about the devastating effects that a full-fledged epidemic could produce. Readers are reminded that earlier in this century, during the "pandemic of 1918 to 1919," a pathological strain of influenza indeed "killed twenty-five million people worldwide" (291). Echoing the concerns that have inspired such recent books as Laurie Garrett's *The Coming Plague*, or Richard Preston's *The Hot Zone*, Cook's novel cautions readers that medical science has by no means succeeded in mastering infectious disease. While *Contagion* is primarily attentive to the dangers that arise from malicious human actions, the threats posed by natural forces serve as backdrop for its plot.

PLOT DEVELOPMENT

Contagion transports readers who are familiar with Robin Cook's thirteenth novel, *Blindsight*, back to a familiar setting. The central action occurs in New York City, where the novel's protagonist, Dr. Jack Stapleton, has joined the staff at the Office of the Chief Medical Examiner. Although a few years have passed since Laurie Montgomery stirred up her department by independently investigating a rash of puzzling cocaine overdose deaths, she still works at the morgue, and Dr. Harold Bingham, the politically motivated administrator, still presides over this public institution. (Other characters from *Blindsight*, including policeman Lou Soldano, also appear within *Contagion*'s pages.) Although the coroners' offices are still housed within the aging building first described by Cook in *Blindsight*, some interesting changes have nonetheless occurred: in the autopsy room, the medical examiners are now equipped with protective "moon suits," fully enclosed, impervious garments that include elaborate ventilation units. This eerily ominous detail speaks to the natural dangers that Cook's plot invokes. In the era of AIDS and other serious infectious diseases, those who practice forensic medicine must observe due precautions.[1]

Pathology, as it happens, has become Dr. Jack Stapleton's second medical career. *Contagion*'s prologue informs readers that Stapleton, now forty-one, was a highly successful ophthalmologist living in Champaign, Illinois before the gigantic conglomerate, AmeriCare, swept into his hometown. After his patient base was all but eradicated, Stapleton elected to retrain in a completely different branch of medical science. (He purposefully chose a specialty that appeared to be in no immediate danger of falling under the jurisdiction of the omnipresent medical corporations.) Yet another personal tragedy soon befell him, however, when his wife and two daughters, after visiting him at the site of his new residency, died in the crash of a small commuter plane. Understandably embittered, Stapleton is therefore gleeful when, as the novel's central action opens, he discovers that a man upon whom he has conducted an autopsy has died of a mysterious infection acquired at a hospital owned by AmeriCare. Not sorry to see trouble appear for his nemesis, Stapleton admits that he cannot "think of anything more enjoyable than giving AmeriCare heartburn. I'd love to see that corporation squirm" (18).

Jack Stapleton's initial sense of grim satisfaction quickly changes to alarm when tests reveal that AmeriCare's patient has succumbed, quite inexplicably, to an airborne form of plague. Fears of contagion are quickly realized when a member of the hospital's staff also dies of plague, and Stapleton therefore responds to the immediate imperative of trying to determine the source of the infection. Although the city epidemiologist and the hospital's own Infection Control Committee are both working on the case, Stapleton, spurred on by his antipathy for AmeriCare, persists in conducting his own investigation.

Very quickly Jack Stapleton runs into the same kind of trouble that Laurie Montgomery encountered when she set out in *Blindsight* to find the answers to troubling questions. The bureaucratic Dr. Bingham, who strongly believes in administratively defined divisions of labor, reprimands his employee, cautioning him to stay away from Manhattan General, AmeriCare's hospital. Nevertheless, when another outbreak of infectious disease (this time, most oddly, tularemia) occurs at the same hospital, Stapleton becomes convinced that the episodes are more than coincidental. This suspicion, in fact, is deepened when he learns that many of the hospital staff members who have become ill worked in the central supply room. Wondering how people who had no contact with the index cases might have become infected, Stapleton decides that this mystery is unlikely to be solved unless he chooses to ignore Dr. Bingham's orders.

Contagion's narrative scenes move back and forth between accounts of Jack Stapleton's experiences and those of Terese Hagen, the ambitious young advertising executive who is, unbeknownst to readers, the primary villain in the plot. Jack Stapleton clearly has a mystery to solve, but so do readers, who have been offered in the novel's prologue descriptions of three disparate events that predate the story's main action by nearly five years. Readers are told that the incidents recounted in the prologue are "totally unrelated," but that they nevertheless are "to cause a tragic intersection of the lives of three of the people involved'' (1). As noted earlier, one of the accounts presented by the prologue supplies readers with information about Jack Stapleton's past life. Another introduces them to Terese Hagen, who undergoes an emergency hysterectomy after suffering complications from an ectopic pregnancy. The third portrays a scene in Alaska. There, within the Arctic Circle, near Prudhoe Bay, two young men explore the site of an ice-covered hut revealed when bulldozers have been used to clear land for an oil pipeline. The hut contains three frozen corpses, all covered in ''frozen pink froth'' (6), and a newspaper on the floor bears the date April 17, 1918. Explaining that he desires a sample of lung tissue from one of the corpses ''for my own collection'' (7), the man named Dick busies himself with a saw. Readers, of course, are implicitly invited to keep the ''unrelated'' events of the prologue in mind as they encounter the puzzles that *Contagion* rapidly unfolds.

Recognizing that the characters and events portrayed in the opening vignettes will prove significant to the novel's subsequent action, readers are not surprised when Stapleton and Hagen meet, and even begin to establish a friendship. Jack Stapleton is openly skeptical about advertising in general and downright critical of advertising in medicine, but Terese Hagen, who is looking for new ideas for National Health Care's ad campaign, appears to value the opportunity to discuss her concepts with a practicing physician. Their differences of opinion notwithstanding, the two characters seem to have in common a mutual sympathy; each senses that the other carries an unspoken burden of grief from the past, and each recognizes in the other a singular dedication to a profession. It is only at the novel's climax, when Hagen's identity as villain is finally revealed, that Stapleton and readers clearly see that Hagen, aware of the investigation that Stapleton has been relentlessly conducting, has encouraged the relationship so that she can keep a watchful eye upon the doctor's activities.

The significance of the remaining scenario from the prologue, the one set in Deadhorse, Alaska, begins to become apparent late in the novel when yet another outbreak of nosocomial disease occurs at Manhattan General. This time the patient and hospital workers die of influenza, and officials at the Centers for Disease Control suspect that the strain they are testing is none other than the one that caused the terrible pandemic of 1918 to 1919. Jack Stapleton, who has long assumed that the outbreaks have been precipitated by someone working at the hospital, figures out that the deadly bacteria and viruses were transmitted to patients through

the humidifiers installed in their rooms. Recognizing this, he understands that the infected hospital workers from central supply were those
who later cleaned the contaminated humidifiers. Having established how
the diseases were introduced, it remains for Stapleton to determine the
identity of the criminal and, of course, the reason for the crime. It does
cross his mind that AmeriCare itself might be engaged in eliminating
particularly costly patients, but the risks of possible epidemic seem to
argue against that conclusion.

As *Contagion* nears its suspenseful climax, Jack Stapleton realizes that
he, too, has contracted influenza. Determined, however, to persist in
playing amateur detective, he treats himself with rimantadine. Using a
ruse to discover the identity of the malefactor at Manhattan General, he
trails Richard Overstreet, head technician at the hospital's lab, back to
his apartment. (Richard, as readers can now see, must be the "Dick"
introduced earlier in the prologue.) When he soon observes Overstreet
leaving the apartment building, Stapleton decides to break in, hoping to
discover proof of incriminating activity. The proof he seeks is clearly
present, in the form of an extensive private laboratory, but in true thriller
fashion Stapleton is caught in his act of intrusion and held at gunpoint
while Overstreet telephones his mysterious coconspirator.

Eager to learn why the lab technician has murdered patients at the
hospital where he works, readers, along with Jack Stapleton, await the
revelation of Overstreet's partner in crime. When, shockingly, it is Terese
Hagen who appears, readers learn that Overstreet and Hagen are, in fact,
brother and sister. Responding to his sister's request that he devise a
way to draw unfavorable media attention to AmeriCare's most important city hospital, Overstreet, an avid microbiologist who, for years, has
privately collected specimens of bacteria and viruses, finds occasion to
make use of his secret stock of microbes. As the novel's climax moves
to its conclusion, Hagen and Overstreet shape plans to get rid of Jack
Stapleton once and for all. Their parents own a somewhat remote vacation cottage in the Catskill mountains of New York State, and this
seems to them to offer the best place to dispose of their intended victim's
body. What they do not realize is that Stapleton's case of influenza has
reached a highly contagious stage; enclosed with him in the car, the
villains themselves become infected (and they have no supply of rimantadine). Employing, therefore, a device similar to the one he also used
in *Fatal Cure* (where murderers were irradiated by the same bed they
used to poison others), Robin Cook metes out retribution appropriate to
the crimes his villains have themselves committed.

CONTAGION'S USE OF THRILLER CONVENTIONS

Contagion's central plot is spiced with plenty of action. Whereas in *Blindsight* Cook offered readers a sociological reading of New York's mobster-run underworld, in this novel he focuses on the network of gangs that exists among communities of inner city blacks. When Terese Hagen and her brother fear that Jack Stapleton's investigations are leading him close to the truth, they immediately take out a contract on his life. Instead of hiring a Mafia hitman, Richard Overstreet makes his arrangements with the leader of one of the neighborhood gangs. What Overstreet does not know is that Stapleton in fact enjoys associations with members of a rival gang. Indeed, Stapleton (who has, since he first moved to the city, lived in an apartment in Harlem) regularly plays pick-up games of basketball with members of his own gang. Because he has learned through careful observation many of the niceties of traditional playground protocol, Jack Stapleton's presence on the basketball court is tolerated by his neighborhood companions. When these casual team-mates learn, however, about the designs of the cross-town gang, they rally quickly to defend what they consider to be a violation of their turf. Thus, without formally requesting it, Stapleton is afforded protection against the assaults of the gang known as the Black Kings.

Suspense in *Contagion* is heightened by Robin Cook's use of episodes typical of thriller action. In addition to his other consuming preoccupations, Jack Stapleton must keep a wary eye upon the gang members who are stalking him. In two of the three attempts made upon his life, Stapleton is rescued by members of his own neighborhood gang. Because one member from each gang is killed in the shoot-outs depicted in these scenes, police begin to fear that a full-fledged gang war might break out. The tension created by this possibility is only relieved through the skillful negotiations conducted by Stapleton's friend Warren, leader of the Harlem gang.

Warren and his comrades come to Jack Stapleton's aid in one final suspenseful scene. At the end of the novel, greatly weakened by his illness, Stapleton is trapped in the Catskills' cottage with the corpses of Hagen and Overstreet. Chained to the kitchen sink, he is anticipating the arrival of the Black Kings, earlier summoned to finish him off. (Hagen and Overstreet, quite capable of indirectly murdering people with the use of microbes, are nonetheless unable to directly shoot their captive.) Managing to break free of the sink when he hears the sound of a car in the driveway, Stapleton hides in a fertilizer box stored in the barn. There, in his "malodorous" surroundings, he is discovered by Warren, who explains that the gangs indeed "called a truce so there'd be no more brothers shooting brothers. Part of the terms were that they wouldn't ice you. . . . So here we are: the cavalry" (425).

CHARACTER DEVELOPMENT

Because *Contagion*'s central characters—protagonist Jack Stapleton and antagonist Terese Hagen—have both suffered personal tragedies, it is interesting to compare the different ways in which they have responded to those terribly significant events in their pasts that have closed off certain realms of their emotional lives. Although these differences are crucial to the outcome of the novel's action, readers nonetheless note, early in the story, certain similarities between the strategies these characters employ to manage the grief that continues to haunt them. Both characters, for example, are extraordinarily reticent about the experiences of their past lives; to their colleagues, who know little about their histories, they are somewhat mysterious figures, remote and self-contained. Moreover, in the absence of particular social interests or commitments, both characters' lives appear to be centered on their work. This seeming similarity, in fact, turns out to mark an important difference between Stapleton and Hagen—as readers will discover by the end of the novel. Not only is Hagen's life centered on her work, but she has, in fact, come to define her whole identity in terms of her professional ambitions. As she tellingly informs a colleague, "I want to be president [of the firm]. It's been my goal for five years" (71). The five years of which she speaks signal, quite clearly, the interval of time that has elapsed since loss and disappointment changed the direction of her life.

Readers can easily see the ways in which Jack Stapleton's life has also changed over the course of several years. During his family days, as pictured in the prologue, Jack was known as John. A staid and confident physician, husband, and father before he lost his practice to AmeriCare, his general transformation began to occur at the time of that first tragedy. During this period he appeared to his wife to turn "bitter and insecure" (8). Worried and beleaguered, he quickly lost twenty-five pounds, giving him, as she observes, "a lean, haggard look consistent with his new personality" (8). By the time *Contagion*'s central action opens, some of these early changes have grown more marked: Stapleton has, for example, exchanged suits and ties for jeans and tennis shoes. The insecurity and bitterness his wife noticed have been subdued, the bitterness only occasionally surfacing—as witnessed, for instance, in the pleasure Stapleton obviously takes in learning of AmeriCare's internal problems.

If the Jack Stapleton who works with Laurie Montgomery is by no means insecure, he is, as she and others both notice and remark, a strangely reckless man. His choice to live in Harlem strikes colleagues as a dangerous one, and his habit of riding his bicycle through the crowded city streets (dodging traffic and bellowing curses) practically guarantees that he must defy death every day. Stapleton has no qualms about venturing alone into Central Park at night, and it is this behavior that presents the occasion for one of the attempts made upon his life. Although he is unquestionably a brilliant pathologist, Stapleton is often acerbic or flippant at his workplace; Laurie Montgomery, who greatly admires her colleague's skill, nevertheless fears (rightly) that his attitude might cause him trouble with his bosses.

The portrait of Jack Stapleton that emerges early in the novel presents readers with a vision of a man who is headstrong, impetuous, and obviously reluctant to seek emotional engagement. *Contagion*'s protagonist, in other words, is slightly eccentric and something of a loner. As the novel's action unfolds, however, readers catch glimpses of Stapleton's wry and subtle nature. Particularly interesting is his relationship with Warren and the other denizens of the neighborhood basketball court. It is through his sensitive attention to nuances of gesture that he earns his acceptance within this special social circle. And, as Laurie Montgomery and Terese Hagen both make overtures of friendship, Stapleton begins to imagine the possibility of broadened horizons in his life. Indeed, as he grows increasingly conscious of his connection to other people, he starts to contemplate some of the implications of his proclivity for risky behavior. A character who changes over the course of the novel, Stapleton finally comes, when Warren rescues him, to an acknowledgment of the degree to which "one's fate" is "in the hands of others" (425).

In contrast to Jack Stapleton, Terese Hagen is a static character. Because she cannot acknowledge, as Stapleton finally does, her dependence upon any relationships with other people, she is convinced that she can secure her own destiny through manipulation of circumstances within her environment. The desperate measures to which she resorts can be seen by readers as arising from the arena of her workplace: all the scenes that feature activities at Willow and Heath underscore an atmosphere of ruthlessly cutthroat competition. In fact, not only do the advertising firms compete with one another, but executives within Willow and Heath itself vie with each other for power and position. (Hagen's original ad campaign for National Health Care is undermined by enemies in her own firm.)

Because readers cannot fully recognize the depth of Terese Hagen's single-minded ambition until it is unmasked at the novel's climax, they are called on to revise their readings of this figure's character. In this light, sympathy for the plight of someone who has experienced an overwhelming disappointment is transformed into suspicion. That the loss depicted in the prologue was of major consequence in Hagen's life there is no doubt. When she hears that she will never have children, she is benumbed: "All her life she had assumed she would have children. It had been part of her identity" (12). Nevertheless, the fact that her husband leaves her at this point takes on new meaning in the context of her subsequent actions. Was this an act of cruelty, or, as he suggests, had Terese Hagen manipulated the circumstances that led to their marriage? In either case, the true nature of Hagen's character is laid bare: having lost one image of herself, she has replaced it with another, one she is determined this time not to lose. Unlike Jack Stapleton, whose remaking of himself remains in flux, Terese Hagen, fixed as she is on her singular objective, is unable to imagine the possibility of realizing new directions in her life.

Although Laurie Montgomery does not play a central role in *Contagion*, readers who remember *Blindsight* are delighted to meet up with her again. Tempered, perhaps, by wisdom and experience, Montgomery nonetheless remains a sympathetic character. Although she does not initially subscribe to Stapleton's suspicions about a conspiracy (and herein lies an irony, since he assumes in *Contagion* the very position she occupied in *Blindsight*), she does remain open to persuasion. Readers who are curious about her relationship with Lou Soldano learn that although there once had been the thought that they "could have had a future together" (312), this has not worked out. There were, it seems, "Too many differences in their backgrounds" (312). She and Soldano do remain good friends, and *Contagion* closes with the suggestion that in Laurie Montgomery Jack Stapleton will also find a loyal friend.

Finally, to address the matter of characterization from a slightly different angle, Robin Cook offers in this novel a fascinating account of the social milieu of the inner-city basketball court. Cook's portrait, filled in with appropriate jargon and explanations of both playground etiquette and court ritual, presents readers with a memorably vivid slice of New

York City life. Hoping to master the intricate conventions of this special form of social interaction (involving exuberant play, but also much more complicated elements of cultural performance), Jack Stapleton wonders "if any psychologist had ever thought about studying it from an academic point of view" (268). Cook's own point of view, as represented in his main character's appreciative attention, seems remarkably perceptive. Indeed, this informal study of social organization (wherein the terms of competition are expressly delineated by the same rules that govern participation) can well be seen as one of the most interesting features of this book.

THEMATIC ISSUES

While Robin Cook's recurrent interest in the theme of corporate greed is played out on one level of the novel's action, his antagonist, in the instance of *Contagion*, is finally more obsessed with acquiring symbolic status and personal power than she is with directly realizing financial gain (though material gain will undoubtedly be one of the trappings of a position of power). In thus focusing on the allure of privilege and status—on, as it were, the desire to be important—Cook extends in an interesting way his ongoing critique of capitalist competition. As he has shown in others of his novels, a ruthlessly competitive environment (such as the one in which Terese Hagen works) places an extraordinary premium on the will to succeed. When, as it plainly does with Hagen, the desire for success surpasses any other considerations, corruption is born of vanity. Although he has previously delineated the pattern wherein overweening ambition leads to an enactment of violence, in this novel Cook seems to pay particularly close attention to the ways in which corporate competition fuels the will to succeed.

Because the power and status that Hagen seeks are dependent upon her ability to promote the self-interested goals of her corporation (the original contract with National Health Care is worth $40 million, and this amount is expected to increase by 20 percent with the new account), the kind of success that she hopes to achieve can itself be seen as a commodity of competition. In other words, if Hagen can distinguish herself within business's own competitive game, she will enjoy the chance to be crowned a winner. In her world, the economy of success is based upon an economy of competition; in the language of business's revealing metaphor of the game (aptly based on its concern with strategies for winning), success can be understood to be a symbolic form of trophy.

In attempting to isolate what Terese Hagen's (and, for that matter, the business world's) abstract formulation of success fails to take into account, *Contagion* poses provocative questions about the value of the very services or products that generate the competition. Hagen might be very good at what she does, but is there value in the doing of it? In the specific case of advertising in corporate medicine, Cook poses his questions in the form of a debate that is conducted, naturally enough, by Stapleton and Hagen. Stapleton's objections articulate a couple of challenging points; as he notes, "the ads have no legitimate function except to increase profits by expanding enrollment. They're nothing but exaggerations, half-truths, or the hyping of superficial amenities. They have nothing to do with the quality of health care. Secondly, the advertising costs a ton of money, and it's being lumped into administrative costs. That's the real crime: It's taking money away from patient care" (85). Rejecting, then, the idea that this form of "service" possesses any sort of value, Stapleton in fact sees only a negative effect resulting from the entire enterprise. Hagen, however, responds with the confident expression of her belief that "all advertising draws distinctions and fosters a competitive environment which ultimately benefits the consumer" (86). This argument, one that assumes that the rigor of competition itself will work to enhance, or possibly even to guarantee, the high value of a product, offers justification for the cost of advertising service. Readers, of course, are invited to evaluate the merits of these radically different perspectives.

To further demonstrate what might be lost when massive enterprises succeed in business's game of competition, Robin Cook presents readers with a little scenario that cleverly echoes Jack Stapleton's original fate at the hands of AmeriCare. In need of his rimantadine, Stapleton stops in at a drugstore whose seemingly numberless aisles lend it the appearance of a supermarket. When he is finally waited on at the pharmacy counter, he is curtly informed that his order will require twenty minutes to be filled. This order, as it happens, is never filled—while Stapleton is aimlessly wandering around the store, one of the ubiquitous Black Kings makes an attempt to gun him down. Later, at a different pharmacy, he asks the druggist how long he must wait. At this small drugstore there is no wait. The prescription, instantly filled, is delivered along with the pharmacist's rueful observation that "Those chain stores don't care a whit about service. . . . And for all their poor service, they're still forcing us independents out of business" (317). If the independents do, in fact, go out of business, and the value of personal service is lost, then Terese Hagen's assertion that competition fosters value appears to become essentially moot. Cook's parable of the drugstores thus exposes a tremendous irony: large-scale success in the arena of competition can result in the effacement of precisely those distinctive values that the fact of competition has implicitly promised to promote.

By no means, then, unequivocally opposed to competition, Robin Cook is, on the contrary, wary about precisely those circumstances that would seem to threaten it. Fearful that the unchecked success of big business (and, particularly, the large-scale success of medicine as big business) might well culminate in the de facto creation of the kinds of monopolies whose hegemony permits no useful form of competition, Cook is in reality calling for some kind of leveling of the playing field, some kind of societal commitment to a common practice of fair competition. In the specific case of medicine, he consistently argues—and has done so for many years—that the corporate playing-field ill serves the purposes of the health-care profession. Making this claim, he disavows the legitimacy of the game metaphor as an appropriate one for medicine: in this field, he repeatedly asserts, there must be more at stake than the goal of winning profits. In the case of drugstores or those other small, independent enterprises whose existence is threatened by the power of corporate structure, he simply takes occasion to remind readers that certain values can be lost when there is no competitive pressure to preserve them.

Although *Contagion* can provide no easy formula for unraveling the "market-driven mess" depicted in its pages, Cook counters his portrayal of Terese Hagen's monstrous obsession with winning her company's corporate game with a striking vision of a very different way to play a game. A wonderful model of fair competition, inner-city pick-up basketball is played round-robin style. Potential participants each make individual arrangements to join a new team composed of "winners." (These five fresh winners will challenge the team that wins the game in progress, for there is always a game in progress.) Playing is called "running," and participants run with heady abandon, passing and shooting and constantly adjusting their roles to draw upon the strengths of the other members of their teams. Team membership itself is always in flux, as new combinations of winners challenge the winners on the court. Playing their game for the pleasure of playing, participants win, and lose, and play again another day.

ALTERNATIVE PERSPECTIVE: GENRE CRITICISM

As outlined in Chapter 10, genre criticism focuses on locating mean-ingful ways to classify categories of literary works. (For an extended discussion of issues relevant to genre theory, see page 176.) Because Robin Cook's seventeenth novel readily can be seen as offering a reprise of several of the features most characteristic of his fiction, a brief analysis of both *Contagion*'s plotting strategies and of its use of mixed generic conventions can serve to leave readers with a general overview of this popular writer's work.

One of a series of novels that Cook himself has played a significant role in ultimately defining, *Contagion* clearly claims a place among the subset of popular suspense narratives that have in recent years come to be known as medical thrillers. As discussed earlier, the medical thriller is most distinctive in its use of the specialized world of medicine as setting. Cook is by no means alone in choosing to situate his narratives within a particular terrain. Indeed, many popular contemporary novel-ists have staked similar claims, sometimes to locale (Sara Paretsky, for example, sets her detective stories in the city of Chicago), and sometimes to other kinds of social landscapes (Tony Hillerman's suspense novels draw readers into the realm of traditional Navajo culture).[2]

In situating tales of intrigue within the medical profession, Cook shrewdly appeals to a reading audience whose general interest in his subject matter has grown significantly as tremendous changes, both tech-nological and economic, have dramatically reshaped medical treatment and practice. Documenting many of these changes, his medical thrillers offer suspenseful and adventure-filled action that centers on two differ-ent kinds of danger: on the one hand, Cook is interested in analyzing those social forces that seem to him to pose a threat to the integrity of medicine's own historical traditions, and, on the other hand, he is quite willing to expose those dangers that appear to arise from within the structure of the medical establishment. (In other words, his plots feature instances wherein the medical profession is victimized by outside forces and instances wherein the profession itself violates its public trust.) *Con-tagion*'s plot incorporates both of these scenarios. While the medical in-stitution, in the form of AmeriCare, is undeniably undermined by an agent of the advertising industry, it is by dint of medicine's own com-plicity in the affairs of business that this tragedy occurs. Furthermore, it is worth noting that AmeriCare, a victim of the profit motive, is itself not blameless on this score: readers will remember that this corporation, also acting out of profit motive, has earlier victimized people like Jack Stapleton.

As is his common practice, Cook draws upon a range of narrative traditions to construct *Contagion*'s plot. Its thrilling chase scenes and shoot-outs are fashioned from the standard conventions of the novel of suspense. Its portrayal of the use of microbes as a deadly form of weapon introduces elements of science fiction's horrific "mutant-disaster" motif. Its focus on Stapleton's pursuit of the identity of culprits guilty of mass murder borrows from the "whodunit" tradition of the mystery/detective genre. Mixing these classic conventions of the popular genres with his idiosyncratic studies of institutional organizations (that of business, the hospital, the medical examiner's office, and the basketball court), Cook writes a popular novel that is carefully designed to entertain its readers in a variety of ways.

NOTES

1. Plots that feature the services of forensic scientists have recently enjoyed a certain popularity, especially in detective fiction. Patricia Cornwell, for example, has written a series of popular novels based upon investigations conducted by a coroner's office.

2. Hillerman is one of the contemporary writers featured in this series.

Bibliography

WORKS BY ROBIN COOK

Novels

Acceptable Risk. New York: Putnam, 1994.

Blindsight. New York: Putnam, 1992. (Edition cited in text: *Blindsight*. New York: Berkley, 1993.)

Brain. New York: Putnam, 1981. (Edition cited in text: *Brain*. New York: New American Library, 1982.)

Coma. Boston: Little, Brown, 1977. (Edition cited in text: *Coma*. New York: New American Library, 1977.)

Contagion. New York: Putnam, 1995.

Fatal Cure. New York: Putnam, 1994. (Edition cited in text: *Fatal Cure*. New York: Berkley, 1995.)

Fever. New York: Putnam, 1982. (Edition cited in text: *Fever*. New York: Penguin, 1983.)

Godplayer. New York: Putnam, 1983. (Edition cited in text: *Godplayer*. New York: New American Library, 1984.)

Harmful Intent. New York: Putnam, 1990. (Edition cited in text: *Harmful Intent*. New York: Berkley, 1991.)

Mindbend. New York: Putnam, 1985. (Edition cited in text: *Mindbend*. New York: Penguin, 1986.)

Mortal Fear. New York: Putnam, 1988. (Edition cited in text: *Mortal Fear*. New York: Berkley, 1989.)

Mutation. New York: Putnam, 1989. (Edition cited in text: *Mutation*. New York: Berkley, 1990.)

Outbreak. New York: Putnam, 1987. (Edition cited in text: *Outbreak*. New York: Berkley, 1988.)

Sphinx. New York: Putnam, 1979. (Edition cited in text: *Sphinx*. New York: Penguin, 1980.)

Terminal. New York: Putnam, 1993. (Edition cited in text: *Terminal*. New York: Berkley, 1994.)

Vital Signs. New York: Putnam, 1991. (Edition cited in text: *Vital Signs*. New York: Berkley, 1992.)

The Year of the Intern. New York: Harcourt Brace Jovanovich, 1972. (Edition cited in text: *The Year of the Intern*. New York: New American Library, 1973.)

Essay

"My Turn: The New Doctor's Dilemma." *Newsweek*, 14 May 1973: 24-25.

WORKS ABOUT ROBIN COOK

General Information and Interviews

Aldridge, Susan. "Medical Mystery Tour." *Interzone*, September-October 1991: 35-37.

Blumenthal, Ralph. "Publisher Sued on Novel Citing Chemical Leak." *New York Times*, 5 April 1982: B3.

Bryant, Edward. "Dateline 1999." *Omni*, January 1989: 22+.

Contemporary Authors, s.v. "Cook, Robin." vol. 111. Detroit: Gale Research, 1984.

Contemporary Authors, New Revision Series, s.v. "Cook, Robin." vol. 41. Detroit: Gale Research, 1994.

Contemporary Literary Criticism, s.v. "Cook, Robin." vol. 14. Detroit: Gale Research, 1980.

"Deadly Obsession." *TV Guide*, 6 May 1995: 20+.

"Doctor Fear." *American Health*, September 1989: 83-87.

Grossmann, John. "Dr. Robin Cook, Novelist." *Health*, June 1983: 56-57.

Heldenfels, R. D. "*Virus* Adds to Epidemic of Medical Thrillers." Rev. of *Virus*, by Robin Cook. *Santa Rosa Press Democrat*, 5 May 1995: D1.

Jennes, Gail. "Dr. Robin Cook Has an Rx for Success." *People*, 6 April 1981: 64-66.

Koncius, Jura. "One for the Books." *Washington Post*, 8 April 1981: B8.

Latimer, Leah Y. "*Post* Book and Author Luncheon." *Washington Post*, 25 March 1981: B9.

Miller, Julie Ann. "Beyond Brain Scan: Science Fact vs. Science Fiction." *Science News*, 7 March 1981: 156.

Reginald, Robert. "Cook, Robin." *Science Fiction and Fantasy Literature, 1975-1991.*
     Detroit: Gale Research, 1992.
Who's Who in America, 48th ed., s.v. "Cook, Robin."
World Authors, s.v. "Cook, Robin."

REVIEWS AND CRITICISM

Sphinx

Mertz, Barbara. "Nancy Drew in Egypt." Review of *Sphinx*, by Robin Cook.
     Washington Post, 18 May 1979: C4.
Sullivan, Jack. "*Sphinx*." Review of *Sphinx*, by Robin Cook. *New York Times*, 13
     May 1979, sec. 7: 22.

Fever

Campbell, Don G. "Drama of Degrees, Fury, Confrontation." Review of *Fever*,
     by Robin Cook. *Los Angeles Times*, 28 February 1982, sec. 9: 9.
McLellan, Joseph. "The Topic of Cancer." Review of *Fever*, by Robin Cook. *Wash-
     ington Post*, 20 February 1982: C4.

Fatal Cure

"*Fatal Cure*." Review of *Fatal Cure*, by Robin Cook. *Publishers Weekly*, 13 Decem-
     ber 1993: 64.

Coma

Newlove, Donald. "Medical Villains and Heroes." Review of *Coma*, by Robin
     Cook. *New York Times Book Review*, 8 May 1977: 14.
Watkins, Mel. "Hospital Horrors." Review of *Coma*, by Robin Cook. *New York
     Times Book, Review*, 14 May 1977: 17.

Terminal

Callendar, Newgate. "*Terminal*." Review of *Terminal*, by Robin Cook. *New York
     Times Book Review*, 13 December 1992: 17.

Taylor, Brian. *"Terminal."* Review of *Terminal*, by Robin Cook. *Library Journal*, 15 March 1993: 126.

"Terminal." Review of *Terminal*, by Robin Cook. *Publishers Weekly*, 9 November 1992: 72.

Brain

Hogan, William. "Surgical Thriller." Review of *Brain*, by Robin Cook. *San Francisco Chronicle*, 9 February 1981: 41.

Nolen, William A. "Plugging the Brain Drain." Review of *Brain*, by Robin Cook. *Washington Post*, 8 March 1981, sec. 3: 1.

Smith, Rosalind. "Computer as a New Clue to Murder." Review of *Brain*, by Robin Cook. *Los Angeles Times*, 28 August 1981, sec. 10: 1.

Godplayer

Abrams, Garry. "Nudging the Needless into the Nether World." Review of *Godplayer*, by Robin Cook. *Los Angeles Times*, 28 August 1983, sec. 9: 1.

Dooley, Susan. *"Godplayer."* Review of *Godplayer*, by Robin Cook. *Washington Post Book World*, 3 July 1983: 6.

Ober, Doris. *"Godplayer."* Review of *Godplayer*, by Robin Cook. *San Francisco Chronicle*, 24 July 1983, sec. 5: 1.

Mutation

Hunt, Adam Paul. *"Mutation."* Review of *Mutation*, by Robin Cook. *Library Journal*, 1 March 1993: 124.

Kaufman, Jackie. *"Mutation."* Review of *Mutation*, by Robin Cook. *New York Times Book Review*, 19 February 1989: 20.

Steinberg, Sybil. *"Mutation."* Review of *Mutation*, by Robin Cook. *Publishers Weekly*, 11 November 1988: 40.

Sweeting, Paul. *"Mutation."* Review of *Mutation*, by Robin Cook. *Publishers Weekly*, 7 April 1989: 107.

Mindbend

Barry, Dave. *"Mindbend."* Review of *Mindbend*, by Robin Cook. *New York Times Book Review*, 3 March 1985: 22.

Geeslin, Campbell. *"Mindbend."* Review of *Mindbend*, by Robin Cook. *People Weekly*, 25 March 1985: 16.

"Mindbend." Review of *Mindbend*, by Robin Cook. *Library Journal*, 15 March 1985: 71.

Steinberg, Sybil. *"Mindbend."* Review of *Mindbend*, by Robin Cook. *Publishers Weekly*, 25 January 1985: 84.

Harmful Intent

Adelson, Bernard H. *"Harmful Intent."* Review of *Harmful Intent*, by Robin Cook. *Journal of the American Medical Association*, 11 July 1990: 266.

Lee, Linda. *"Harmful Intent."* Review of *Harmful Intent*, by Robin Cook. *New York Times Book Review*, 11 February 1990: 15.

Steinberg, Sybil. *"Harmful Intent."* Review of *Harmful Intent*, by Robin Cook. *Publishers Weekly*, 10 November 1989: 48.

Outbreak

Fitzpatrick, Donovan. *"Outbreak."* Review of *Outbreak*, by Robin Cook. *New York Times Book Review*, 22 February 1987: 28.

Geeslin, Campbell. *"Outbreak."* Review of *Outbreak*, by Robin Cook. *People Weekly*, 2 March 1987: 11.

"Outbreak." Review of *Outbreak*, by Robin Cook. *Time*, 30 March 1987: 73.

Smothers, Joyce. *"Outbreak."* Review of *Outbreak*, by Robin Cook. *Library Journal*, 15 February 1987: 160.

Steinberg, Sybil. *"Outbreak."* Review of *Outbreak*, by Robin Cook. *Publishers Weekly*, 5 December 1986: 64.

Vital Signs

Brombacher, Susan. *"Vital Signs."* Review of *Vital Signs*, by Robin Cook. *Library Journal*, July 1991: 156.

Queenan, Joe. *"The Shark Ate Wendy."* Review of *Vital Signs*, by Robin Cook. *New York Times Book Review*, 16 December 1990: 12.

Smith, Kristen L. *"Vital Signs."* Rev of *Vital Signs*, by Robin Cook. *Library Journal*, 1 June 1991: 222.

Steinberg, Sybil. *"Vital Signs."* Review of *Vital Signs*, by Robin Cook. *Publishers Weekly*, 23 November 1990: 55.

Mortal Fear

Fuller, Richard. "*Mortal Fear*." Review of *Mortal Fear*, by Robin Cook. *New York Times Book Review*, 10 April 1988: 32.

Steinberg, Sybil. "*Mortal Fear*." Review of *Mortal Fear*, by Robin Cook. *Publishers Weekly*, 27 November 1987: 71.

Sweeting, Paul. "*Mortal Fear*." Review of *Mortal Fear*, by Robin Cook. *Publishers Weekly*, 4 November 1988: 55.

Taylor, Brian. "*Mortal Fear*." Review of *Mortal Fear*, by Robin Cook. *Library Journal*, 15 May 1993: 116.

Toepfer, Susan. "*Mortal Fear*." Review of *Mortal Fear*, by Robin Cook. *People Weekly*, 11 January 1988: 15.

Blindsight

"*Blindsight*." Review of *Blindsight*, by Robin Cook. *Publishers Weekly*, 15 November 1991: 62.

Acceptable Risk

Madrigal, Alix. "Robin Cook Goes Gothic." Review of *Acceptable Risk*, by Robin Cook. *San Francisco Chronicle Book Review*, 29 January 1995: 4.

OTHER SECONDARY SOURCES

Aisenberg, Nadya. *Ordinary Heroines: Transforming the Male Myth*. New York: Continuum, 1994.

Dove, George N. *Suspense in the Formula Story*. Bowling Green, Ky.: Bowling Green State University Press, 1989.

"Ethics and Embryos." *Newsweek*, 12 June 1995: 66-67.

Ferguson, Mary Anne. *Images of Women in Literature*. 5th ed. Boston: Houghton Mifflin, 1991.

Garrett, Laurie. *The Coming Plague*. New York: Farrar, Straus & Giroux, 1994.

Gilbert, Sandra M. "What Do Feminsit Critics Want? A Postcard From the Volcano." In *The New Feminist Criticism*. Edited by Elaine Showalter. New York: Pantheon, 1985. 29-45.

Girard, René. *Violence and the Sacred*. Translated by Patrick Gregory. Baltimore: Johns Hopkins University Press, 1977.

Greene, Gayle, and Coppelia Kahn, eds., *Changing Subjects: The Making of Feminist Literary Criticism*. New York: Routledge, 1993.

Iaccino, James F. *Psychological Reflections of Cinematic Terror*. Westport, Conn.: Praeger, 1994.

Jung, Carl Gustav. *The Basic Writings of C. G. Jung*. Edited by Violet Staub De Laszlo. New York: Modern Library, 1959.

Kassirer, Jerome P. Managed Care and the Morality of the Marketplace. (Editorial). *The New England Journal of Medicine* 333, no.1 (6 July 1995): 50–52.

Klein, Kathleen Gregory. *Great Women Mystery Writers*. Westport, Conn.: Greenwood, 1994.

Nelson, Cary, Paula A. Treichler, and Lawrence Grossberg. "Cultural Studies: An Introduction." In *Cultural Studies*. New York: Routledge, 1992.

"Outbreak of Fear." *Newsweek*, 22 May 1995: 48-55.

Panek, LeRoy Lad. *Probable Cause: Crime Fiction in America*. Bowling Green, Ky.: Bowling Green University Press, 1990.

Preston, Richard. The Hot Zone. New York: Random House, 1994.

———. "Why Viruses Push Our Hot Buttons." *Newsweek*, 22 May 1995: 54.

Reeves, Charles Eric. "Myth Theory and Criticism." In *The Johns Hopkins Guide to Literary Theory and Criticism*. Edited by Michael Groden and Martin Kreiswirth. Baltimore: Johns Hopkins University Press, 1994. 520-523.

Roberts, Thomas J. *An Aesthetics of Junk Fiction*. Athens: Universtiy of Georgia Press, 1990.

Todorov, Tzvetan. *The Poetics of Prose*. Translated by Richard Howard. Ithaca: Cornell University Press, 1977.

Wood, Michael. "Horror of Horrors." *New York Review of Books*, 19 October 1995: 54-58.

Index

About the Author

LORENA LAURA STOOKEY is a lecturer in the English department at the University of Nevada, Reno, where she teaches courses in mythology, poetry, and British literature. She is also interested in writing in the sciences and in language theory.